TRADITION
and
REVOLT

TRADITION

and

REVOLT

Historical
and
Sociological
Essays

Robert A. Nisbet

University of California, Riverside

[RANDOM HOUSE NEW YORK]

ACKNOWLEDGMENTS

It is a pleasure to thank my friend Charles Page for his counsel in assembling these essays and for valuable suggestions drawn from his rich store of sociological wisdom. He is not a conservative or traditionalist and cannot therefore be held for any of the book's heresies or errors. For these, if they exist, I am alone responsible.

ROBERT A. NISBET

Riverside, California

CONTENTS

Introduction   3

[1]   Rousseau and the Political Community   15

[2]   The Politics of Pluralism: Lamennais   31

[3]   Leadership and Social Crisis   51

[4]   Conservatism and Sociology   73

[5]   History and Sociology   91

[6]   The Decline and Fall of Social Class   105

[7]   Moral Values and Community   129

[8]   Sociology as an Art Form   143

[9]   Power and the Intellectual   163

[10]   The Impact of Technology on Ethical
Decision-Making   183

[11]   Kinship and Political Power
in First Century Rome   203

[12]　The Permanent Professors:
A Modest Proposal　225

[13]　Project Camelot
and the Science of Man　247

[14]　Conflicting Academic Loyalties　283

TRADITION
and
REVOLT

Introduction

Whatever unity may lie in this volume is the consequence of a single perspective, one that has served me during the past two decades as both philosophy of history and framework of analysis. This perspective is the historical conflict between traditionalism and modernism. The conflict erupted at the end of the eighteenth century, given form by the two great revolutions, democratic and industrial. Almost immediately it became the concern of intellectuals in Western Europe, and it has remained this ever since. If today the conflict of traditional and modernist values is most vivid in the new nations of the world, it is far from dead in the West and in our own country. The most dramatic evidence of the continuing conflict is, of course, the Negro rights movement, followed closely in importance by the political upsurge of youth. But, as I have tried to show in some of these essays, the conflict is to be seen in the contexts surrounding technology, social class, family, and community.

In the final three essays I have dealt with the university essentially in these terms.

There are many ways to describe the modernist revolt against traditional values. What else indeed has literature, criticism, and much philosophy been about for the past century and a half? But I must limit myself to the way in which this revolt and conflict seem important to a historical sociologist. The conflict is one between two sets of dialectically opposed values: on the one hand, hierarchy, community, tradition, authority, and the sacred sense of life; on the other hand, equalitarianism, individualism, secularism, positive rights, and rationalist modes of organization and power. It was the eruption of the latter set of values at the end of the eighteenth century that was the beginning of the modernist revolt. The eruption has continued ever since—in life and literature, in politics and culture, in macrocosm and microcosm. Its tensions have provided motive power for one of the great cultural efflorescences in human history. That it has produced some of the crowning moral virtues of our civilization is plain. That the same revolt and conflict have also produced cankers—vast power, social dislocation, anomie—is equally plain. If preoccupation with both aspects of modernism has made the contemporary intellectual more troubled and confused than his predecessors were a generation ago, it has to be admitted that this preoccupation has also made him more humble—and civilized. He has acquired something of a tragic sense of life.

That most of the essays in this volume have a conservative cast I acknowledge freely and readily. I use the phrase "conservative cast" advisedly. Conservatism is a structure of thought, a style, it seems to me, as well as a set of political dispositions toward state and society. Thirty years ago, while still a graduate student at Berkeley, I came across the writings of the post-Revolutionary conservatives in Europe: Louis de Bonald, Joseph Marie de Maistre, Edmund Burke, Georg Friedrich Hegel, Ludwig von Haller, and, somewhat later, the greatest of them, Alexis de Tocqueville (in whose genius, to be sure, lay both liberalism and conservatism.

History has made the latter dominant, however.) It seemed to me then, and still does now, that these works told me things about the nature of power and society that I had not gotten from my more or less conventional education as an undergraduate and that the basic perspectives of the conservatives are useful to historical and social analysis irrespective of whether one is himself conservative, liberal, or radical. (In this latter reflection I was, as I learned later, but repeating the reflections of such men as Karl Marx, Pierre Proudhon, and Georges Sorel.)

The conservatives were not merely philosophers and scholars; they were embattled and militant intellectuals. For them the touchstone of social excellence was the feudal order—the combination of aristocracy, corporatism, and hierarchy that left its stamp upon posterity as few orders ever have in history. The conservatives eulogized and glorified this order out of recognition, but in the act of glorifying it they identified it, and made it vivid as a type. Conservative hatred of modernism exceeded all reason, but in the act of hating it the conservatives identified it too. Today, reading Burke's or Bonald's idealizations of the traditional order—of the gentleman, honor, patriarchal family, commune, and guild—we tend to forget that such idealizations were weapons that the conservatives used in their war with the soldiers of modernism: the Jean Jacques Rousseaus, Jeremy Benthams, and Adam Smiths, who, of course, had their own weapons in this ideological struggle.

The conservatives, as we know, lost their ideological war, lost it to those who were more nearly on the track of modern history. To lose is usually to ensure posterity's indifference or hostility. And such has indeed been the fate of the conservatives—with the exceptions of Burke, Hegel, and, more recently, Tocqueville, each of whom is usually treated as an individual rather than as a part of the rather remarkable anti-Enlightenment movement that post-Revolutionary conservatism actually was. Yet, as I have tried to show in several essays, the conservatives had their due share of influence on strands of thought that have survived into the twentieth century.

In reading their works today, one can discern the outlines of a curse that, in Parthian fashion, they hurled at their
victors. Like the Dark Witch of the Evil Forest, who was
defeated in all her undertakings but who revenged herself
by the curse of misery she placed upon those who had
bested her, the conservatives said in effect:

"You have defeated our hopes for the revival of the old
regime. Europe will become, as you have chosen, ever more
democratic, equalitarian, affluent, rational, and secular. So
be it. But our curse upon posterity is this: However democratic society becomes, it will never seem democratic enough;
the sense of relative undemocracy will incessantly enlarge.
However broad and popular the base of political power, the
sense of relative powerlessness will only spread. No matter
how equal men become in rights and opportunity, the sense
of relative inequality will grow and fester. Spreading economic affluence will only leave men haunted by the specter
of relative poverty. Individualism and secularism, far from
buoying up the sense of creative release, will shortly leave
many of them with the agonizing sense of estrangement—
first from community, then from self. And over the whole
wondrous achievement of modern technology and culture
will hover the ghosts of community, membership, identity,
and certainty."

Lest the curse I have described seem fanciful, let me
refer the reader to a single work written in the early nineteenth century by a conservative: the second volume of
Tocqueville's *Democracy in America*, from which I have
drawn it almost word for word.

But our proper concern is with neither prophecy nor
curse. Movements of ideas in history are important to us
chiefly for the degree of perspective they provide in the
understanding of the world around us. The conservatives
were prophets of the past. They were out of sympathy with
the world that was being born, nostalgic, and frequently the
victims of romantic archaism. So much is true. But they had
two overriding excellences that their rationalist-liberal contemporaries did not have: First, they began not with an
imaginary natural order—with a set of natural rights, liber-

ties, and harmonies—but with the actual institutions, groups, and social roles that they found around them. As I noted above, the conservatives, in attacking modernism, identified it; in cherishing traditional society, they made its physiognomy plain. Second, the conservatives had a profound sense of historical development and, with this, a sense of the ineffaceability of the historical record that lies in traditions and customs. Man's identity, they declared, almost in the words of contemporary historical psychology, has roots in time as well as in space.

What are the specific perspectives that we may draw from our reading of the conservatives? I will limit myself to four. First, a tragic view of history. Far from seeing the work of modern history—the Reformation, the Age of Reason, capitalism, nationalism, and democracy—as progressive, they saw it as containing forces that man, finite man, would be unable to control, that would in time desolate culture and personality. Second, the conservatives saw forming in modern society, on the very ruins of the ancient authorities of class, kinship, church, and monarchy, new and more awful forms of power than had ever been known before—forms of power at once centralized, bureaucratized, and popular. Third, the conservatives viewed the new order as one of social dislocation, disorganization, and anarchy: it was the result of such forces as technology, romantic individualism, and, above all, the penetration of political power into the social structure. Fourth, they had a vision of man's alienation from self once he had gotten loose from the accustomed "inns and resting places" (as Burke called them) of family, community, and class.

What is important in this is not prophecy but perspective. That contemporary society is not the midden of bones and shards that some of the early nineteenth-century conservatives foresaw for the twentieth century is of no importance. Neither, really, are the more specific questions of whether contemporary culture is in fact irredeemably bureaucratized, mechanized, commercialized, and alienated (as today the Left, not the Right, is prone to say). What is important, for the scholar and the reflective mind at least, is whether such perspectives are useful in understanding history and society. It is not necessary to believe in the existence of a colossus of power to recognize that within modern democracy power over human life has indeed become greater—more systematized, more penetrating, more pervasive—and equally important, that there is a negative relation between the structure and intensity of *power* in a society and the structure and vitality of *certain types of social organization* (my essay on kinship and political power in first-century Rome is no more than an elaboration of this idea). It is not necessary to plunge one's self perceptually into a sea of social anarchy to be made aware of the reality and importance of certain processes of disintegration, of entropy, in our social system—processes that one would never discover in the works of the rationalist-liberals until a decade or two ago. And, finally, it is not necessary to take an undilutedly pessimistic or tragic view of history to be aware that in the midst of modern affluence, popular sovereignty, equality in civil rights, and rational technology there are indeed elements of human alienation, obsessive quest for identity, and search for community. These elements may not constitute the whole picture, but they are plainly important and flow directly—as the conservatives foresaw—from these very forces we pronounce good.

It is in this context, then, that I refer to the conservative cast of the essays. It would be tedious and gratuitous to comment on all of them, but comments on several are perhaps in order.

The first of the essays, and earliest written, is the one on Rousseau. He seems to me now, as he did a quarter of a century ago, the very archetype of the political modern, the embodiment of the modernist revolt in politics. In its original form this essay was a statement of Rousseau's relation to the totalitarian tradition in the West. I have modified it, deleting the rather long sections on the popular roots of totalitarianism, for two reasons: first, because this subsequently became the subject of J. L. Talmon's far more penetrating and exhaustive *The Origins of Totalitarian Democracy* and the idea is now a familiar one; second, because Rousseau's lasting and most fundamental significance is to the *political community*—of which totalitarianism in its German and Russian forms is but a single and corrupt type. Rousseau is the political intellectual par excellence. It is clear, as one reads the tracts and manifestoes of the Left today, that he is as naturally their exemplar as Marx was when the enemy seemed to be capitalism alone. What gives Rousseau undiminished relevance to any political Left is his exciting (and infinitely adaptable) combination of social nihilism and political absolutism. Rousseau remains, even after two centuries, the most brilliant, persuasive, and powerful advocate (and also metaphysician) of the monolithic political community in the Western tradition—with perhaps the single exception of Plato, whom Rousseau revered. It is Rousseau, more than any other modern, who has given the political state the guise of community, who has made it the image of a fortress and a refuge against the tyrannies and injustices that seem always to be a part of traditional society. The medieval philosopher was prone to see the church as this fortress, and there are those today who still see in Christianity a vanguard for the attack upon social ills. But it would appear that the role of the religious intellectual of the Middle Ages has been taken today by the contemporary political intellectual. In Rousseau the political intellectual has his prototype.

I have decided to reprint the essay on Felicité Robert de Lamennais because there have recently been signs of renewed interest in this generally neglected and tragic figure and because he is, in a sense, the first of those in modern history (Tocqueville was the greatest) to suffer the torments involved in trying to reconcile the values of traditionalism and modernism. In my essay I have dealt with Lamennais primarily as the real founder of what later came to be known as political pluralism. Were I writing the essay today I would give greater stress to the conflict element in Lamennais than I did originally. Of Lamennais, as of Tocqueville, it could be said that he ceased to be traditionalist without ever becoming modern. His life, following his excommunication, was one long quest—in labor organization, in politics, and in philosophy—for the refuge he had known earlier when his powerful and widely read *Essay on Indifference* had made him the hero of all those dedicated to Catholic dogma, monarchy, and traditionalism.

"The Decline and Fall of Social Class" had two intents when I wrote it ten years ago. The first and more important was simply to emphasize that social class, in any substantive sense of the phrase, has no more significance as a motivating context of human behavior today than does any other survival of preindustrial, predemocratic society. The second, and related intent was that of trying to persuade fellow sociologists that their compulsive efforts to reduce complex community, ethnic, and religious patterns of behavior into the shopworn (if familiar and comforting) trinity of "lower class," "middle class," and "upper class" made about as much sense as trying to use the model of the kindred in studies of American family life. It seemed plain to me that continued use of these hoary concepts was made possible only by heroic and Procrustean acts of redefinition on the one hand, and, on the other, by methodological subtleties and convolutions that put one in mind of Roy Campbell's famous lines on some contemporary poets: "They use the snaffle and the curb all right. But where's the bloody horse?"

Matters have improved greatly, it seems to me, over the past ten years. Although an aura of almost Puritan predestinarianism still clings to many uses of "middle class" and "lower class"—company for the psychiatrist's even more predestinarian use of such words as "schizophrenic"—we have come a long way from the days when the conceptual trinity of classes governed social thought about the complex, infinitely varied styles and structures of social stratification in this country. Stratification studies today seem to me much more sophisticated than they were ten years ago. Sociological perspectives of stratification in the study of power, elites, status styles, and economic levels are far more reflective of the fact that in modern history there has been a disengagement of status, as well as of power and affluence, from the historic three layers of traditional class society.

Two of the essays, "Conservatism and Sociology" and "Sociology as an Art Form," are efforts to show the ideological and also the humanistic roots of sociology. Despite wide misunderstanding within as well as outside the discipline, sociology is far from an upstart in contemporary thought. Its roots and also its principal manifestations in the nineteenth century are intimately involved in some of the profoundest movements of modern intellectual history. Of all the sciences born in the nineteenth century, sociology, I believe, came the closest to full anticipation of those moral problems of man and society that are so distinctively twentieth century in shape and mood. Whatever else men like Max Weber, Emile Durkheim, and Georg Simmel were (and I readily concede that they were scientists), they were humanists—even artists—and they never made the mistake of thinking that science could ever be reduced to propositions and formulas in methodology. The humanistic character of such perspectives as *rationalization, metropolis,* and *anomie* is plain enough from the role that these have in contemporary literature and letters. It is in sociology that they had their first clear-cut exposition in the nineteenth century. The major insights of sociology have been refractions of the same moral and intellectual forces that have gone into the making of the modern mind.

The final essays of the volume deal with the contemporary university. Nowhere, it seems to me, has the conflict between traditional and modern values become so strikingly apparent to observers, so influential in the shaping of policy, so frequently agonizing to participants, as in the university. For all its adaptation to modern life, for all its influence in our culture, the university is medieval, not only in origin but in continuing structure. Ceremonial plumage at commencements serves as well as anything to remind us that not only its internal division into "colleges," "faculties," and "curricula" is medieval but also its jealously guarded internal hierarchy, its claimed faculty authority over students, its insistence upon corporate privilege and autonomy, and, perhaps above all, its obsessive concern with matters of internal government. These qualities were more honored in medieval life (which was a rich complex of such matters) than they were to be honored in the imaginations of the founders of the modern temper—such men as Rousseau, Bentham, and Herbert Spencer, all three of whom, characteristically, detested the university, as they did the guild and the monastery.

It may well be that recent attacks by students on the structure of the university—including the idea of faculty governance—have in them a kind of dimly realized but powerful sense of being on the main line of modern history. The student Left might argue that just as an economic system survived without the guild, the political system without estates, wealth and status without hereditary class, marriage without the extended family, why should not intellect and knowledge be able to survive without the reinforcement of that equally medieval structure, the university? More excitingly, why should not intellect be liberated from the academic corporation as it was once from the churchly corporation?

Nothing in today's university would suggest either weakness of structure or moribundity of aim—or, for that matter, diminution of strength of scientist and scholar. The power of the university in America today is perhaps greater than it has been in Western society since the Middle Ages. "Guild" is the word frequently used to describe it. We might better see university power as an image of feudalism itself, with powerful and competing autonomies, claims of privilege and immunity, and a rich aristocracy towered over by Nobel Prize barons. It extends across the land from fief to fief, barely acknowledges the existence of president-monarchs, and forces even congressional committees into the unwonted attitude of diffidence. No industrial or political tycoon would dare today to take on the university directly. The late Senator Joseph McCarthy was the last to do so, and it is possible to see his abortive attack on Harvard as the beginning, if not the cause of, his political downfall. The university comes very close to being *imperium in imperio*.

Long may this happy state continue! But if it does not

continue—if it becomes gradually transformed, as did the medieval guild, into a set of diverse, scattered functions represented by private enterprise and government agency—it will be because of precisely the same set of forces (drawn from the Left as well as from the Right) that earlier dislodged kindred, guild, social class, and local community from importance in society.

(1)

Rousseau and the Political Community

It is doubtful whether any political theorist, with the possible exception of Plato, has more often been charged with inconsistency than has Jean Jacques Rousseau. How, it is asked—and has been asked since the age in which Rousseau wrote—can the individual be absolutely free, as Rousseau declares him to be in the *Social Contract*, and, at one and the same time, under the absolute dominion of the General Will? How can there be in fact what Rousseau described as "a form of association which will defend and protect with the whole common force the person and goods of each associate, and in which each, while uniting himself with all, may still obey himself alone, and remain as free as before"? How is it possible for there to be "the total alienation of each associate, together with all his rights, to the whole community" and, despite this, indeed *because* of it, the achievement by the individual of a degree of inde-

This article, in a slightly different version, originally appeared as "Rousseau and Totalitarianism," *Journal of Politics* (May 1943).

pendence that he had known in the earliest phases of his history but had lost through the rise of inequality and injustice.[1] Answers to these questions are doubtless impossible in terms of strict logic, but it is at least possible, I think, to clarify what Rousseau was trying to do.

The individualism of Rousseau's thought is not the individualism of a William Godwin; it is not the libertarian assertion of absolute rights against the *state*. Rousseau's passionate defense of the individual arises out of his opposition to the forms and observances of *society*. "What excites Rousseau's hatred," Professor Vaughan has commented, "is not the state, but society of any sort, quite apart from the civic ties by which in fact it is held together. His ideal, alike in the *Discourses* and in *Émile*, is no doubt individual freedom: freedom, however, not in the sense of immunity from control of the state but in that of withdrawal from the oppressions and corruptions of society."[2] It is this ideal which animates the educational philosophy of *Émile*, the belief in the goodness and perfectibility of the individual when he is protected from the corruption of society. It is, perhaps above all others, the basic theme of the *Confessions*. The splendidness of isolation from society is a *leitmotif* which recurs again and again in the passages of that work.[3] The ideal lies implicit in the *Discourse on Inequality* where each stage of advancement that removes the individual from the isolation which was his existence in the conditions of nature is marked as a point on the way to degeneration. It is not the political state which inspires Rousseau's hostility, but the harshnesses, inequalities, and dissensions of civil society. In a letter to Mirabeau, he writes: "It is of the essence of society to breed a ceaseless war among its members; and the only way to combat this is to find a form of government which shall set the law above them all."[4]

The traditional bonds of society, the relationships we generally speak of as social, are the ties which to Rousseau symbolize the chains of existence. It is from these that he desires to emancipate the individual, and to replace their gross inequalities with a condition of equality approximating as nearly as possible the state of nature. "Each citizen would then be completely *independent* of all his fellow men, and absolutely *dependent* upon the state: which operation is always brought by the same means; *for it is only by the force of the state that the liberty of its members can be secured.*"[5] There is no other single statement in all Rousseau's writings which better serves as the theme of his political philosophy than this. In it is incorporated the essential argument of the two *Discourses* and of the *Contrat social.* His ideal is independence for the individual, but independence, it will be observed, not from the state but from fellow members of society.

The function of the state is made apparent by the same statement. Its mission is to effectuate the independence of the individual from society by securing the individual's dependence upon itself. The state is the means by which the individual can be freed of those restrictive tyrannies which compose society. It is the agency of emancipation which permits the individual to develop the latent germs of goodness heretofore frustrated by a hostile society. By entering into the pure state, Rousseau declares, "Man's actions receive a moral character which was wanting to them before," and "from a stupid and limited animal he now for the first time becomes a reasoning being and a man."[6] The state is thus of the essence of man's potential being, and far from being a check upon his development, it is the sole means of that development. Through the power of the state, man is spared the strife and tyranny which arise out of his selfish and destructive passions. But in order to emerge from the dissensions of society, and to abide in the spiritual peace of the state, there must be "an absolute surrender of the individual, with all of his rights and all of his powers, to the community as a whole."[7]

Rousseau's emphasis upon the community has been too often interpreted in a sense that is foreign to his own aim. Commentators have occasionally written of his "community" as the revival of a concept which had disappeared with the Middle Ages. The mystic solidarity which Rousseau preaches is not, however, the solidarity of the community existing by custom and unwritten law. The social community, as it existed in the thought of Thomas Aquinas or, later, in the theory of Althusius, is a community of communities, an assemblage of morally integrated minor groups. The solidarity of this community arises out of the moral and social observances of the minor groups. Its unity does not result from being permeated with sovereign law, extending from the top through all individual components of the structure. Rousseau's community, however, is a *political* community, one which is indistinguishable from the state and which shares all the uniformitarian qualities of the state. It is, in his mind, a moral unity, but it is a unity conferred by the sovereign will of the state, and directed by the political government. Thus the familiar organic analogy is used to indicate the unitary structure of his political community.[8] The same centralization of control which exists in the human body must dominate the structure of the community; unity is conferred by the brain which in Rousseau's analogy represents the sovereign power. The General Will is the analogue of the human mind, and as such must remain as unified and undiversified as the mind itself. The *Volonté générale*, as he is careful to indicate, is not synonymous with the *Volonté de tous*, the will of all. It is the will of the political organism, an entity which has a life of its own quite apart from that of the individual members of which it is built.

In its supra-human reality it is always right, and while the *Volonté de tous* may be often misled, the General Will never deviates from the strictest rectitude. The General Will is indivisible, inalienable, and illimitable. It demands the unqualified obedience of every individual in the community, and implies the obligation of each citizen to render to the state all that the state sees fit to demand. This preeminence of the state in the life of the individual is not, however, despotism; it is the necessary basis of true individual freedom. "In order that the social contract shall be no empty formula it tacitly implies that obligation which alone can give force to all the others: namely that anyone who refuses obedience to the general will is forced to it by the whole body. *This merely means that he is being compelled to be free.*"⁹ In this last phrase is revealed clearly the relationship between individualism and authoritarianism in the thought of Rousseau. The same rationale of values which leads him to restrict morality to life within the state, compels him similarly to regard the state as the sphere of freedom. The individual lives a free life only within his complete surrender to the omnipotent state. The state is the liberator of the individual from the toils of society.

The totalitarian implications of Rousseau's thought do not arise merely out of the severity of his theory of sovereignty. The most common form of criticism—that the theory sets up an illimitable power—is applicable to all monistic theories of sovereignty. In any social theory where the sovereign state exists as a concept there is implicit at least the idea of potentially unrestricted power. What gives uniqueness to Rousseau's doctrine is not so much its severity as its subtle but explicit identification with freedom. What has connoted bondage to the minds of most men is exalted as freedom by Rousseau. To regard the power structure of the state as a device by which the individual is only being compelled to be free is a process of reasoning that sets Rousseau apart from the tradition of liberalism. The phraseology of liberalism in this case merely intensifies the authoritarianism which underlies it. What Rousseau calls freedom is at bottom no more than the freedom to do that which the state in its omniscience determines. Freedom for Rousseau is the synchronization of all social existence to the will of the state, the replacement of cultural diversity by a mechanical equalitarianism. Other writers have idealized such an order in the interests perhaps of justice or of stability, but Rousseau is the first to invest it with the value of freedom. Therein lies the real distinctiveness of his theory of sovereignty.

It is, however, in the bearing of Rousseau's General Will upon traditional society that the full sweep of its totalitarian significance becomes manifest. It has been made clear that the object of Rousseau's dislike is society, and the special merit of the state lies in its power to emancipate the individual from traditional society. The relationship among individuals which forms the General Will, and which is the true state, is obviously an exceedingly delicate one. It must be unitary and indivisible for its nature fully to unfold. In short, it must be protected from the operations of extraneous channels of constraint. "For the same reason that sovereignty is inalienable, it is indivisible," he writes; "the Will is general or else it is nothing."[10] To achieve a pure sovereignty, one which will be untrammeled by social influences, one which will encompass the whole of man's personality, it is necessary that the traditional social loyalties be abrogated. A unified, *general*, Will is incompatible with the existence of minor associations; hence they must be banished.

> When the people, having been adequately informed, hold its deliberation, and the citizens have had no communication among themselves, the whole number of individual opinions will always result in the General Will, and the decision will always be just. But when factions arise, and partial associations are created at the expense of the great association, the will of each of these associations becomes general so far as its members are concerned, and particular in its relation to the state: it may then be said that it is no longer a number of votes equal to the number of men, but equal only to the number of associations. . . . It is therefore essential, if the General Will is to be able to express itself, that there should be no partial society within the state, and that each citizen should think only his own thoughts.[11]

The proscription of all forms of association except that which is identical with the whole being of the state: such is Rousseau's drastic proposal. This is not to be regarded as one of these hasty, ill-considered remarks for which Rousseau is famous. Nor is it true that his banishment of associations is out of harmony with the rest of his thought. We have seen that Rousseau's animus is against society, against those ties which make individuals dependent upon one another. We have seen, further, that his conception of sovereignty demands the attributes of unity and indivisibility; the General Will is *general* or else it is nothing. Is it not then logical that the right of non-political association should be sharply restricted? In his earlier *Économie politique*, Rousseau, in almost the same words, had presented this analysis of the relation of associations to the state.[12] There is to be no bond of loyalty, no social affiliation, no interdependence, save that which is embodied in the General Will. This will, as we have seen, is meticulously distinguished by Rousseau from the mere "will of all." The latter is the collective opinion or judgment reached by the people in their ordinary social roles; in their roles of businessman, soldier, cleric, family member, and so on. This will is *not* the "voice of God"; it is *not* necessarily just, right, and equitable. But the General Will is. What makes the General Will, in Otto von Gierke's words, a process of permanent revolution is that by its very nature it must seek to dissolve away all of the social roles in society which, by their very existence, militate against both the individual's freedom and his capacity to enter into the absolute political community.

The genius of the idea of the General Will lies in its masterful utilization of the ancient distinction between appearance and reality. We must, Rousseau is saying, beware of the *apparent* will of the people—the will that simple majority vote may make evident—for this is the will of the people still incompletely emancipated from the private authorities and the separate roles that are given them by history. The *real* will of the people is that will which lies latent in man and that requires as its condition man's liberation from these authorities and roles. *This* is the General Will and is alone "the voice of God."

How, in practical operation, is the General Will to be ascertained? Representation through parliamentary institutions is out of the question, for, we are told, the General Will cannot be represented. To seek to represent it is to distort it. Moreover, representative institutions are themselves a part of the hated legacy of the Middle Ages. Balloting will not do, for, as we have seen, balloting may yield only the spurious and deceptive "will of all." Rousseau's answer to his question is a fascinating one:

> But how, I shall be asked, can the General Will be known in cases in which it has not expressed itself? Must the whole nation be assembled together at every unforeseen event? Certainly not. It ought the less to be assembled, because it is by no means certain that its decision would be the expression of the General Will; besides, the method would be impracticable in a great people, and is hardly ever necessary where the government is well-intentioned: for the rulers well know that the General Will is always on the side which is most favourable to the public interest, that is to say, most equitable; so that it is needful only to act justly, to be certain of following the General Will.[13]

How can the ruler be certain of acting justly? He must be, above all things, virtuous. Only "the most sublime virtue," Rousseau writes, "can afford sufficient illumination for it"—that is, for the distinction between the real will and the apparent will. But what is virtue? And here we come full circle back to the General Will.

> If you would have the General Will accomplished, bring all the particular wills into conformity with it; in other words, as virtue is nothing more than this conformity of the particular wills, with the General Will, establish the reign of virtue.[14]

Was ever a doctrine, in the whole history of political theory, more beautifully tailored, more ingeniously complected, than the doctrine of the General Will? In it, at one and the same time, lie ideas of widest range: liberation from social tyranny; emancipation from self and its egoistic demands; the achievement of a form of spiritual communion that had previously been reserved for heaven; the attainment of virtue. And withal a conception of power as absolute as it is sealing and providential. Others in history, from the Roman lawyers through the great Hobbes, had justified the power of the state in terms of order. Rousseau is the first to justify absolute power in the name of virtue, community, and freedom. Power is more than power: it is refuge from the inequities and uncertainties of ordinary society.

In a host of ways the practical implications of the doctrine of the General Will are made evident by Rousseau. I shall confine myself to but two of them: his treatment of religion and of the family. A socially independent church, like any form of non-political loyalty, would constitute an interference with the functioning of the General Will. It would represent a flaw in that spiritual unity which Rousseau prizes so highly in his political order. Yet it would not do to repress the religious propensities of man, for "as soon as men come to live in civil society they must have a religion to keep them there. No nation has ever endured or ever will endure without religion."[15] But, argues Rousseau, it is not enough that a nation should have a religion. The religion must be identified in the minds of the people with the values of national life, else it will create disunity and violate the General Will. It is not enough that a religion should make good men; it must make good citizens. Religion has a responsibility toward civic or political ends before any others. It must reflect, above all, the essential unity of the state, and find its justification in the measures it takes to promote that unity.[16]

In light of these criteria, Christianity must be rejected as the religion of the true state. "For Christianity, as a religion, is entirely spiritual, occupied solely with heavenly things; the country of the Christians is not of this world." There are even greater objections to Christianity. "Christian charity does not readily allow a man to think hardly of his neighbors. . . . Christianity preaches only servitude and dependence. Its spirit is so favourable to tyranny that it always profits by such a régime. True Christians are made to be slaves, and they know this and do not much mind: this short life counts for too little in their eyes." It cannot be overlooked that it is the essential humanity in the Christian faith that Rousseau despises. Its very virtues, he tells us, are its vices, for a society of Christians

with all its perfections would be neither the strongest nor
the most lasting. The very fact that it was perfect would
rob it of its bond of union. The disregard of the Christian
mind for secular law, for the values of the nation, would be
the undoing of that unity which is indispensable to the true
state.[17] The spirit of subserviency which Christianity em-
bodies would prevent any real flowering of the martial
spirit. "Set over against Christians those generous peoples
who were devoured by ardent love of glory and of their
country; imagine your Christian republic face to face with
Sparta or Rome; the pious Christians will be beaten,
crushed, and destroyed before they know where they are."
The ancient Romans were possessed of military valour until
Christianity was accepted, "but when the Cross had driven
out the eagle, Roman valour wholly disappeared." Christianity, then, because of its pacifism, its depreciation of
the state, and because of its concentration upon men rather
than citizens, must be replaced by another religion, one
which will perfectly embody the measure of nationalist
ardor necessary to the state.

There must be instituted a purely civil religion, of which
the Sovereign should fix the articles of faith. "While it
can compel no one to believe them, it can banish from the
state whoever does not believe them . . . ; if anyone after
publicly recognizing these dogmas behaves as if he does
not believe them, let him be punished by death: he has committed the worst of all crimes, that of lying before the
law." Other faiths will be permitted to exist along side of
the Civil religion providing there is nothing in their articles
which is deemed by the Sovereign to be inimical to the development of citizenship. "Tolerance should be given to
all religions that tolerate others, so long as their dogmas
contain nothing contrary to the duties of citizenship." It
will be remembered, however, that the criteria of good
citizenship are far reaching. Rousseau's prior criticism of
Christianity on the ground of its intrinsic irreconcilability
with good citizenship should serve as the grain of salt with
which to take the protestations of tolerance. The articles
of faith of the Civil religion as fixed by the Sovereign have

as their fundamental objective the cementing of the social contract. We have already seen that the most basic values of Christianity at least are not regarded as compatible with the state. One may perhaps speculate on the extent to which tolerance as a practical policy would be deemed commensurate with Civil religion.

It is political religion which Rousseau extolls, one which in essence is indistinguishable from the law of the land. Like his forerunner Hobbes, Rousseau holds sin to be no more than a transgression of civil law, and in that fact lies the inspiriting aim of *la religion civile*. Respect for the Sovereign, allegiance to the state alone, and subordination of all interests to the law of the realm: these are the primary attributes of the Civil religion proposed by Rousseau. The symbol of *patrie* is uppermost; religion and patriotism will be but two aspects of the same thing.[18] "If it is good," Rousseau wrote in his *Économie politique* "to know how to deal with men as they are, it is much better to make them what there is need that they should be. The most absolute authority is that which penetrates into a man's inmost being, and concerns itself no less with his will than with his actions." So had declared the Church's militants in the Middle Ages. So would declare Dostoevski's Grand Inquisitor.

The family, too, must be radically altered, especially in its hold over the young. This follows inevitably from the demands of the General Will and from the nature of virtue which, as we have learned, is nothing more than conformity with the General Will. To form citizens is not the work of a day, nor is it a responsibility that can be left idly to the influences of traditional society. The unitary state calls for a remodeling of human nature so that there shall be no irritants to the body politic. According to Rousseau:

> He who possesses the courage to give a people institutions, must be ready to change human nature, to transform every individual, who by himself is a complete and separate whole, into a part of a greater whole from which this individual in

a certain sense receives his life and character; to change the constitution of man in order to strengthen it, and to substitute for the corporeal and independent existence which we all have received from nature a merely partial and moral existence. In short, he must take from man his native individual powers and equip him with others foreign to his nature, which he cannot understand or use without the assistance of others. The more completely these natural powers are annihilated and destroyed and the greater and more enduring are the ones acquired, the more secure and the more perfect is also the constitution.[19]

It is necessary to inculcate from infancy in the minds of the people the surpassing claim of the state to their loyalty. "If, for example," Rousseau writes, "the people were early accustomed to conceive their individuality only in its connection with the body of the state, and to be aware, of their own existence merely as parts of that of the state, they might in time come to identify themselves in some degree with the greater whole. . . ."[20] The family should not be granted the all important duty of education, for too great a responsibility hangs in the balance. The traditional educative function should be transferred from the family to the state, so that, as Rousseau states it, the "prejudices" of the father may not interfere with the development of citizens. However, the disintegration of this age-old basis of the family should in no wise create alarm. "Should the public authority, in assuming the place of father and charging itself with this important function, acquire his rights in the discharge of his duties, he should have little cause to protest; for he would only be altering his title, and would have in common, under the name citizen, the same authority over his children, that he was exercising separately under the name of father, and would be no less obeyed when speaking in the name of the law than when he spoke in that of nature."[21] Family-relationship is transmuted subtly into political relationship; the molecule of the family is broken into the atoms of its individuals, who are coalesced afresh into the single unity of the state.

Just as the religious bond is transformed into a spiritualized patriotism, the family tie is in effect disintegrated, and its members re-unified in the tissue of the state. Underlying this proposal to eradicate the social unity of the family is Rousseau's encompassing desire to replace the natural diversity of society with the mechanical equalitarianism of the state.

If the children are reared in common in the bosom of equality, if they are imbued with the laws of the state and the precepts of the General Will, if they are taught to respect these above all other things, if they are surrounded by examples and objects which perpetually remind them of the tender mother who nourishes them, of the love she bears them, of the inestimable benefits they receive from her, and of the return they owe her, we cannot doubt that they will learn to cherish one another mutually as brothers. . . .[22]

NOTES

1. *Contrat social*, Bk. 1, Ch. 6. Wherever possible I have followed G. D. H. Cole's notable translation in the Everyman edition of Rousseau's political writings.

2. *Contrat social*, ed. by Charles E. Vaughan (Manchester, 1918), Preface, p. xiv.

3. See especially the closing pages of the *Confessions*.

4. *Correspondance générale de J. J. Rousseau* (Paris, 1932), Vol. 17, p. 156.

5. *Contrat social*, Bk. 2, Ch. 12 (italics mine).

6. *Contrat social*, Bk. 1, Ch. 8. In the *Confessions*, Rousseau tells us he had come to see that political action was the only means of furthering morals.

7. *Contrat social*, Bk. 1, Ch. 6. See also Bk. 2, Ch. 4.

8. See the *Économie politique* where the analogy is developed in detail. (Everyman ed., p. 252.)

9. *Contrat social*, Bks. 1, 7 (italics mine).

10. *Contrat social*, Bk. 2, Ch. 2. Rousseau had only contempt for those who thought in terms of divided sovereignty.

11. *Contrat social*, Bk. 2, Ch. 3. Rousseau cites, with admiration, the "sublime system" of Lycurgus, and, in a footnote, quotes Machiavelli approvingly on the proscription of associations. That Rousseau tempers the severity of this decree by adding a brief sentence on a "second best" system does not mitigate the effect of his unitary preference.

12. *Loc. cit.*, pp. 253–4. Alfred Cobban in his *Rousseau and the Modern State* (London, 1934), has attempted to exculpate Rousseau, to some extent, on the ground that others in that age expressed the same sentiments, and that many of the gilds and religious societies deserved banishment. Mr. Cobban might also have mentioned that the development of the whole theory of sovereignty from the fifteenth century was based upon a limitation of the social group. Hobbes' comparison of associations to "worms in the entrails of natural man" illuminates the restrictive effect his *Leviathan* has upon the social group. But Rousseau's theory of sovereignty by its very nature is based upon the complete *dissolution* of the smaller loyalties.

13. See Sections I and II of the *Économie Politique*.

14. *Ibid.*

15. See the first draft of the *Contrat social* in the *Political Writings of J. J. Rousseau* (ed. by Charles E. Vaughan, Cambridge, 1915), Vol. 1, p. 499.

16. Rousseau singles out Hobbes for praise as the one who "has dared to propose the reunion of the two heads of the eagle . . . ; it is not so much what is false and terrible in his political theory as what is just and true that has drawn down hatred on it." (*Contrat social*, Bk. 4, Ch. 8.) As will shortly be made evident the absorption of religion by the state is a more drastic process in Rousseau than Hobbes.

17. Professor Vaughan has observed that the complaint of Rousseau against Christianity is that it is social to the excess. "It knocks down all the barriers which the state sets up and without which the state must fall in ruins: the bond it weaves is not between citizens but between men." See the "Notes" to the *Contrat social* (Manchester edition), p. 162.

18. Rousseau's treatment of the Civil Religion is to be found chiefly in the *Contrat social*, though there are highly relevant passages on the subject in the *Économie politique*.

19. *Contrat social*, Bk. 2, Ch. 7. The political psychology of totalitarianism is here revealed in terms whose clarity and forcefulness are not surpassed in any contemporary document.

20. *Économie politique, loc. cit.,* p. 268.

21. *Ibid.,* p. 269.

22. *Ibid.,* p. 269, a true believer in his doctrines, Rousseau delivered his own children to a foundling asylum, and in his *Confessions* tells us that when he did so he felt as if he were behaving as a citizen and considered himself a member of Plato's republic. In many respects Rousseau's political community deserves comparison with Plato's, and it is hardly surprising to learn from Rousseau that he considered Plato his strongest influence.

(2)

The Politics
of
Pluralism:
Lamennais

I

It has been the singular misfortune of Felicité Robert de Lamennais that much more attention has been paid to the beliefs that he came to abandon late in life than to those by which he himself would have chosen to be remembered by posterity. Much has been written by historians of his early political conservatism, his Catholic ultramontanism, and his theology of the common reason. His break with Rome has been the substance of a number of studies, as well it might have, given the high drama of that event.[1] Less attention has been paid, however, to his social philosophy, to the ideas on freedom, authority, association, and pluralism that emerged first in his single-minded defense of the Church in secular society and then widened to include trade union, cooperative, and other elements of the new society that was being formed in the first half of the nineteenth century. This disproportion of regard would

This article, in a slightly different version, originally appeared as "The Politics of Social Pluralism: Some Reflections on Lamennais," *Journal of Politics* (November 1948).

be more understandable if the ideas of the later period of his
life were lacking in either the brilliance or the influence
which marked his early works. But in clear fact they are
not. It is possible indeed to assert that in his social theory
lay a relevance, both to his own time and ours, that was
never true of his ecclesiastical lucubrations.

The thought of Lamennais is invariably treated in terms
of its ascent to and fall from the peak of Catholic ultramontanism in the nineteenth century. His break with the
Church is regarded as the occasion of a no less violent
break in his philosophy, and too often his fall from Catholic eminence is seen as a fall also from intellectual distinction. From the high point of his inspired Catholicism he is
said to have passed to socialism or "red democracy." But
these are labels of vagueness and can offer no insight into
the essential principles which dominated his life and influenced his contemporaries during the last quarter century
of his life.

The frequent neglect of the later, social, phase of Lamennais' life is the consequence of his brilliant early relationship with the Catholic Church and of his dramatic rise and
fall in ecclesiastical eminence. The story has been written
often enough, and only the highlights need to be retold
here. He was born in 1782, the son of a prosperous and
devout Breton family. The impact of the Revolution upon
the Church appears to have left a lasting impress on his
mind, and throughout his life he was to remain preoccupied by religious questions and by the problem of the relation of religion to secular society. In 1816 he was ordained
to the priesthood, and in the next year published the first
volume of his *Essai sur l'indifférence*. With it a notable
religious author had made his appearance. By 1824 when
the last volume appeared, Lamennais was regarded by
many as the foremost Catholic in Europe and the leader
of the Catholic ultramontane movement then struggling to
restore the Church to its medieval glory. No man stood
higher in the regard of Rome than Lamennais when, in
1824, he made his first pilgrimage to the Vatican to receive the assurances of Leo XII. His picture hung on the

wall of Leo's private sitting room, and he was even offered, so the report spread, membership in the Sacred College.

Yet, but eleven years hence, Lamennais had drawn upon his head two papal encyclicals and, soon after, exile from the Church. In 1834, like a thunderbolt, appeared his *Paroles d'un croyant*, one of the most devastating criticisms of organized government and religion ever written, a book which Gregory XVI, Leo's successor, described as "small in size but immense in perversity."[2] Lamennais' religious faith remained profound throughout the rest of his life, but he never re-joined the Church. On his death bed he refused to see representatives of the Church, resisting the entreaties of even those with whom he had remained on friendly terms, lest the significance of their visit be misunderstood by the public. The instructions of his will were: "I wish to be buried among the poor, and like the poor; nothing shall be placed on my grave, not even a simple stone; my body shall be carried direct to the cemetery, without being presented in a church previous to burial."[3] To the last was maintained separation from the Church in whose militant defense Lamennais had first risen to international renown.

It is an extraordinary development, with few parallels in the religious history of Europe, and there is little wonder in the fact that historians have been prone to subordinate Lamennais' philosophy to the dramatic phases of his ecclesiastical career. His life must remain one of the thrilling biographies of modern times, and none of his numerous biographers can be said to have exhausted its mystery and wonder. The eloquence of his writing competes reluctantly with the magnetism of his personal history, and it is tempting always to discuss his writings merely as a series of footnotes upon a public career. To do so however is to miss one of the most interesting and significant social philosophies in the nineteenth century.

II

The background of his social thought is the Revolution. The significance of Lamennais like the significance of such men as Tocqueville, Taine, and LePlay must be seen against the theory of power that the Enlightenment had given pen to and the Revolution had made effective. It would be difficult to find any other event in the modern history of Europe so productive of intellectual controversies, so fertile in philosophical problems, as the Revolution of 1789. It is hardly an exaggeration to say with Taine that for every problem solved by the Revolution ten new ones were created. From the vantage point of the present it is hard to find any significant issue of nineteenth century France— in politics, economics, sociology, even in literature and art —that was not strongly affected by one or more of the partisanships and animosities which grew out of the Revolution. The beginnings of social pluralism derive plainly from the issues that were raised by the impact of the Revolution on traditional society.

The legislators of the Revolution, in their devotion to the rights of the individual and the sovereignty of the rational state, did much to destroy or weaken the assemblage of groups that were identified with the hated feudal order. Family, church, guild, community, all suffered the impact of a revolution that was concerned with rationalizing the political order and emancipating the individual. Rousseau's earlier declaration that "it is our business to make every individual member absolutely independent of his fellow members and absolutely dependent on the state" came very close to being a guiding principle at the height of the Revolution.[4]

The roots of Revolutionary legislation are of course in the Enlightenment. Despite the emphasis upon "freedom" and "natural rights" in the writings of the Philosophers it is difficult to discern any clear conception of freedom against the state for either group or individual. Their attack was against not the idea of the State, but the intermediate network of associations that were the legacy of medievalism. When Rousseau wrote, "it is only by the force of the State that the liberty of its members can be secured" he was giving epigrammatic strength to a view that was prevalent among all the philosophers of the Enlightenment. For men like Voltaire, Holbach, Diderot, and even the Physiocrats, with their desire for a natural economic order, the prime necessity was a strong, centralized state tempered only by the enlightenment of its rulers. The real enemies of the rationalists were the frequently corrupt and inefficient authorities of religious and local society.[5]

The tremendous contribution of Rousseau to the theory of freedom was his insistence that freedom is not the *immunity* of the individual or group from political power but the *sharing* of that power. What matter if the state become omnipotent, providing only that the citizen shall be constitutionally a part of that omnipotence. Out of this seminal thought came not only the nineteenth century theory of equalitarian democracy, so closely allied to nationalism, but also the more recent theories of the mass state with its all-powerful executive resting on the passive acquiescence of the multitude. Out of it too came much of the practical legislation of the Revolution.

The Revolution marked the triumph of the political order over all social groups in France. The centralization and gradual politicalization of society which had begun in the sixteenth century reached its apogee under the Jacobins. The abolition of the guilds and the prohibition of new forms of economic association, the extinction of cultural localism, the depredations against the corporate Church, the weakening of the patriarchal family, all this was the work of the successive governments of the Revolution. With the advent of Napoleon these measures were given added strength by the extensive legal reforms in the direction of administrative centralization and by the concentration of all education in the machinery of the State. The effect of the Revolution, as Tocqueville and Taine were to see so clearly, was in no sense to limit the power of the state.

By its act of broadening the base of political power, the Revolution expanded the State's actual power to an extent undreamed of by any divine right monarchist.

It was the Church that had suffered most grievously the impact of the Revolution, and it is this body that forms the subject of Lamennais' earliest thinking. For him religion is no abstract body of dogma, set apart from the structure of society. Like Bonald, from whom he drew so much, he sees religion as the constituent principle of society. The dissolution of the corporate Church is symbolic of the destruction of society itself. In the rehabilitation of the Church lies the only possible means of a regeneration of society. But the first step must be an emancipation of the Church from the state, the restoration of ecclesiastical autonomy, and the reestablishment of religion as *society*. Thus Lamennais was drawn, as Bonald before him had been, to a concern with the problems of the relation of the religious association to the secular state. It was his continued reflection upon this problem that led him to expand his interest to include the problem of all associations in their relations with the state. And it was along this intellectual route that Lamennais passed from his early traditionalism to the social philosophy that characterized his later years.

In political centralization he found the source of most of the ills from which society was suffering. "Centralization," he wrote in a famous sentence, "breeds apoplexy at the center and anemia at the extremities." Almost from the beginning of his public career he waged war on "the fatal system of centralization, the deplorable and shameful offspring of imperial despotism" which he saw in the France of his day. He did not make the mistake of his fellow traditionalists in attributing political centralization to the Revolution alone. Long before Tocqueville's *L'Ancien régime et la révolution* appeared, with its scholarly demonstration of the monarchical roots of Revolutionary legislation, Lamennais pointed out the essential continuity of French political history from Louis XIV to Napoleon. In Gallicanism he found the beginnings of the political theory which reached its climax in the Revolutionary legislation on the Church and traditional society. As Michel points out, for Lamennais the guilt of Louis XIV is almost equal to that of the men of the Revolution. "The origin of Gallicanism," writes Lamennais, "goes back to the time when princes, having affranchised themselves from the authority of the Church, which imposed as a check upon their power the law of universal justice, no longer recognized any but their own pleasures and interests; and after knocking over the ancient barriers which protected the rights of each and the liberty of all, they transformed the Christian monarchy into despotism."[6]

If Lamennais' early preference was for monarchy, along with ultramontanism in religion and traditionalism in morals, it was not therefore because of any failure to understand the monarchical background of Revolutionary centralization. His early repudiation of republicanism was based chiefly upon his conviction that more extreme tendencies toward omnicompetence lie in popular government than in monarchy. The Revolution had been proof of this. Expand the base of political power, and you widen the limits of state intervention in social institutions. "Monarchie," Bonald had written in his *Theorie du pouvoir,* "considère l'homme dans ses rapports avec la société; la république considère l'homme sans rapport avec la société . . . despotisme est la démocratie dans la camp, comme la démocratie est le despotisme dans la cité."[7] Among all the Traditionalists there was the view, developed later in such detail by Taine in his *Origins of Contemporary France,* that democracy leads the more easily to despotism by its promotion of social equality and its desire to level the social barriers that interpose between the individual and the state. Lamennais shared this view, and even after his disillusionment with kings and popes led to an espousal of republican government he never lost his conviction that political power must be checked by non-political associations.[8]

The cause for which Lamennais fought was at bottom never the monarchy or papacy as such; it was the regeneration of *society.* If kings and popes become false to their

charge, as Lamennais understands it, then let them be discarded. His support of monarchy was based on prior
assumptions regarding society. His early crusade for ultramontanism and papal infallibility emerged from his conviction that because Rome was the last remaining symbol
of universalism in European society, its faith could be
independent of and even dominant over the various national
sovereignties that threatened society. Always he saw in the
Church no mere religious autarchy but the inspiration of a
social reformation for France and for all Europe that would
lead to freedom and justice. In the beginning he thought
the state to be his only enemy. It was the climax of his life
when he reached the conclusion that the monistic Church
is no more compatible with a free society than is the
monistic state.

III

Lamennais' opposition to the omnicompetent state must
not be confused with the ordinary laissez-faire doctrines
which had developed out of the eighteenth century's faith
in the individual and the natural order. Unlike such liberals as Guizot and Royer-Collard in France and Mill and
Spencer in England, Lamennais holds no brief for individualism. For him the Revolution had been calamitous
testimony to the fact that individualism, by its atomizing
effects upon traditional society, will lead inexorably to the
authoritarian state. It must be so. The individual draws
not only his sense of security, but also his desire for freedom from the social group. The Rights of Man as promulgated by the revolutionaries were the rights of abstract
individuals and could offer little protection against the
French government when it became authoritarian in the
later phases of the Revolution. It is not enough to begin
with the individual, for, apart from his membership in
society, man is weak and helpless. "The individual has only

an ephemeral, fugitive existence, the shadow of a dream."
All efforts to create for man a condition of individual
autonomy are foredoomed to tyranny. Individualism in
thought which Lamennais found exemplified in Cartesian-
ism and Protestantism is directly related to the individualism
of action which the Revolution so fatally embodied.

Like Tocqueville, Lamennais saw in the individualism
of his time an augury of social dissolution that must finally
leave the state alone as the sphere of order and association.
That which inclines men to live separately, and celebrates
man's independence rather than his interdependence, must
be seen as the foundation of the despot's easy access to
the masses. "Despotism," Tocqueville wrote, "which by its
nature is suspicious, sees in the separation among men the
surest guarantee of its continuance, and usually makes every
effort to keep them separate . . . Equality places men side
by side, unconnected by any common tie; despotism raises
barriers to keep them asunder; the former predisposes men
not to consider their fellow creatures, the latter makes
general indifference a sort of public virtue."[9] Nearly a decade before these words were published Lamennais wrote:
"From equality is born independence, and from independence, isolation. As each man is circumscribed, so to
speak, in his individual life, he no longer has more than
his individual strength for defending himself if he is at-
tacked; and no individual strength can offer a sufficient
guarantee of security against the abuses of that incomparably
greater force which is called sovereignty and from which
arises the necessity of a new liberty, the liberty of association."[10]

It is neither the individual nor the state that forms the
basis of Lamennais' philosophy of freedom. It is the intermediate association. Not natural man but social man is the
unit of society, and man is made social only by his membership in the smaller associations of family, church, community and guild. "If one wants to get a just idea of our
present condition, one must first understand that no government, no police, no order, would be possible if men were
not united beforehand by ties which already constitute them

in a state of society . . ."[11] The moment that the primacy
of society is denied is the moment that the individual is
left precariously exposed to the state. Destroy the multiplicity of society and you destroy the foundations of a free
political order. Bonald had rediscovered the importance of
the autonomous social group, but he made it only the basis
of a theory of order. Lamennais, like Tocqueville, made the
group the basis of liberal pluralism. Each saw that far
from there being irreconcilable hostility between individualism and statism there is in fact mutual dependence; and the
enemy of each is intermediate society.

The essence of the problem of freedom is thus put by
Lamennais into the realm of non-political association.
Whether under monarchy or republic "where there exist
only individuals there is no possible protection against
arbitrary authority without freedom of association."[12] The
ancien régime had afforded the individual some measure of
protection from political power by its hereditary nobility,
its communes, guilds and the Church. But the laws of the
Revolution, in the name of individual freedom, had weakened or destroyed these. Now, Lamennais writes, "there
exist in France only individuals. All the particular centers
of political influence founded on special rights and distinct
interest, all the hierarchies, all the corporations, have been
dissolved . . ."[13] This is an intolerable condition. For "it
is within human nature to draw together and to associate;
because it is a natural right, because one does nothing except by association, for weak, poor, and wretched is man as
long as he is alone."[14]

In 1830, Lamennais, together with such followers as Montalembert and Lacordaire founded the newspaper, L'Avenir,
in order to propagate his ideas. This journal is generally
recognized as the foundation of nineteenth century liberal
Catholicism, and it must be seen too as one of the main
sources of the pluralist movement in non-Catholic thought.
In an early issue Lamennais set forth the following as the
basic needs of France: (1) total separation of the Church
and state, that the Church might govern its own affairs; (2)
freedom of education and an end to the government's

monopoly of this important social function; (3) freedom
of each association to publish communications to its members; (4) freedom of all associations; (5) extension of suffrage; (6) decentralization of government.[15] The contrast
between Lamennais and the orthodox liberals of the nineteenth century is made striking by the omission here of any
reference to *individual* freedom. The emphasis is on association.

This emphasis never left Lamennais' writings. He was
among the first in France to see the profound importance
of free associations among workers as a protection against
both state and industry. In his *Le Livre de Peuple,* published in 1837, he wrote:

> You have to create in the material order a less precarious,
> a less difficult existence; to combat hunger, to see to it that
> your wives and children are assured the necessities which are
> lacking to none among all creatures, but only to man. Now
> why are you in need? Because others absorb the fruits of
> your labor and grow fat on it. Whence comes this wrong?
> From the fact that each one of you, deprived in his isola-
> tion of the means of establishing and maintaining a real
> concurrence between capital and labor, is delivered without
> protection to the avidity of those who exploit you. How
> will you get out of this fatal dependence? By uniting, by
> forming associations. And what one cannot do, ten can, and
> thousand can do still better.[16]

Despite his profound concern for the condition of the
working classes under industrialism, Lamennais had little
sympathy with the socialism of his time. He was repelled
by the socialist insistence upon collective ownership of property; in this he could see ominous possibilities of state
centralization and omnicompetence. "All questions of freedom reduce themselves in practice to questions of property,"
he was fond of saying, a statement which led some of
the Socialists to accuse Lamennais of deifying property.
"If by socialist," he wrote in 1848, "one means the doctrines of such men as Saint-Simon and Fourier . . . which
are based on the negation of property and the family, the

answer is no; I am not a socialist. But if by socialism one understands instead the principle of association . . . the answer is yes; I am a socialist."[17] It is his pluralistic envisagement of the problem of freedom and order that separates Lamennais as definitely from the orthodox socialists of his time as from the liberals.[18]

His defense of the principle of property was not rooted in any belief in the anteriority of property to human rights but in the conviction that in the right of private property lay the security of the family. For Lamennais the family is the most important group in society. This is not simply because of its procreative function but because it is the source of all the social values upon which social order rests. The family is society in small, and, like Comte, Lamennais can see in the family the only medium through which individual consciousness is enlarged into a truly social entity. It is in this association that the child gains his sense of the continuity of past generations and of the solidarity of the living. "The principle which constitutes the family by regulating the union of man and wife is a vital law of humanity. It is the entire order of duties and rights without which no society would endure."[19]

He cites bitterly the statement of Danton, made during the Revolution, that children belong to the state before they belong to their parents. Such a declaration, argues Lamennais, "signifies that one recognizes no other authority at all, that domestic society is a chimera or an abuse which should be reformed; that the sole object of the family is to furnish the state with the young whom it may rear as it pleases." Under Napoleon the family came to be conceived simply as the source of individuals "to replenish the vast ranks of his army," in short, as a mere instrument of the state. No external authority can rightfully "interfere under any pretext in the affairs of the family . . . without violating its natural indefeasible liberties." The authority of the family in its own realm must be supreme.[20]

It is centralization of any sort that Lamennais opposes. Not only must decentralization prevail between the state and such non-political groups as family, church and workers' association, but it must become the very principle of government itself. The proper political relation is not between the central government and the individual, but between government and the commune. "The commune is the state in small; we are more or less free or more or less enslaved by the state according as the commune is more or less enslaved, more or less free."[21] When the state takes upon itself the task of governing all details of a society and absorbs the traditional rights of the smaller units, it imposes a rationalistic uniformity upon the naturally differing customs and institutions that must, in the long run, remove all sources of a desire for freedom. The claims of freedom and order can meet harmoniously only in the pluralist society where the internal stability of each association is the measure of its freedom from the state. "Because each place has its own interests distinct from the general interest of the state, each locality, that is, each commune, each arrondissement, each province has the natural and imprescriptible right to administer its interests freely, just as the family has the right to administer its interests freely without the state interfering except to protect the rights of other families in the event they are violated."[22]

At the outbreak of the Revolution in 1848 Lamennais was elected to the Constituent Assembly. His election was the culmination of more than fifteen years devotion to the cause of social and political reform during which he had edited journals and written numerous articles, pamphlets and books. Once he had even been prosecuted by the government and suffered a year's imprisonment in St. Pelagie. Such was Lamennais' popularity in the Assembly that he was elected to membership on the *Commission de constitution*, receiving the third largest number of votes in a list that included such names as Tocqueville, Barrot, and Beaumont.[23]

During the meetings of the Constitutional Commission Lamennais, together with Tocqueville and Barrot, attempted to make the principle of decentralization uppermost in the new constitution of France and to reassert the rights of the commune. He had already, in the pages of his journal, *Le*

Peuple Constituant, drawn up the outline of a constitution, and he now presented its principles to the members of the commission. The projected constitution repeated the ideas of his earlier works, freedom of association, separation of Church and state, freedom of education, and autonomy of the commune; to these were now added proposals for the direct election of the President by the people, a graduated income tax, and universal male suffrage. He also set forth, in a separate work, a plan for the financial reorganization of France, one which was based upon a system of communal banks from which all credit would emanate for the undertakings of the people. In this plan too decentralization was the keynote.[24]

Despite his personal popularity, it cannot be said that Lamennais' ideas seriously affected the actual constitution that was adopted in 1848.[25] There was little enthusiasm either in the Commission or in the Assembly for any relaxation of administrative centralization. Lamennais' ideas were regarded as too radical and impractical. Moreover he possessed few of the temperamental endowments that make for success in the realm of practical politics. "By fanatics," Charles Kingsley wrote in his essay on Sir Walter Raleigh, "whether military, commercial, or religious, and not by 'liberal-minded' men at all has the world's work been done in all ages." Fanatic, Lamennais certainly was. The brilliance of his ideas won him followers from afar, but the intensity of his own faith in these ideas cost him the support of comrades. Loath to compromise, quick to take offense, bitter, restless, he had more of the zeal of the prophet than the organizational sense of the leader. The philosopher of association, he was himself the incarnation of the individualism that he condemned.

His relationship with Rome illustrates this perfectly. Few would deny the logic of his intellectual development from traditionalism to liberal pluralism. Yet one may justly marvel at the dramatic sequence of events which led to his separation from the Church. Even on the basis of the account written by Lamennais himself[26] it is difficult to avoid the conclusion that temperamental rather than ideological influences underlay the rift. As Edward Dowden has written, "Lamennais possessed sympathies too wide for his cause, and by them was carried into opposition to his party, his friends, and his former self." There is much irony in Gregory's condemnation of *L'Avenir* and in Lamennais' renunciation of the Church. For the ideas that were disseminated by *L'Avenir* were to become, through such men as Montalembert and Lacordaire, the principal elements of the social program that has characterized the Catholic Church down to the present. Viewed in light of its background there is much less originality than is commonly supposed in such a document as the *Rerum Novarum*, promulgated by Leo XIII in 1891. In its major arguments the encyclical is but a restatement of Lamennais' platform of 1830. Contemporary ideas of Catholic social reform owe much to the early nineteenth century efforts of Lamennais to "liberalize society and Catholicize liberalism."[27]

It would be folly however to explain the failure of pluralism at the meetings of the Constituent Assembly in 1848 by the temperamental limitations of one man or of any group of men. The disinclination of the Assembly to reorganize France along pluralist lines stemmed from a practical recognition of the realities of the time. The tactical advantages of the unitary state are manifest in the struggle for power, both within and without national borders. Even Tocqueville could write: "I do not deny that a centralized social power may be able to execute great undertakings with facility in a given time and on a particular point." In a world increasingly haunted by the threat of war and personal insecurity, the state looms up as the hope not only of the conservative nationalist but also of the nationalistic radical. The major forces of social action have chosen the state as the area of reconstitution and political sovereignty as the instrument. By comparison the claims of pluralism have remained weak. As Magid has written, "Pluralism is not a satisfactory fighting philosophy for those whose aim is to make society over all at once and on a grand scale. By its very nature, pluralism does not point to any all-embracing end that can be used to rally the people . . .

Although a pluralistic analysis of society may be closer to the facts of political life, it is much farther from the principles of mass manipulation than is monism."[28]

The tactical disadvantages of pluralism however need not blind us to the true nature of the problem of freedom. "All liberty," wrote Lord Acton, "consists *in radice* in the preservation of an inner sphere exempt from state power." The contemporary liberal may boggle at this, but the proposition is irrefutable. Freedom does not emerge from the state, nor from any of its agencies. Freedom is not the consequence of any biological instinct. Freedom emanates from the autonomous social unities that are "exempt from state power." Destroy or weaken these unities and the desire for freedom must wither in the individual. The way to the total state is made easy when the non-political loyalties of church, trade union, family and community are allowed to become weak. Out of the destruction of society, in all its specific manifestations, comes the incoherent and distracted mass whose anonymous particles gain cohesion in Leviathan.

Pluralism, as Lamennais saw vividly, is both fact and ideal. The distinction between the two is crucial. Not a little of the theoretical difficulty of recent doctrines of pluralism in politics has been the result of a failure to keep this distinction in mind. Moreover, pluralists have attempted to prove too much and have become lost in the subtleties of reasoning about sovereignty. With their demonstration of the associational nature of the state and their proof of the unreality of the Austinian sovereign, they have thought their work complete. But to argue from the diversity of society and the metaphysical unreality of sovereignty to the point of denying the actual power of the modern state, democratic or otherwise, is a piece of reasoning that is likely to land the reasoner in a totalitarian order, the while denying the reality of sovereignty.

Historically, the distinction between society and the state has been real, and this is indeed the basis of the pluralist's position. But the distinction has become increasingly tenuous in the modern world, and it is not likely to be maintained at all by mere semantic depreciations of the state, by adjurations against its worship, or by learned arguments proving that since the precise locus of sovereignty cannot be established, sovereignty is therefore a chimera. Whatever else we give heed to in the modern world, we must start from the fact of the state in all its power. A genuine philosophy of freedom is inseparable from some kind of pluralism; it is inseparable from a distinction between state and society. If the distinction between society and state is to remain the basis of freedom, and, if present tendencies toward the depletion of social power and the maximization of political power are to be counteracted, there must be a more exact knowledge of the specific social relationships which compose society, their connection with individual personality, with the industrial economy, and with the state itself.

NOTES

1. The best full study of Lamennais is by F. Duine, *La Mennais* (Paris, 1922). See also Duine's valuable *Essai de bibliographie de Felicité Robert de La Mennais* (Paris, 1923). Harold Laski's study of the political implications of Lamennais' theology, Chapter 3 of Laski's *Authority in the Modern State* (New Haven: Yale University Press, 1919) remains the best appreciation in English of Lamennais as social thinker. See also Waldemar Gurian, "Lamennais," *Review of Politics* (April 1947).

2. For an account of the sensational impact of this book on the European public see F. Duine, *La Mennais* (Paris, 1922), pp. 192 ff.

3. Duine, *op. cit.*, pp. 344 ff. He died in 1854 in Paris.

4. *Contrat social*, Bk. 2, Ch. 12.

5. On this aspect of the Enlightenment see Henry Michel, *L'idée de l'etat* (Paris, 1896), p. 17. Also J. Paul-Boncour, *Le Fédéralisme économique* (Paris, 1901).

6. *Oeuvres complètes de F. de La Mennais* (Brussels, 1839), Vol. 2, p. 250.

7. Bonald, *Oeuvres complètes* (Paris, 1859–64), Vol. 1, p. 358 and Vol. 2, p. 357. It was of course Burke who first developed this insight. His *Reflections on the Revolution in France* was read widely among French conservatives. What the Traditionalists in France added to Burke's insight was a clear distinction between state and society.

8. Freedom, for Lamennais, is not something intrinsically identified with any form of government. It is a result of the relationship *between society* and *government,* irrespective of the form of the latter. Lord Acton's words are pertinent here. "The modern theory, which has swept away every authority except that of the State, and has made the sovereign power irresistible by multiplying those who share it, is the enemy of that common freedom in which religious freedom is included. It condemns, as a state within the State, every inner group and community, class or corporation, administering its own affairs." *History of Freedom* (London, 1919), p. 151.

9. *Democracy in America,* Vol. 2, p. 102. Elsewhere Tocqueville expresses his fear of "that cool reflection that induces each citizen to become isolated from the mass and to draw himself aside, that individualism which begins by drying up the fountain of public virtues, then goes on ultimately to dry up all others and to become absorbed into sheer egoism."

10. *Oeuvres,* Vol. 2, p. 440. These words first appeared in Lamennais' journal *L'Avenir* in January 1831. It will be remembered that Tocqueville too saw in free associations the surest guarantee of liberty.

11. *Ibid.,* Vol. 2, p. 241.

12. *Ibid.,* Vol. 2, p. 415. "Without freedom of association no democracy could survive for two days; it would transform itself immediately into despotism" (p. 440). On this point Tocqueville later wrote: "There are no countries in which associations are more needed to prevent the despotism of faction or the arbitrary power of a prince than those which are democratically constituted." *Democracy in America,* Vol. 1, p. 195. See also the words of Lord Acton, *Letters of Lord Acton to Mary Gladstone* (London, 1908), p. 124: "Liberty depends on the division of power. Democracy tends to unity of power. To keep asunder the agents, one must divide the sources; that is, one must maintain, or create, separate administrative bodies."

13. *Oeuvres,* Vol. 2, p. 414.

14. *Ibid.,* Vol. 2, p. 430. Not until 1848 was there any relaxation of the laws against autonomous associations. See

Duguit, *Traité de droit constitutionnel* (Paris, 1921–5), Vol. 5, p. 198.

15. *Oeuvres*, Vol. 2, pp. 29–30.

16. *Ibid.*, Vol. 2, p. 650. In his *Du passé et de l'avenir du peuple* (1941) he wrote: "Now who says association says liberty, liberty of each with regard to the others, liberty of all with regard to the public power. Is there association between the ox and the one who harnesses him to the plow? And what difference whether the one who does the harnessing is called Peter or is called the State? No free association is possible unless there is a moral tie . . ."

17. J. Poisson, *Le Romantisme social de Lamennais* (Paris, 1932), p. 303. See also Lamennais' *De l'Absolutisme et de la liberté* (Brussels, 1836). Despite his criticisms of Fourier the latter's emphasis upon *association* frequently suggests comparison with Lamennais.

18. Between Proudhon and Lamennais there is perhaps the closest affinity. Each favored decentralization, free association and a strong family system. Each was relentlessly hostile to all schemes of centralized collectivism.

19. One of the most important contributions of the nineteenth century to social theory was its revival of interest in the family. The whole sociological tradition in France, from Bonald to Durkheim rests upon its recognition of the social and psychological influences of the primary groups. On this see the valuable study by Jeanne Duprat, "La famille et la société dans la sociologie française," *Zeitschrift für Sozialforschung*, Vol. 2 (1933).

20. See *Du passé et l'avenir du peuples*, Ch. 15. Also *Oeuvres*, Vol. 2, pp. 269 and 461. Throughout his works are scattered discussions of the family.

21. *Politique à l'usage du peuple* (1839), p. 37.

22. *Oeuvres*, Vol. 2, p. 440. "No man ever was attached by a sense of pride, partiality, or real affection, to a description of square measurement . . . We begin our public affections in our families. No cold relation is a zealous citizen. We pass on to our neighbourhoods, and our habitual provincial connexions. These are inns and resting-places." Burke, *Reflections on the Revolution in France* (Everyman), p. 193.

23. Duine, *op. cit.*, p. 283. For an account of the meetings of the Commission see De la Gorce, *Histoire de la seconde république française* (Paris, 1904), Vol. 1, pp. 432 ff.

24. *Projet de Constitution de Credit Social* (Paris, 1848).

25. On the 11th of July, 1848 his journal, *Le Peuple Constituant,* appeared with a black border, and the words, "Le Peuple Constituant a commencée avec la république, il finit avec la république."

26. "Affaires de Rome," *Oeuvres,* Vol. 2, pp. 515–566.

27. On this see Parker T. Moon, *The Labor Problem and the Social Catholic Movement in France* (New York, 1921), pp. 31–32 and 159 ff.

28. Henry M. Magid, *English Political Pluralism* (New York, 1941), pp. 63–64.

[3]

Leadership
and
Social
Crisis

Moral crises in civilization are less often the consequence of right against wrong or truth against error than they are of right against right and truth against truth. The present crisis of freedom and order in Western society—and all that is implied in the problem of leadership—would be easier to resolve were it plainly the outcome of antagonistic forces of good and evil. But who can doubt that the present premonitions of disaster and the whole tragic sense of life so evident in modern literature arise from a cultural condition in which we see the things we value destroyed or weakened by elements we also value. Thus on the one hand we prize equalitarian democracy, individualism, secularism, science, and the liberating impersonalities of modern industrial life. On the other hand, however, we continue to venerate tradition, the corporate moralities of family, church, and community,

This article, in a slightly different version, originally appeared in *Studies in Leadership*, Alvin Gouldner, ed. (New York: Harper & Row, 1950).

close personal involvement in clear moral contexts, and secure social status. Conflicts between these values in the
modern Western world symbolize our deepest social conflicts and make difficult the perspective of leadership.

To regard all evil as a persistence of the past has been
until recently a favorite conceit of the progress-nurtured
liberal. But the contemporary intellectual, without wholly
losing his faith in the future and his distrust of the past, is
nevertheless coming to see a more and more enigmatic
shape to those elements of the present that point most
clearly to the future.

In the literature of moral revaluation that has spread so
widely in recent years one theme stands above all others: the
glaring discrepancy between morality and power. It is this
which has disillusioned and alienated a generation of thinkers
from cherished ideas of economic and political reform. If
there is one inference to be drawn from this literature, it is
that *moral purpose has been sacrificed to technical excellence
and power.* Heretofore valued norms of human uplift have
become tragically irrelevant to the social and psychological
demands of the time. A more subtle inference might be the
perception of widespread failure to bridge the gulf between
moral ends and institutional realities by intermediate norms
and procedures based upon knowledge.

What is the social vision that gives meaning to the
varied processes of contemporary society? Is it democracy
that we in the West would sight as our guiding star? Russia,
much like Hitler's Germany, stridently reiterates its popular and democratic foundations. Each nation has been able
to document its reiterations by reference to many of the
same revolutionary forces in nineteenth-century Europe that
we in the West continue to celebrate. Is it the Common
Man? There is no country in the modern world that does
not defend its most despotic invasions of liberty or security
by an appeal to the sanctity of the common man. Is it
Reason? Only the naïve persist in treating either the Communist or Fascist Leviathan, with their far-flung and
"progressive" schemes of scientific management, as mere
irruptions of the irrational. Immoral, if we like, but not

irrational. Nor would we dare claim, in painful memory of the superb assurance with which the Russian, the German, and the Japanese fought in the recent war, that spiritual faith alone is the touchstone of the cultural salvation that each of us continues to hope for.

Few moderns would reject any of these values—democracy, reason, faith, the individual—for they are clearly the heritage of all that is most distinctive and noble in the Western heritage. Yet few would deny that in each of them there is something for modern man that is elusive and curiously irrelevant. As symbols none of them seems to stand in clear relation to the actual problems of the culture we find ourselves in. It is not that either democracy or rationalism is obsolete. *It is rather that the embedded meanings of each lack that sharp relevance to immediate circumstances that is the condition of effective symbolism.* And the problem of symbolism is indeed at the very heart of the problem of leadership in the modern state.

> *Now when we examine how a society bends its individual members to function in conformity with its needs, we discover that one important operative agency is our vast system of inherited symbolism. There is an intricate expressed symbolism of language and of act, which is spread throughout the community, and which evokes fluctuating apprehension of the basis of common purposes. The particular direction of individual action is directly correlated to the particular sharply defined symbols presented to him at the moment.*[1]

But in our own time, as many observers have pointed out, more and more of this "vast system of inherited symbolism" has become dim to the vision and weak to the touch. Inherited symbolism does not now afford so secure a foothold to reason, nor to leadership. Two centuries of individualism in ethics, religion, economics, and politics have acted to weaken the symbolism upon which both reason and leadership have traditionally relied. In short, we are dealing with a difficulty that is social in the broadest sense.

Contemporary interest in the problem of leadership is closely related to inquiries into the nature of the social bond, to studies of group identification, social role, and other problems of interpersonal relations. All of these are, to a significant degree, theoretical reflections of the basic moral preoccupation in our age with the adjustment of the individual to a complex political and economic order. Future historians of Western society are not likely to miss in their intellectual inquiries the present compelling importance of the problem of insecurity. "The most obvious symptom of the spiritual disease of our civilization," an English scholar has written recently, "is the widespread feeling among men that they have lost all control of their destinies. . . . It is not new for men to be cogs in the machine; it is new for them to be frustrated by the fact."[2]

Not a few of the contemporary mass movements in politics are directed to the people for whom society has become cold and unapproachable, to the disinherited and the disenchanted. Those who professed wonder that the crude and fantastic doctrines of Hitler could have enlisted the intellectual support of millions of otherwise intelligent human beings missed, in the phenomenon, the deep urge of Germans to become morally identified, to escape from a world in which economic mechanism and caprice combined to create feelings of frustration and insecurity. If moral security came with conversion to Nazism, the convert could agree perversely with Tertullian that intellectual absurdity might be the crowning appearance of truth.

In his classic account of the religion of ancient Greece, Sir Gilbert Murray has described the period following the Peloponnesian Wars as one "based on the consciousness of manifold failure, and consequently touched both with morbidity and with that spiritual exaltation which is so often the companion of morbidity. . . . This sense of failure, this progressive loss of hope in the world, threw the later Greek back upon his own soul, upon the pursuit of personal holiness, upon emotions, mysteries and revelations, upon the comparative neglect of this transitory and imperfect world for the sake of some dream world far off, which shall subsist without sin or corruption, the same yesterday, today, and forever."[3]

Murray uses the phrase "failure of nerve" to describe the collapse of the moral ties which had bound the individual to others and given him a warming sense of direction of his own destiny. A collapse which left the external world as something hostile, cold, and fortuitous. The failure of nerve in declining Athens was an intellectual transformation, but it accompanied the steady disintegration of the cementing bonds of the old community. The ties of family, community, and religion, the ancient conveyors of Athenian values, had grown weak under the incessant impact of war and economic tensions. Increasingly the outer world of society took on a harsh and formidable appearance; a world at best to tolerate, not to participate in. Out of social disintegration emerged the undifferentiated, atomized masses. Out of it, too, came the solitary, inward-turning ego.

In the present age, as many writers bear witness, signs abound that point to the spreading incidence of analogous conditions. It is not necessary to succumb to fatalism or sterile determinism to perceive that we, too, face a society, especially in Europe, composed in ever-increasing numbers of amorphous and incoherent masses of people who have seen spiritual meanings vanish with the forms of traditional society and who struggle vainly to find reassimilation. This is an age of the omnicompetent state and of economic interdependence, but it is also an age of bewildered masses and of solitary, obsessed individuals.

Anxiety, a contemporary novelist has written, is the natural state of twentieth-century man. At the very least, anxiety and frustration have become the natural state of the contemporary novel, and of much poetry and drama as well. The hero in the contemporary novel, it has been said, is not the man who does things, but the man to whom things are done. The morbid, normless being, twisted into passive neuroticism by the conflicting compulsions of an incomprehensible world, bids fair to become the reigning literary type of the age—a kind of inverted Tom Jones. In much contemporary fiction there is vagueness and indecisiveness of intent, accompanied by a belief that the exterior world is a vast scene of purposeless and inexplicable forces. The notion of the impersonality of society is a pervasive one; a society in which all actions and motives seem to have equal value and to be perversely detached from human direction. Widespread, too, is the vision of irresistible fate, before which the mind and spirit of the individual are helpless. Nor can one miss the ethical implications of those literary works in which the most intense individual spirituality is set in conditions of rotting social circumstances. The ancient quest for spiritual ecstasy through mortification of the flesh has been transposed, it would seem, into the same quest but through mortification of circumstances.

It would be difficult to exaggerate the importance in contemporary writing of the problem of the individual in his relation to the social and moral world. The spectacle of the individual caught treacherously in a world of shifting norms is not merely a widespread theme in literature; it has become a basic theoretical problem of the humanities and the social sciences. The "lost individual," to use Dewey's phrase, is a creature of as much concern to the politics of a Lasswell, the anthropology of a Mead, and the psychology of a Horney, as to the theology of a Niebuhr or Demant.

The problem of the individual and his relation to society is an old one. Quite apart from the concern with the problem in the ancient and medieval worlds, it has been a continuous theme of the social sciences since the seventeenth century. Present concern with the bases of order is not wholly new. But it is important to observe some of the differences between present and earlier inquiries. From the seventeenth through the nineteenth centuries the dominant perspectives of order were essentially *political* and *economic*. The rise of the theory of secular sovereignty in the sixteenth century became the major response to the problem of stability and, indeed, has remained the most influential. From Bodin to Rousseau the chief objective of political theory was the reconciliation of man and the secular state. The rise of formal economics at the end of the eighteenth century did not significantly change this objective. The origins of political economy rested on the assumption of self-sufficient individuals bound together by the impersonal ties of a mechanical system. The main effort of economists went toward the ascertainment of the theoretical conditions under which a state based upon aggregates of free and discrete individuals could achieve economic stability.

But now it is the *social problem* that has come to the fore. What was in the first instance an exclusive interest of sociology has become a more and more influential and characteristic aspect of all the social sciences. The very shift in terminology is instructive. Concepts of sovereignty, contract, equilibrium, and instinct, to be sure, have not disappeared. But increasingly they are rivaled in theoretical interest and empirical inquiry by such terms as *status, identification, group, anomie, interpersonal relations, security, role,* and *leadership,* terms which reflect vividly the transfer of attention to an area of association that heretofore has been indifferently regarded if not neglected altogether. It is not necessary to describe in detail the separate lines of investigation associated with the names of such contemporary students as Mayo, Bakke, Lasswell, Fromm, Murphy, Warner, Moreno, Parsons, Merton, and many others in the front ranks of social science, to bring pointedly to attention the fact that in all of the social sciences at the present time *there is a gathering momentum in the whole study of social cohesion,* interpersonal relations, call it what we will. Where the solid fact of the individual was the basis of analysis and the unit upon which systems of theory were based a generation ago, it is now the primary *relationships* among men that are becoming central. They provide the guiding perspective of studies of industry, community, race, and nation. In these relationships is found the clue not only to cultural stability but to the stability of the individual himself. The "individual" has become for both conceptual and therapeutic purposes a kind of unity of social memberships and intensities of participation.

The scientific nature of many of these inquiries into the conditions of association and dissociation, and the relation of the individual to the group, is apparent. On all sides, particularly in sociology, applied anthropology, and social psychology, the basic elements of the associative process have become subjected to experimental and comparative studies. Controlled studies of the intensities of social relationships, the processes of leadership, depictions of social position in factory and community, measurements of tensions within and among groups—all of these are to be regarded as among the most hopeful signs on the horizon for the revitalization of human relations—in industry and community.

But there is a quickly reached limit to both the theoretical value and the practical utility of studies in human relations that lose sight of the historically given institutional realities of our time. Thus, an experimentally controlled study of the effects of varying kinds of leadership upon groups of children, or a study of associational spontaneity in an isolated workroom in a factory, has, in each case, a true value that can be perceived only when these contrived situations are interpreted in the light of their larger surroundings and in light of the historical position of these surroundings. In their efforts to uncover "natural" social relationships certain contemporary students are likely to wander into the same blind alley that the classical economists were led into —a blind alley that can be described most tersely as doctrinaire universalism.

To deal with problems of social structure and personal identification, however scientifically, without recognition of their historical background, without regard for their institutional setting, is at once to underestimate the complexity of these problems and to make almost impossible any practical utilization of the answers. It is not possible to regard problems in social relations in the same perspective in which the physicist or chemist regards his problems. Concepts such as function, structure, identification, dissociation, and leadership have theoretical and practical relevance only when their referents are regarded as the outcome of historical processes. Not that the narrative method of the academic historian points the way here. What is important is to see the present as a *historical* stratification of elements, some new, some old, all in varying patterns of interaction.

Now all of this is related closely to the problem of leadership. For the interest in leadership, so pronounced at the present time, is a manifestation of the same intellectual pattern that contains the interest in problems of association and dissociation. And beneath this total pattern of ideas lie the psychologically and morally baffling institutional circumstances in which more and more individuals find themselves in contemporary society. These circumstances are in a real sense the very materials of the practical problem of leadership. It is important to remind ourselves continuously that leadership is inseparable from specific, environing conditions.

What Livingston Lowes has written on the creative process is relevant in a consideration of the relation between leadership and the materials of leadership:

> "Creation" like "creative" is one of those hypnotic words which are prone to cast a spell upon the understanding and dissolve our thinking into haze. And out of this nebulous state of the intellect springs a strange but widely prevalent idea. The shaping spirit of Imagination sits aloof, like God, as He is commonly conceived, creating in some thaumaturgic fashion out of nothing its visionary world. . . . [But] we live, every one of us—the mutest and most inglorious with the rest—at the center of a world of images. . . . Intensified and sublimated and controlled though they be, the ways of the creative faculty are the universal ways of that streaming yet consciously directed something which we know (or think we know) as life. Creative genius, in plainer terms, works through processes which are common to our kind, but these processes are superlatively enhanced.[4]

In leadership there is something of the same combination of imagination and experience that goes into the creative process; Leadership indeed is one manifestation of the creative proclivity. To draw organization out of the raw materials of life is as much the objective of the leader as it is of the artist. *Structure or organization is the primary concern of the leader, as form is the concern of the artist.* Leadership is no more comprehensible than any other type of imaginative creation except in terms of the materials.

> Every great imaginative conception is a vortex into which everything under the sun may be swept. . . . For the imagination never operates in a vacuum. Its stuff is always fact of some order, somehow experienced; its product is that fact transmuted. . . . I am not forgetting that facts may swamp imagination, and remain unassimilated and untransformed.[5]

Whether we consider the leader as planner, policy maker, ideologist, or as exemplar, we are dealing essentially with an imaginative conception, a vortex, into which the materials of the environing culture are swept, assimilated, and expressed. And even as the creative urge in literature, art, drama, and religion expresses itself selectively, so to speak, in history, taking note now of one theme, now of another, forming thus distinguishable ages or periods, even so does leadership. For there are configurations of leadership, from age to age, even as there are historic configurations in the arts and sciences. It is difficult not to believe that leadership presents itself, as do poetry and painting, in historical types, each given form and illumination by some distinctive theme.

Now the theoretical problem of leadership in contemporary democracy must be seen in light of the conditions which have produced the widespread scientific interest in problems of social structure and function, identification, role, and status. All of these problems are intellectualizations of a social crisis created by certain changes in the relation of individuals to institutions. From these changes has come the obsessive problem of insecurity. And, more than anything else, it is insecurity that gives the unique color to leadership in our time.

The modern release of the individual from the traditional ties of religion, class, family, and community has made him free—free at least in the negative sense of disenchantment with, and aloofness from, the old moral certainties. But for many individuals this emancipation from the traditional fetters of custom and prejudice has resulted not in a creative sense of independence but in a stultifying feeling of aloneness and irresponsibility. For generations after the dissolution of the legal bonds of medievalism the social ties remained to bind individuals. But the same forces which led to the breaking of the legal bonds began to dissolve the psychological bonds and to smash the sense of lateral and vertical interdependence.

Our social crisis is essentially a crisis within the same order of social relationships that is undergoing disintegration in the civilizations peripheral to the West, societies indeed that have received the full impact of Western civilization. Even as the ancient loyalties and allegiances—to caste, family, village community—are weakening in such areas as India, China, and Burma, thus creating in almost painful intensity the problem of leadership, so have the analogous loyalties become weak in our own society. Basically, ours is also a crisis in transferred allegiances. In any society the concrete loyalties and devotions of individuals—and their typical personality structures—will tend to become oriented toward those institutions which in the long run have the greatest perceptible significance to the maintenance of life. In earlier times, the family, church, class, and local community drew and held the allegiances of men, not because of any indwelling instinct to associate, not because of greater impulses to love and befriend, but because these were the chief security-providing and authority-giving agencies in the personal lives of individuals.

Leadership—actual leadership—was so subtly and so delicately interwoven into the fabric of kinship, guild, class, and church that the conscious problem of leadership hardly existed. So far as the bulk of people were concerned leadership came not from distant political rulers but from the innumerable heads of families, villages, guilds, and parishes. Between the individual and the highest ruler in the land there lay a continuous hierarchy of intermediate orders and intermediate leaders. There was indeed a kind of chain of leadership in society even as in philosophic imagination there was a "great chain of Being" that connected the lowest inorganic substance to God.

Contemporary interest in leadership in mass society, like the related interest in social cohesion, has been *precipitated* by the growing irrelevance of traditional centers of association and authority. As modern events make plain, the older primary centers of association have been superseded in institutional importance by the great impersonal connections of property, function, and exchange in modern society. *These connections have had a liberating influence upon the individual.* Through them he has been able, not only in Europe but also in parts of India, China, and Latin America, to shake off the restraints of patriarchal and hierarchical servitude. But the impersonal relations have had an isolating influence, for they are in no broad sense social relationships. As Park has written:

> Everywhere in the Great Society the relations of man, which were intimate and personal, have been more or less superseded by relations that are impersonal and formal. The result is that in the modern world, in contrast with earlier and simpler societies, every aspect of life seems mechanized and rationalized. This is particularly true in our modern cities, which are in consequence so largely inhabited by lonely men and women.[6]

The moral and social isolation, the increasing individual insecurities, the rash of tensions that characterize so many areas of modern life, should not be dismissed as merely urban phenomena. For, as recent studies have shown, the old stereotype of the rural area must be discarded and replaced, in the United States at least, by a picture which contains in an increasing number of localities these same phenomena. When agriculture becomes dominated by the principles of organization that have characterized industrialism, the social consequences are the same.[7]

The point that is crucial here is that the basic decisions in modern mass society have become vested increasingly in organizations and relationships that operate with technical and essentially nonsocial procedures. Vital activities have thus been removed from the competence of the older traditional areas of practical decision-making. In consequence, their sheer institutional importance has waned. Their growing economic and administrative irrelevance has been the basis of their decline in symbolic importance, a fact of the utmost significance to the social basis of leadership in modern society.

Thus in industry, as A. D. Lindsay has written,

> the tendency is to specialize planning and organization in a few hands and to ask unskilled repetition work of the great mass of work-people. . . . The factory manager is primarily a technician. He has to contrive an organization of human effort which in conjunction with the operation of machinery will produce the most efficient results. He does not treat his factory as a real society, but as a collection of forces or powers. He is not a leader and does not consider the problem of leadership. A leader has power because he is trusted and believed in; no man can lead or govern without somehow winning the confidence of those whom he leads. Business management is a much more impersonal business. . . . The odd result is that 'the management'—whether employers or managing directors—do not lead the men they control. They have enormous power over men's lives but they are not their leaders. The men choose their own leaders to defend them against management.[8]

But even in trade unions, those at least which have also become large-scale organizations, the problem of social cohesion and leadership is a pressing one. For the forces of impersonality and rationalization have entered here also, even as they have entered into many of the larger political, charitable, and educational organizations in the contemporary world. Nor have these forces been absent in religion, especially Protestantism. There is in consequence a disinclination among many Protestants to stand now, as did their forefathers, on the primacy of individual faith to organization, of conscience to institutional membership. The widening implications of the problem of the lost individual in modern society have not been lost on those for whom the answer is to be found within Christianity. There is growing awareness that ecclesiastical leadership, if it is to be decisive, must be rooted in social structure, not merely in faith.

Much has been written about the gigantic Manhattan Project during the second World War, the extraordinary and unprecedented spectacle of tens of thousands of individuals working for several years upon a product the nature of which few of them knew or were permitted to discover, and who were forbidden even to look too closely into the identities of their fellow workers. Such an organization is manifestly extreme, but in retrospect the Manhattan Project may with some justice be viewed as a kind of extension of the scene in which more and more workers find themselves in modern industry. The impersonalism and mechanization of relationships in many areas of industry and government, the frustrations that come from noninvolvement in even minor decision-making, and the consequent feelings of anonymity, cannot help but react disastrously upon the almost universal desires of men for status and for intelligible leadership.

The impersonalization of social relationships in modern Western society can be seen also in the rise of formal public and private administration. We are most indebted to Max Weber for perceiving the historical importance of bureaucracy. Weber saw in the development of bureaucracy the same exclusion of qualitative social differences and the same reduction of cultural diversity to mechanical uniformity that distinguished philosophical rationalism of the seventeenth and eighteenth centuries:

> It is decisive for the specific nature of modern loyalty to an office that in the pure type it does not establish a relationship to a person, like the vassal's or the disciple's faith in feudal or in patrimonial relations of authority. Modern loyalty is devoted to impersonal and functional purposes. . . . The fully developed bureaucratic mechanism compares with

other organizations exactly as does the machine with the nonmechanical modes of production.

In bureaucracy, as Weber saw, there is created a kind of abstract regularity of authority which is at once the fulfillment of equalitarianism and of impersonality. "Its specific nature, which is welcomed by capitalism, develops the more perfectly the more bureaucracy is 'dehumanized,' the more completely it succeeds in eliminating from official business love, hatred, and all purely personal, irrational, and emotional elements which escape calculation."9

It is obvious that an extraordinary number of activities which in earlier times were the functions of smaller unities and their leaderships have undergone a transforming rationalization of procedure. There has been a transfer of responsibilities and custodianships from the vast plurality of primary, close relationships to a diminishing number of great, bureaucratically administered agencies which operate with a maximum of technical efficiency. The administration of such functions as charity, hospitalization, unemployment assistance is manifestly more dependable, more regular, and more pervasive when so organized. *But the gains in technical efficiency and diffusion of service do not offset the resulting problems of identification and security among individuals.*

At bottom, social organization is a pattern of basic identifications in which feelings of reciprocity and intimacy are interwoven. Only thus does the individual have a sense of status. Only thus is communication established which makes effective leadership possible. But if social stability is rooted in personal identification and in groups and associations small enough to provide a sense of participation, then, plainly, there is a serious problem presented by the vast increase of forces of impersonality and anonymity; especially when in these forces there are lodged the basic economic and political decisions affecting the individual's existence.

It is a problem in security, but it is also a problem in the perspective of freedom. For there is evidence that people tend "to react favorably to authoritarian leadership when they are emotionally insecure or when they find themselves in an ambiguous and critical social position."[10] Leadership then becomes invested with a sacred significance that offers surcease from the frustrations and anxieties of society. Studies of the National Socialist movement in Germany suggest strongly that the greatest appeal of Hitler lay in those areas or spheres of society in which feelings of moral isolation and social anonymity were strong.[11] As Drucker has written:

> The despair of the masses is the key to the understanding of fascism. No "revolt of the mob," no "triumphs of unscrupulous propaganda," but stark despair caused by the breakdown of the old order and the absence of a new one. . . . Society ceases to be a community of individuals bound together by a common purpose, and becomes a chaotic hubbub of purposeless isolated nomads. . . . The average individual cannot bear the utter atomization, the unreality and senselessness, the destruction of all order, of all society, of all rational individual existence through blind, incalculable, senseless forces created as result of rationalization and mechanization. To banish these new demons has become the paramount objective of European society.[12]

The leadership of Hitler was no simple revival of ancient forms of force, nor was it based upon any of the traditional ritualizations of remote mastery or domination. Kolnai has told us that the word *Führer* has the meaning, among others, of "guide":

> The intimacy implied in modern "Fuhrertum" corresponds to the idea that the Leader is—in a particular sense—congenial to the People, linked to it by special bonds of affinity. . . . In an address delivered by Hitler at the Nürnberg Party Congress in 1934, we find the definition: "Our leadership does not consider the people as a mere object of its activity; it lives in the people, feels with the people, and fights for the sake of the people!" . . . It is even suggested, much in the spirit of Schmitt, that the Führer system guarantees the only real "democracy," for it alone secures an effective "representation of the people."[13]

We are deceiving ourselves if we refuse to see that behind the appearance of Nazism lay, on the one hand, widening areas of social disintegration produced by many of the individualistic forces that we ourselves celebrate, and, on the other the popularization of the State as a spiritual area of salvation for the disinherited.

The modern intellectual has been, on the whole, the political intellectual. In his eyes the apparatus of formal government has appeared the most desirable medium of social and moral reform. The result has been to throw the greater weight of attention upon the creation and utilization of *political* leadership, upon *political* administration, leaving other types of leadership in society—and their fate in modern history—unexamined. Only in the most recent years has the problem of leadership in industry, in trade unions, in all the essentially nongovernmental forms of association, come to assume respectable significance. This fact, to be sure, has various explanations, but not least among them is the suspicion that however crucial the State may be in modern civilization, political leadership is not enough. For political leadership plainly becomes capricious and inadequate to the demands of freedom and order unless it is rooted deeply in the variety of social and economic and cultural leaderships in society.

The historic significance of political democracy has resulted not so much from its insistence upon individual freedom as from its proffer of the State as an area of psychological participation and integration. Democracy arose at a time when the older social unities were undergoing a radical displacement caused by industrialism, urbanism, and the various other individualizing and secularizing forces of modern history. In the inspired utterances of its advocates, democratic freedom came to be envisaged not as the preservation of immunity from the State but as full participation in the power of the State. Democracy popularized and in a significant sense sanctified the State relationship. The continuous expansion of political power and responsibility that has been inherent in the democratic state would be inexplicable were it not for the underlying, popular, emotional acceptance of the State as a haven and provider even as the Church held this role in earlier Europe.[14]

The socialist tradition which followed Marx accepted at its full value the theory of the omnicompetent state. It has, however, contributed little to an adequate conception of the management or the administration of the society envisaged by socialists. The naïveté which underlay Marx's own view of the state was expressed in his curious statement that "when, in the course of development, class distinctions have disappeared, and all production has been concentrated in the hands of a vast association of the whole nation, the public power will lose its political character."[15] A half a century later Lenin could write, in the same vein, of the "simple" transition to socialism:

> The bookkeeping and control necessary for this have been simplified by capitalism to the utmost, till they have become the extraordinarily simple operations of watching, recording, and issuing receipts, within the reach of anybody who can read and write and knows the first four arithmetical rules. . . . When most of the functions of the State are reduced to this bookkeeping and control by the workers themselves, it ceases to be the "political" State. Then the public functions are converted from political into simple administrative functions.[16]

As the result of an uncritical attitude toward political power and of a mechanistic view that organizational and leadership problems are settled by history itself, contemporary socialists have been found disastrously short in the kind of administrative knowledge that is needed in the planned state. It is a striking commentary on the history of modern socialism that nearly all of the actual techniques utilized in contemporary national planning—in England and the United States, as well as in Soviet Russia—are the product chiefly of experience by capitalist nations in wartime.[17] The manifold problems of bureaucracy and leadership, of social incentives, of autonomous areas of responsibility, and of the preservation of group freedoms in the planned state have no readier answer in traditional socialist thought than they have in the orthodox theory of public administration.

The planned state we must have in one degree or another. The alternative in the economic, military, and political society that we have developed is simply chaos. But we need not assume, as many technicians have assumed, that planning merely with a view toward economic and political processes is sufficient. For our main problems are *social*— social in the exact sense that they pertain to the personal relationships among human beings and to the status of individuals. To refer to the social problem in any concrete sense is to refer to the actual groups and associations in which human beings live—to families, trade unions, local communities, churches, professions, and all the other forms of association in a complex civilization.

To suppose that these centers of leadership will remain vital and symbolically important when they have become institutionally irrelevant in our economic and political order is to indulge in fantasy. The decline of kinship as an important psychological sphere within Western society has been, at bottom, no more than the diminution or disappearance of those institutional functions which formerly gave the kinship group centrality in the life of the individual. It would be naïve not to see that the loss of institutional functions by other groups—groups now central in our industrial civilization—may have analogous consequences. Social groups thrive not upon moral fervor or ritual enchantment but upon what they can offer their members institutionally in the way of protection and well being. Thus, as more and more liberals have come to realize, there is a profound social difference between a State that seeks to provide a legal scene within which trade unions and coöperatives themselves can raise their members' standard of living, and a State that seeks, however benevolently, to make this its own direct and exclusive responsibility.

The demands of effective leadership, like the demands of freedom and security, necessitate a large amount of autonomy and functional significance in those spheres of society which are *intermediate* to the individual and the

State. In one of his most perceptive passages Tocqueville wrote: "It must not be forgotten that it is especially dangerous to enslave men in the minor details of life. For my own part I should be inclined to think freedom less necessary in great things than in little things, if it were possible to be secure of the one without the other."[18] The implications of this statement are more relevant to our own age than they were a hundred years ago when Tocqueville wrote. For it is only in the present age that the technical command of communication and the psychological knowledge of attitudes have made it possible in any full sense to invade, politically, the private areas of existence.

The assumption that centralized power must carry with it centralized administration was tenable only in a day when the range of governmental activities was limited. It is no longer tenable. As government, in its expanding range of functions, comes ever closer to the spheres of primary social existence, the need is intensified for a theory of public administration that will be alive to social and psychological values and to the relationship between political power and cultural associations and groups. In this connection, Karl Mannheim has written that "It is obvious the modern nature of social techniques puts a premium on centralization, but this is only true if our sole criterion is to be technical efficiency. If, for various reasons, chiefly those concerned with the maintenance of personality, we deliberately wish to decentralize certain activities within certain limits, we can do so."[19]

We cannot be reminded too often that the stifling effects of centralization upon leadership are as evident in large scale private industry as in political government. Big government and big business have developed together in Western society, and each has depended upon the other. To these two has been added more recently a third force in society, big labor. In all three spheres there has been a strong tendency to organize administration in terms of ideas of power inherited from the seventeenth and eighteenth centuries. In all three spheres there are perplexing problems created by the widening gulf between, on the one hand, a technically trained and experienced managerial group who lead and, on the other, the rank-and-file membership.

"Centralization in administration," David Lilienthal has written, "promotes remote and absentee control, and thereby increasingly denies to the individual the opportunity to make decisions and to carry those responsibilities by which human personality is nourished and developed.

"I find it impossible to comprehend how democracy can be a living reality if people are remote from their government and in their daily lives are not made a part of it, or if the control and direction of making a living—in industry, farming, the distribution of goods—is far removed from the stream of life and from the local community. 'Centralization' is no mere technical matter of 'management,' of 'bigness versus smallness.' We are dealing here with those deep urgencies of the human spirit which are embodied in the faith we call 'democracy.' "[20]

The larger problem of society and leadership at the present time is not that of the devolution of administrative authority within formal political government. It is the division of powers and responsibilities between political authority, wherever lodged, and the whole plurality of autonomous social groups in our society. These are the areas of psychological security, as they are the areas within which practical freedom unfolds. They are also the primary spheres of leadership. So long as public opinion is confronted with the choice between insecure individualism in these areas of existence and political collectivism, the trend toward centralization will not be arrested, and the moral attraction of Leviathan will become irresistible.

NOTES

1. A. N. Whitehead, *Symbolism, Its Meaning and Effect* (New York, 1927), p. 73.

2. Robert Birley, *Burge Memorial Lecture for 1947*.

3. Gilbert Murray, *Five Stages of Greek Religion* (New York, 1930), p. 18.

4. J. Livingston Lowes, *Road to Xanadu* (Boston, 1930), pp. 428, 429, 430.

5. *Ibid.*, pp. 426–427.

6. Robert Park, "Modern Society," cited by S. de Grazia, *The Political Community* (Chicago, 1948), p. 107.

7. See the valuable study by Walter Goldschmidt, *As You Sow* (New York, 1947).

8. A. D. Lindsay, *The Modern Democratic State* (New York, 1943), pp. 184–185.

9. Max Weber, *Essays in Sociology*, ed. Gerth and Mills (New York, 1946), pp. 199, 216.

10. Krech and Crutchfield, *Theory and Problems of Social Psychology* (New York, 1948), p. 429.

11. See, for example, H. Peak, "Observations on the characteristics and distribution of German Nazis," *Psychological Monographs*, 59, No. 276. Also, Loomis and Beegle, "The Spread of German Nazism in Rural Areas," *American Sociological Review*, 1946.

12. Peter Drucker, *The End of Economic Man* (New York, 1939), p. 67.

13. Aurel Kolnai, *The War Against the West* (London, 1938), pp. 150, 153, 156.

14. Tocqueville, Ostrogorski, and Max Weber, among others, have dealt with this fully.

15. *Communist Manifesto* (Chicago, Ill., Charles H. Kerr and Co., 1940), p. 42.

16. *The State and Revolution* (New York, 1939), p. 205.

17. This point has been stressed by E. H. Carr in *The Soviet Impact on the Western World* (New York, 1946).

18. *Democracy in America* (New York, 1945), II, 230.

19. Karl Mannheim, *Man and Society in an Age of Reconstruction* (New York, 1940), p. 319.

20. *T. V. A. Democracy on the March* (New York, 1944), p. 139.

[4]

Conservatism
and
Sociology

To the contemporary social scientist, to be labeled a conservative is more often to be damned than to be praised. After all, does not the *New International Dictionary* define "conservatism" as the "disposition and tendency to preserve what is established" and, in effect, accuse the conservative of "tending to maintain existing institutions or views" and of being "opposed to change or innovation"? Put in this light the social scientist is likely to conclude that those qualities most essential to the humanist or scientist—originality, independence, audacity, and disdain for tradition—are the very opposite of conservatism.

But conservatism, in any full view, cannot be restricted to the psychological terms of attitude and evaluative response. In the contextual terms of history there are also conservative *ideas*. Such ideas as *status, cohesion, adjustment, function, norm, ritual, symbol*, are conservative ideas not merely in the superficial sense that each has as its referent an aspect of society that is plainly concerned with

First published in the *American Journal of Sociology* (September 1952), 167–175.

the maintenance or the *conserving* of order but in the important sense that all these words are integral parts of the intellectual history of European conservatism.

They are also integral concepts in the contemporary study of human behavior. More than one observer has been recently struck by the profound change that has taken place during the last generation in the general orientation of American sociology. Until a generation ago the principal interests of American sociologists lay in the study of *change*. Those aspects of society which Spencer and Ward had categorized as dynamic were foremost objects of study, and in almost all such studies the essentially organizational character of historical change was taken for granted. Allied with this faith in the beneficence of change was the conviction that the real unit of sociological investigation was the individual, regarded typically as self-sufficing in nature and as the most solid element of social reality. With very few exceptions, problems and hypotheses reflected a widespread moral conviction of the organizational direction of history and of the self-sufficing nature of the individual.

Today, we plainly find a radically different orientation. The major orientation is not change but *order*. Gone is the rationalist faith in the power of history to solve all organizational problems, and gone also is the rationalist myth of the autonomous, self-stabilizing individual. In the place of these older certainties there now lies a widespread preoccupation with phenomena of institutional dislocation and psychological insecurity. More than any other, it is the concept of the social group that has become central in contemporary sociology. As a concept it covers the whole set of problems connected with integration and disintegration, security and insecurity, adjustment and maladjustment. It contrasts sharply with the primacy of the individual in earlier American sociology.

Doubtless, present theoretical interests in the social group and its psychological properties may be seen as manifestations of the moral imperatives of community which dominate so many areas of belief and longing at the present time. Theoretical problems in the social sciences always have a significant relation to the moral aspirations of an age. When, in the eighteenth and nineteenth centuries, there was widespread faith in moral and social progress and in the emancipation of individuals from old ways of action and belief, the prime theoretical problems of the social sciences were those of change, process, evolution, and the varied concepts of the self-driven, autonomous individual. In our own day, when a preoccupation with community and a fear of insecurity pervade almost every area of civilized life, it is not strange that the social sciences should deal so preponderantly with theoretical problems of group integration and disintegration.

But current ideas are related not only to current moral contexts; they have also a genetic relationship to earlier sequences of ideas. An idea system which possesses no decisive importance in one generation or century frequently provides the materials of the dominant intellectual perspective of the generation or century following. Such is the historical significance of the idea system of conservatism. As a historical structure of ideas, conservatism had received much less attention in the history of ideas than have individualism and rationalism, systems which so notably held the intellectual field in the nineteenth and early twentieth centuries. Yet, from an essentially minor position in the nineteenth century, conservatism has come to exert a profound influence upon the contemporary mind.

Three major perspectives stem from the writings of the early nineteenth-century conservatives in Europe. The first is the perspective of the *masses:* of populations relentlessly atomized socially and morally by the very economic and political forces which the liberals and radicals of the nineteenth century hailed as progressive. The second perspective is that of individual *alienation:* of widening aggregates of individuals rendered steadily more insecure and frustrated as the consequence of those moral and intellectual changes which the rationalists saw as leading to creative liberation from the net of custom. The third is the perspective of *power:* of monolithic power that arises from, and is nurtured by, the existence of masses of rootless individuals, turning with mounting desperation to centralized authority as a refuge from dislocation and moral emptiness.

These are the major intellectual legacies of conservatism. But within them lies a number of smaller, more specific, interests which can be seen in sharp contrast to the central ideas of nineteenth-century individualist rationalism and which can be seen also as contributing to the very core of a great deal of contemporary sociological thought. It is the argument of this paper that present-day problems and hypotheses of social order, group integration and disintegration, and the nature of personality are rooted much more deeply in the conservative tradition in modern European thought than in the liberal-radical systems of the nineteenth century which are more commonly made the background of modern sociology.

Conservatism, as a distinguishable social philosophy, arose in direct response to the French Revolution, which had something of the same impact upon men's minds that the Communist and Nazi revolutions have had in the twentieth century. In each instance the seizure of power, the expropriation of old rulers, and the impact of new patterns of authority upon old certainties led to a reexamination of ideas of freedom and order. But it was not alone against the Revolution in France that the conservatives revolted. It was more fundamentally against the loss of status that could be seen everywhere in western Europe as the consequence of economic change, moral secularism, and political centralization. For such men as Burke and Bonald, the French Revolution was but the culmination of historical process of social atomization that reached back to the beginning of such doctrines as nominalism, religious dissent, scientific rationalism, and to the destruction of those groups, institutions, and intellectual certainties which had been basic in the Middle Ages. In a significant sense, modern conservatism goes back to medieval society for its inspiration and for models against which to assess the modern world. Conservative criticisms of capitalism and political centralization were of a piece with denunciations of individualism, secularism, and equalitarianism. In all these historical forces the conservatives could see, not individual emancipation and creative release, but mounting alienation and insecurity, the inevitable products of dislocation in man's traditional associative ties.

From this critical view of history the conservatives were led to formulate certain general propositions concerning the nature of society and man which diverged sharply from those views which the rationalists and individualists had emphasized.

The first and most inclusive proposition has to do with the nature of society. Society—what Burke called "legitimate" and Bonald "constituted" society—is not a mechanical aggregate of individual particles subject to whatever rearrangements may occur to the mind of the industrialist or the governmental official. It is an organic entity, with internal laws of development and with infinitely subtle personal and institutional relationships. Society cannot be created by individual reason, but it can be weakened by those unmindful of its true nature, for it has deep roots in the past—roots from which the present cannot escape through rational manipulation. Society is, to paraphrase the celebrated words of Burke, a partnership of the dead, the living, and the unborn. For the conservatives, especially in France, the metaphysical reality of society, apart from all individual human beings, was unquestioned; and this was perhaps the major proposition directed against the social nominalism of the Enlightenment.

Second, the conservatives insisted upon the primacy of society to the individual—historically, logically, and ethically. Bonald was led to work out a complex theory of symbolism and language development in order to prove that man and his ideas could never have preceded the institutions of society, institutions which had been created directly by God. "Man," wrote Bonald, "exists only in and for society. Society forms him only for himself. . . . Not only is it not true that the individual constitutes society, but it is society which constitutes the individual by *l'éducation sociale.*" Hegel wrote critically of rationalist efforts to deal with "the isolated individual" and rejected strenuously what he called "the atomistic and abstract point of view." Apart from the constraints and representations embodied in society and its associative disciplines, there is no morality, and man is intellectually in a void. There are no instincts or prepotent reflexes in man by which thought and morality can be deduced. Only through society and its associative and symbolic manifestations does man become man at all.

From this it follows, in the third place, that society cannot be broken down, even for conceptual purposes, into individuals. The irreducible unit of society is and must be itself a manifestation of society, a relationship, something that is social. The individual, Lamennais declared, is but a fantasy, the shadow of a dream. We can never perceive what the rationalist calls "individuals." We see, rather, members of society—not "individuals" but fathers, sons, priests, church members, workers, masters, and so forth. Not even for purposes of politics, Hegel argued, should the reality of social membership be obscured. "The circles of association in civil society are already communities. To picture these communities as breaking up into a mere conglomerate of individuals as soon as they enter the field of politics is . . . to hang the latter in the air. . . ."

Fourth is the principle of interdependence of social phenomena. Since society is organismic in nature, there is always a delicate interrelation of belief, habit, membership, and institution in the life of any society. Each individual and each social trait are parts of a larger system of coherence. Efforts, however well-intended, to reform or remake one part of society inevitably violate the complex lines of relationship which exist and must exist in any stable society.

Fifth is the principle of needs. Not fictitious natural rights but unalterable *needs* of man, his "wants," as Burke termed them, are primary. Allowance for these, Burke wrote, "requires a deep knowledge of human nature and human necessities, and of the things which facilitate or obstruct the various ends which are to be pursued by the mechanisms of civil institutions." Every society and each of its parts is the response to certain timeless needs of human beings. Disrupt the mechanisms of satisfaction, and disorder and misery are the result.

Sixth is the principle of function. Every person, every custom, every institution, serves some basic need in human life or contributes some indispensable service to the existence of other institutions and customs. Even prejudice, Burke insisted in a striking passage, has, despite the contempt that it arouses in the mind of the rationalist, the indispensable function of holding together the structure of society, of providing a kind of emotional cement for beliefs and habits. There is, in prejudice, an indwelling wisdom that is the product of the centuries and of man's deep needs for security.

Seventh, the conservatives, in reaction to the individualistic Enlightenment, stressed the small social groups of society. The social group, not the individual, is the irreducible unit of society; it is the microcosm, *societas in parvo*. Internal social groups constitute the smaller allegiances of society, within which the whole society becomes meaningful. They are, Burke wrote, "our inns and resting places." The Revolution had exerted its most drastic powers against the traditional social loyalties, against the whole of that area of interpersonal relationships which had descended from the despised Middle Ages. But these are the true sources of society and morality. "No man was ever attached by a sense of pride, partiality, or real affection to a description of square measurements," Burke wrote in a hostile critique of French efforts to create new areas of administration and loyalty. "We begin our public affections in our families. . . . We pass on to our neighborhoods, and our habitual provincial connections."

The religious groups, family, neighborhood, occupational association—these, declared Bonald, are the necessary supports of men's lives. The reformers are in error when they strive to make men forget the values of this sphere of society and to live in terms of the rational dictates of will, based on scientific information. Abstract, impersonal relationships will never support a society; and where these principles tend to prevail in the population, there we find the strongest tendencies toward social and moral disorganization.

Weaken the traditional social relationships of men, whether by commerce or by governmental reform, argued the conservatives, and inevitably legitimate society will be replaced by an incoherent and distracted mass of individual atoms. Once individuals have become separated from traditional ties "and have got themselves loose, not from the restraint, but from the protection of all the principles of natural authority and legitimate subordination, they become the natural prey of imposters," wrote Burke. The conservatives in France made this the essence of a principle: man's reason, his goals, even his individuality, are dependent upon close affiliation with others and upon the structure of external values in society.

Lamennais, in a short essay on suicide,[1] wrote: "As man moves away from order, anguish presses around him. He is the king of his own misery, a degraded sovereign in revolt against himself, without duties, without bonds, without society. Alone, in the midst of the universe, he runs, or rather he seeks to run, into nothingness." To regard community as a check upon individuality is a monstrous error, for it is only within community that individuality can develop and be reinforced.

Eighth, the conservatives were led to recognize the reality of social disorganization. Liberals and radicals were not unmindful of the miseries and dislocations occasioned by the historical process, but they persisted in seeing the nature of history as inherently organizational in basic design. From the point of view of a Condorcet or a Bentham (and this remained true in the rationalist tradition through both the classical and the Marxian economists) there may have been intermittent *disorders*, but never disorganization in the large sense.

But the effects of revolutionary legislation upon traditional institutions created in the minds of the conservatives a deep preoccupation with disorganization. This was, for them, essentially a moral phenomenon, but it was inextricably related to historical dislocations of the legitimate interdependence of the functions and authorities of society. The consequence of revolutionary changes would not be higher forms of organization but rather an intensification of old processes of disorganization, culminating eventually in the atomization of all morality and society.

It was in these terms that the conservatives, especially in France, wrote bitterly of religious individualism. For them religious individualism was to be seen as the opposite side of social disorganization. Protestant depreciation of the corporate, ritualistic, and symbolic elements of religion could lead, like its historic attack upon the supremacy of Rome, only to the eventual sterilization of the religious impulse. The root meaning of the word "religion," Bonald declared, is social. What, indeed, does the parent-word, *religare*, mean but to bind together? To argue the supremacy of individual faith or belief is to argue the collapse of religion as a spiritual society.

The conservative view of urbanism and commerce was not different. All the conservatives were struck by the contrasting effects of town and country upon institutions and groups. Burke could see in urbanism and commerce certain leveling implications which weakened the basic resources of individuality. Hegel observed with alarm the disorganizing effects of English industrialism upon the personalities of men, through its destructive inroads upon family and local community. In a systematic study of the contrasting effects upon the family of urban and rural conditions, Bonald pointed to the dislocative impact upon the kinship ties of urban impersonality and industrialism. The city, he wrote, has the effect of congregating human beings but not of uniting them. The urban family is inherently a less stable form of organization than the rural, and so is the urban community. There is more genuine social solidarity in backward rural areas, despite the greater dispersion of the population than in the city.[2]

Ninth, the conservatives were led to insist upon the indispensable value of the sacred, nonrational, nonutilitarian elements of human existence. To argue that man may ever live by reason alone or by relationships founded solely upon reason is preposterous, the conservatives argued. To attempt to found society upon the purely secular and upon purely individualistic motivations of pure achievement is ruinous. Man lives and must always live through observances of ritual, ceremony, and worship. The onslaught of the Revolution against the *ancien régime* and the celebration of pure reason, both in legislative action and in popular decree, had dangerously weakened the sacred supports of society. Burke's famous words on the rationalist view of the political contract which is the state, his insistence upon the sacred, prerational foundations of all political association, were echoed in the writings of other conservatives. Apart from the *sacredness* of an institution or relationship it will not long hang together. Mere rationality is not sufficient.

Tenth was the principle of hierarchy and status. The revolutionary and rationalist emphasis upon equality must lead quickly, it was argued, to a leveling of social differences which will obliterate the natural channels of transmission of human values. Without hierarchy in society, there can be no stability. Classes of men in the larger society perform the same functions that are performed by ranks in an association, by the unequal status of father and child in the family. The very principle of interdependence of institutions in society carries with it, when one recognizes the different ages and capacities of individuals, the necessity of a similar interdependence of individuals. And this interdependence is necessarily hierarchical. In all associations the principle of hierarchy will assert itself; and, when men become aware of diminishing relationships between themselves and their accustomed status in this large social hierarchy, nothing but unhappiness and despair will be the result.

Finally, the conservatives emphasized the principle of legitimacy of authority. Authority is legitimate when it proceeds from the customs and traditions of a people, when it is formed by innumerable links in a chain that begins with the family, rises through community and class, and culminates in the large society. By its invasions of traditional areas of authority and its exaltation of the rational state, the Revolution had deprived human beings of the secure roots which come from legitimate authority and left them exposed to unstable compromises between chaos and extreme power. The legitimacy of authority proceeds, not from axioms of right and reason, but from beliefs and habits which are imbedded in the needs which are served by authority. Far from being an artificial thing, a necessary evil at best, as the liberals had argued, authority is the substance of every form of relationship. Authority does not degrade; it reinforces. It is force that degrades, the kind of force that must ensue when the normal authorities are dissolved. A generation later, Tocqueville gave perfect expression to the conservative theory of authority when he wrote: "Men are not corrupted by the exercise of power or debased by the habit of obedience, but by the exercise of power which they believe to be illegitimate, and by obedience to a rule which they consider usurped and oppressive."

It can scarcely be argued that conservatism exerted any widespread influence on thought in the nineteenth century. For this was the century of great hope, of faith in what seemed to be the ineluctable processes of history, of faith in the natural individual and in mass government. All the major tendencies of European history—the factory system included —were widely regarded as essentially liberating forces. By them, men would be emancipated from the ancient system of status and from communities within which initiative and freedom were stifled. For most minds in the nineteenth century, conservatism, with its essentially tragic conception of history, its fear of the free individual and the masses, and its emphasis upon community, hierarchy, and sacred patterns of belief, seemed but one final manifestation of that past from which Europe was everywhere being liberated.

Yet conservatism had its influence, and it is only today that we are becoming aware of the real extent of conservative ideas upon nineteenth-century thinkers and policy-makers. Here we can consider but one of these lines of influence, that which is a part of the rise of systematic sociology in France. Sociology may be regarded as the first of the social sciences to deal directly with the problems of dislocation involved in the appearance of a mass society. Economics, political science, psychology, and anthropology long remained in the nineteenth century faithful to the precepts and perspectives of eighteenth-century rationalism. Sociology, however, from the very beginning, borrowed heavily from the insights into the society that such men as Burke, Bonald, and Hegel had supplied. Thus, even in Comte's philosophical celebration of progress, there is a profound note of veneration for the past and of preoccupation with processes of status and security that is lacking in the writings of those for whom the rationalists of the eighteenth century formed the proper point of departure in the study of man.

The traditionalist quality of Comte's new science is not to be missed. His admiration for the structure of the Middle Ages is almost unbounded, and he tells us that the Catholic traditionalists deserve the eternal gratitude of positivists for having awakened men's minds to the greatness of medieval culture. Moreover, he praises the followers of Bonald for having actually used positivist principles in their own analysis of institutions. By their recognition of the inherent instability of individualism and the disorganizing social consequences of such dogmas as equality, popular sovereignty, and individual rights, and by their insistence upon the priority of society to the individual and the social dependence of man upon society's values and institutions, the traditionalists have earned the gratitude of all positivists.

Comte's aim was the creation of a science of society. He regarded his long study, *The Positive Polity*, as a treatise in sociology, as the compendium of the new science of society. The principles of positivism, he declared, when absorbed by everyone, would make forever unnecessary any reliance upon the tenets of historic religion. The science of human relations was to be the great organizing principle in society that would replace traditional Christianity. Comte himself was no scientist; but, through his romantic worship of science, the social structures of family, community, language, religion, and cultural association were removed from the frankly theological and reactionary context in which they lay in Bonald's thought and were given the context and terminology, if not the substance, of science. However absurd many of Comte's ideas may have appeared even to some of his followers in France and England and however difficult it is to distinguish clearly between the positive approach and the conservative approach to human relations, the important fact here is that, by his veneration of science, Comte's work was the means of translating the conservative principles into a perspective more acceptable to later generations of social scientists.

If Comte gave most of the nomenclature and emotional appeal of science to the study of human relations, it was Pierre Frédéric Le Play, who some years later gave it a methodology and set of techniques for empirical investigation. Le Play was a devout Catholic, a reactionary by all standards of his time. Like the earlier conservatives, he found most of the ills in western Europe to be the product of the Revolution. He, too, was concerned with restoring the prestige of the family, church, and local community and correspondingly depreciated the role of the state and direct political action. Ideas of progress, equality, individual rights, popular sovereignty—all these were as detestable to Le Play as they had been to Bonald and Comte.

Yet, despite his outspoken traditionalism on all economic, social, and spiritual matters, the conclusion cannot be avoided that Le Play contributed more to the scientific study of human relationships than the science-worshipping Comte did. It is irrelevant to point out that most of the conclusions which Le Play drew from his massive study of the European working classes were conclusions hardly different from the basic prejudgments which he had inherited from his early environment, hardly different from the frankly reactionary ideas of Bonald and De Maistre. What is important from the point of view of historical analysis is that Le Play transformed the moral insights of the conservatives into a set of concrete problems calling for rigorous field investigation.

Les Ouvriers européens is perhaps the supreme example in the nineteenth century of actual field research into the structural and functional aspects of human institutions. The heralded thinkers of the nineteenth century—Comte, Spencer, and Ward—were content, on the whole, to leave their readers in the terminological suburbs of science; the nomenclature of science was set in contexts alien to techniques of verification. But in Le Play's work we have something decidedly different. Making all allowance for the influence upon his field work of moral presuppositions and objectives which have nothing to do with science strictly regarded, the fact remains that it was Le Play, above all others, who took the study of the family, local community, occupation, and cultural association out of the theological, the romantic, or the evolutionary contexts in which others had set them, robbing them of reality, and put them in the tougher, richer perspectives of comparative research into the actual lives of peoples. With this comparative methodology went a complex of precise techniques for the detailed study of human beings in their institutional environments.

What is important in the present connection is simply to note that in Le Play's work the basic insights and assumptions of philosophical conservatism become translated into an empirical study of human relationships. The essential content of conservatism remains; the methodological approach is changed significantly.

It is in the writings of Durkheim, however, at the very end of the nineteenth century that we find the most important link between conservatism and the contemporary study of human behavior. Durkheim shares with Freud a large part of the responsibility for turning social thought from the classic rationalist categories of volition, will, and individual consciousness to those aspects of behavior which are in a strict sense nonvolitional and nonrational. Until a few years ago Freud's was the more widely recognized influence in this respect. But it is impossible to miss the fact that Durkheim's reaction to individualistic rationalism is more radical than Freud's. Freud was virtually one with the rationalists in his acceptance of the primacy of the individual and of intra-individual forces. Nonrational influences upon behavior proceed, in Freud's system, from elements deeply imbedded in the individual, elements deriving essentially from man's racial past. The individual remains the *terminus a quo* in Freudian explanations. For Durkheim, however, the principal sources of human motivation, thought, and conduct lie in social conditions external to the individual; they lie in society and in the history of society. What we are given in the study of human nature, as Durkheim tirelessly proclaimed, is a set of social facts, facts which stem from the primacy of society to the individual. It is this supreme emphasis upon society and all its mechanisms of constraint that makes Durkheim's reaction against individualistic rationalism more basic than Freud's, and it is this emphasis in all its ramifications that places Durkheim securely in the conservative tradition.

If Durkheim could not accept the basic premise of the French conservatives—the primacy of an omnipotent personal God to all society and culture—he was at least willing, in his final phases of thought, to ascribe to religion a determinative influence in human life that no theologian could improve upon. And it is hard to resist the conclusion that society, for Durkheim as for Bonald, takes on characteristics of exteriority and power that make it almost indistinguishable from a divine entity.

Like Bonald, Durkheim can declare that "society is a reality *sui generis*; it has its own peculiar characteristics, which are not found elsewhere and which are not met with again in the same form in all the rest of the universe." Almost in the words of Burke, Durkheim writes of collective representations that they "are the result of an immense cooperation, which stretches out not only into space but into time as well; to make them a multitude of minds have associated, united, and combined their ideas and sentiments; for them long generations have accumulated their experiences and knowledge. A special intellectual activity is therefore concentrated in them which is infinitely richer and complexer than that of the individual." And when he writes of crime that it is *necessary*, that "it is bound up with the fundamental conditions of all social life, and by that fact useful, because these conditions of which it is a part are themselves indispensable to the normal evolution of morality and law," he might be paraphrasing Burke's celebrated remarks on the necessity of prejudice in society.

We see the elements of conservatism in Durkheim's whole rationale of social constraint; in his demonstration of the noncontractual elements in contract; in his insistence upon the irreducibility of the moral "ought" to utilitarian considerations; in the moral basis that he gives to all social organization; in his dissection of morality into the two cardinal categories of discipline and group attachment; in his momentous division of all social phenomena into the sacred and the secular. We see the philosophical assumptions of conservatism in his profound stress upon the functional interdependence of all parts of society; in his derivation of the categories of human reason from sources in society. Durkheim's view of history is essentially the conservative view, with its stress upon the disorganizational and alienative aspects of modern European development and upon the creation of the masses, lying inert before an increasingly omnipotent state. And, finally, we cannot miss the conservative cast of his most articulate program of reform, the creation of new intermediary occupational organizations to fill the social vacuum caused by revolutionary liquidation of the guilds.

None of this derogates in any way from the scientific achievement of Durkheim. One may agree with many a reader of Durkheim's works that seldom has the scientific union between theory and empirical data been as rigorous and fruitful as it is in *Suicide*. What Durkheim did was to take the conservative view of society out of what was essentially a speculative frame of inquiry and translate it into certain hypotheses, which he sought to verify—at least in the case of rates of suicide—crucially. We assuredly cannot miss the scientific intent and perspective of much of Durkheim's work or the careful relation between theory and existent bodies of data. But neither can we miss the clear historical source of Durkheim's hypotheses regarding suicide

that is to be found in earlier writings on the subject by
Lamennais and Tocqueville and, for that matter, in the
whole structure of the conservative view of society.

NOTES

1. This remarkable essay was published in 1819. See *Oeuvres
complètes* (Brussels, 1839), Vol. II, pp. 150–51. The same
insight is to be found two decades later in Tocqueville's great
study of democracy and at the end of the century in Durkheim's
writings. I am indebted to Cesar Graña for directing my
attention to this passage.

2. "*De la famille agricole et de la famille industrielle*,"
in *Oeuvres complètes*, ed. by Abbé Migne (Paris, 1859–64), II,
238 f.

(5)

History
and
Sociology

I

Until recent years the relationship between history and sociology was a distant one. Before the last decade or two, it was nearly inconceivable that projects could be formed in which members of the two disciplines might work amicably and fruitfully together. Equally inconceivable was the thought that either discipline possessed insights and perspectives that could be of use to the other. Historians were prone to say that what was valid in sociology was already incorporated in their discipline, had been since Herodotus, and what was left in sociology they did not want. Sociologists were only too likely to regard historians as theory-dreading, fact-worshiping, data-collecting antiquarians, concerned with just about everything but the question "Why do human beings behave as they do?"

How do we explain a gulf that for so long separated history and sociology in this country? (In Europe it was never so pronounced: Weber, Durkheim, and Simmel made much use of historical data, and historians, at least those who did not slavishly follow Leopold von Ranke—notably Otto von

This article, in a slightly different version, originally appeared in the *Bucknell Review* (December 1957).

Gierke and Fustel de Coulanges—dealt straightforwardly with sociological problems). Several explanations are possible of course. There was the American historian's early widespread preoccupation with political rather than cultural data; a tendency on the part of historians to conceive of themselves as humanists rather than social scientists; the early concern of sociologists (distasteful to historians) with social uplift, followed, in radical mutation, by sociological modes of empiricism that humanists found even harder to forgive; and, perhaps not least, the usual considerations of status that prevail betwen ancient and modern lineages.

But I think there is a more fundamental explanation than any of these: namely, the sharp contrast that existed between their views of the nature of social reality. Despite the fact that in the early days of the two disciplines there was an almost complete identity of overall objective—a reconstruction of man's past as the means of understanding his present—there was an unbridgeable gulf between their respective conceptions of how the past and the present were to be envisaged.

For sociology the central problem was that of *change*. Almost without exception the works of the pioneers of American sociology—such men as Ward, Sumner, and Giddings—were oriented toward the discovery of laws of development. Reality was conceived by the early sociologists as consisting of social institutions in ceaseless processes of advancement from one phase or stage to another. Change itself was universally held to be the result of immanent forces. The obsessing interest in origins and stages of development arose from a conviction that there was, if only it could be determined, a natural pattern of change for every system and that by a comparative study of societies the natural patterns could be uncovered. Social change was conceived of as duplicating itself from one culture to another.

For history, on the other hand, the central problem was not really that of institutions in the process of change but rather that of the discovery of significant *events* of the past. Now, events are not changes: they are happenings, occur-

rences—call them what we will—represented typically by
such phenomena as victories and defeats, invasions and re-
pulsions, accessions and terminations of rule, and births and
deaths of important personages. Events may indeed be connected with change, but it is important at this juncture to
stress the fact that events, as such, are not themselves
changes. In any case, the point is that early historiography
took the event as its central subject matter and that, as the
means of setting the present into causal relation to the past,
the ingenuity of historians went into the construction of
sequences of events, each flowing ineluctably from the previous one. In addition, and arising from the very nature of
the events, there was the historian's emphasis upon the
uniqueness of all things. To the historian it was inconceivable that events ever duplicated or repeated themselves,
and for all historians particularity of time and place was as
much the essence of human behavior as cell structure is of
human life.

Given fields, then, whose original identity of objective
was accompanied by differences so radical in conceptions of
reality and method, the results are not difficult to imagine.
Among sociologists there developed the strong conviction
that historians were scarcely more than date and fact grub-
bers, their total enterprise resembling nothing so much as
ant-hill industry, worship of uniqueness, and dedication to
narration as one of God's means of revelation. For historians,
on the other hand, sociology took on more and more the
character of a science of Never-Never Land, what with its
bland disregard of particularity and its preoccupation with
universalist schemes of development that seemingly could
never be precisely located in time or space.

So much for the original relationship between history
and sociology in the United States. It is unnecessary to
dwell even briefly on the transformation of American sociology beginning in the period between 1910 and 1920 with
the works of such men as Cooley, Ross, and Thomas and
working on a widening front to the modern conception of
sociology as the study of social systems. It is useful merely
to remember that since approximately 1920 the most fruit-

ful accomplishments of sociology have been in the general area of statics—that is, the analysis of social systems, the elements of social structure, the roles, and the complex patterns of interaction which all human groups embody. With but few exceptions the study of change has been neglected.

But the balance is beginning to shift; for, despite the extraordinary insights that have been gained by structural analysis into the nature of human behavior, it is evident that further development of knowledge along these lines is dependent upon fresh inquiries into the processes of change. It is not surprising, therefore, to note in a number of places at the present time a reawakening of the sociological interest in change. In this respect sociology has company, for in economics and political science also there are clear evidences of a turning away from static models to a study of dynamics of change. It is not simply the intrinsic importance of change as a problem; more to the point is the fact that further additions to our knowledge of structure must come from insights into change.

Now, there is little likelihood that we shall revert to nineteenth-century social evolutionism, but there are already signs that certain older assumptions regarding the nature of change are still with us. I have already said that a cardinal article of faith with the social evolutionists was the conception of change as being immanent, autonomous, and self-generating within all social systems. The vast panoply of stages of development that earlier sociologists created as a superstructure should not blind us to the conception of the process of change which lay underneath.

Without exception there was presented a view of change as the consequence, not of exogenous factors, but of self-resident forces. Change was held to derive from interaction of elements within the system itself—be this system kinship, the state, social class, or religion. In no sense was change regarded as a historical problem by the social evolutionists—that is, a problem calling for analysis of specific changes caused by events occurring outside the social system under consideration.

It is this aspect of the philosophy of change in the nineteenth century that has continued in certain areas of contemporary theory in sociology. There is now, even as there was a half-century ago, a conviction that macroscopic changes of an institution may be considered as merely the cumulative results of microscopic changes within the institution, with external factors disregarded or envisaged as, at best, catalytic agents only. Such a conviction is acceptable provided we are sure of the micro-changes and their accumulation. But it is highly questionable when, instead of verified micro-changes, there are presented for consideration only vaguely defined tensions and strains that are held to be constant elements of a social system.

I can perhaps clarify my remarks by referring briefly to the four major phases of any social change. There is, first, the source of the change, that is, the original impetus which sets into the operation the whole process. Second, there are the means of transmission of the original impetus throughout the social structure. Third, there are the actual alterations of authority, relationship, and social roles within the structure; that is to say, the change of the structure itself. Fourth, there are the complex psychological modifications that are involved in the adjustment—always uneven—of individual life-organizations to new roles and relationships. Here, obviously, we are dealing with psychological phenomena of strain and tension that are inevitably bound up with the crisis of change.

Now, the point I wish to emphasize is that in the writings of a number of contemporary theorists we find the problem of the source of structural change dealt with in an essentially psychological manner rather than in historical terms. Change is approached as an immanent, rather than as an adaptive, process. To say, as Robert Merton has, that "the strains and stresses in a social structure which accumulate as dysfunctional consequences of existing elements will in due course lead to institutional breakdown and basic social change" is excellent as long as there is a clear realization that the dysfunctional elements are products of forces emanating from outside the system. But too often we find the psychological strains and stresses themselves treated as the original causal agents in the process, and structural change is correspondingly dealt with as "autonomous change," as the consequence of "the continuous operation of the individual psyche, with its potential of unsatisfied desires . . . within the universe of its social system."[1] And, again, we are told that "the search for the sources of change must be shifted from the external factors to the social structure itself."[2]

The tendency to search for causes of change *within* the structure is not entirely to be explained through sheer persistence of nineteenth-century assumptions. There is the understandable desire to place the processes of change within the same general theoretical system that contains explanations of structure, even as modern geneticists have done with fair success. But, in dealing with social structures, I doubt very much that we shall successfully incorporate the initiating factors of change within a general system of analysis: not, at least, without subscribing to some *vis a tergo* that is assumed to be built in or to a kind of Hegelian dialectic. Beyond these considerations lies the continued dependence of sociology upon ethnological material. I am not here referring to the kind of materials that have accumulated during the past few years in applied anthropology or that have been represented, let us say, by such a journal as *Ethno-History*. Rather, I am thinking of the more traditional ethnology of primitive cultures, an ethnology necessarily reduced to sheer deduction in its efforts to analyze dynamic elements.

However justified, or at least understandable, the search for internal sources of change may be in primitive peoples, there is little warrant for applying the deductive procedures of ethnology to the kind of materials sociologists deal with. So far as its approach to the sources of change is concerned, sociology must be historical sociology, leaving to structural analysis the immanent processes that follow the initiation of a change and to psychological investigation the tensions and strains that reflect the impact of change upon personality.

Needless to say, I am not suggesting that we borrow the framework of narrative from historiography when I refer to a historical sociology. What is essential is recognition of the specific event in the study of change and skepticism of "built in," or timeless, sources of change. We say that an event is a happening, an occurrence. It may or may not be as casual, adventitious, and sporadic as historians often declare it to be. A slowly arrived-at change in one system may well be the precipitating event for a change in a neighboring system. The crucial point, however, is that the event represents, from the point of view of a social structure, an external force, an intrusion, that has its own context of initiation and one that will not be revealed, predicted, or deduced from a purely internal analysis of the system under study.

Let us turn now to the field of history. Here, as in sociology, there have been notable changes of both content and objective during the past quarter of a century in the United States, changes that have made the prospect of a sociological history more than a faint one. Just as French historians like Granet, Glotz, and Declareuil were stimulated a generation ago to apply some of Durkheim's insights to the study of ancient and oriental history, more than a few contemporary historians in the United States are applying sociological insights to the study of American history. It is not merely that historians are turning increasingly to such interests as social groups, kinship, social class, and local community for the illumination of the past; more to the point is the rising conception of history as a social science rather than one of the humanities, and amenable to the method and techniques of the social sciences.

For it is apparent that a knowledge of the present can be as important to an understanding of the past as that of the past to the present. Concepts of social role, status, reference group, and the like—all forged in terms of present processes —have both an analytical and clarifying function for the historian engaged in the study, say, of the ante-bellum Negro, the western frontier, the New England renaissance, or the public careers of Calhoun or Lincoln.

It is because the discipline of history has become increasingly directed to the study of cultural change, rather than to mere filiations of events, that it can draw as much from the *sociological concept of structure as sociology can draw from the concept of event*. When I referred previously to the phases of any process of change, I dwelt chiefly on the first, or initiating, phase emphasizing the crucial importance of the *event*. But the total process of change involves also transmission of impulses, slow alterations of structure and role, and adaptations of a psychological kind. Change is never simply the mechanical result of an event impacting upon human behavior in direct fashion. Despite the often-times disruptive influence of events, they are nevertheless filtered in their impact by existent norms, authority-relation-ships, and roles. What we have learned is that even the most disruptive of events—for example, a sudden physical catas-trophe or key assassination—is mediated in its change-conse-quences by existent social structures, and inevitably the transmission of the impact of the event is retarded or hastened by social structure.

It was the mediating, or filtering, influence of social groups or communities that diffusionists in anthropology so often overlooked a generation ago in their plottings of the distribution of traits. It was assumed that wherever a trait spread, its acceptance by a people was automatic and that, furthermore, the form, function, and meaning of the trait remained the same that they had been at the time of emanation from the originating culture.

In much the same way historians too often assume that the occurrence of an event is itself the change in an institu-tion and that the change of a structure may be explained simply by reference to the initiating circumstances. There is a tendency to focus attention upon the purely adaptive aspects of change, overlooking the immanent processes which represent the filtered transmission of the change through a social system. Admittedly, there are many areas of historical research in which documents are altogether too scanty to provide even superficial insight into the structural aspects of change. On the other hand, acceptance of a sociological perspective by historians has made suddenly relevant large numbers of documents that would otherwise have been simply neglected. In sum, then, the concepts of structure and process seem to me as important for the historian as the concept of event is for the sociologist.

II

So far I have restricted my comments to interrelationships between the two disciplines of sociology and history insofar as the study of change is involved. I must now refer to another relationship between sociology and history, one that in a real sense involves the emergence of a new discipline: the study of uniformities in time. This is the most fruitful referent of the term *historical sociology* since the methods and insights of two fields conjoin here in results not found in either discipline as it is commonly understood. In the most fundamental sense what is called for is an envisagement of the dimension of time in a manner that is now largely reserved for space.

All sociologists are accustomed to comparisons of uniformities in space, whether such comparisons be of six delinquency areas in a metropolis or six kinship systems selected from different parts of the whole world. In such studies, time is held constant by the limits of the study and does not intrude itself byond making clear whatever is necessary about different dates of analysis by the investigator. So long as a proper allowance is made for contextual differences that are the direct results of different environments, we feel no sense of uneasiness about the possible violation of particularity of place.

How different is the case with time! We have long conceived time as unilinear and, as such, built into the very nature of reality. It is more than a matter of dealing with past, present, and future. Commonly we think of time as we do the flow of a river; minutes flow into hours, hours into days, etc., giving imagination the spectacle of an irreversible flow of time, onrushing and unabstractable, from a point infinitely remote in the past to a point similarly remote in the future. Each moment is unique—not to return any more than a drop of water can return and flow down the same river bed again.

On the whole, historiography has been built around this conception of time as unilinear flow, and narrative has been the means by which all the past's multiplicities of circumstances and pluralities of sequence have been compressed into an apparently unitary perspective. But problems of selection and arrangement have been formidable. How are we to deal, for example, with the history of Europe as a unity when what we are actually given is not one but a whole congeries of local, institutional, and national histories, each with its own identity, each coming in uninterrupted fashion right down to the present day? The result has been to reify the concept of Europe, to give it an identity greater than the sum of its parts, and to convert some of the actual histories into mere life-phases of the conceptualized whole; hence, the familiar practice of treating Greece only in the early chapters of a book on Europe, chopping off its history arbitrarily when Rome forges into prominence, and doing the same with Rome when feudalism begins to appear in France.

All this is difficult enough on the scale of European civilization; it becomes absurdly impossible on the world scale unless one follows the Hegelian procedure of tracking a *Zeitgeist* through its different resting places on earth. But the difficulties of operating with narrative in a single time perspective are not really obviated by reducing the scope of the subject to the nation or even the local community. Always we are dealing with plurality that unilinear narrative cannot easily absorb.

It is not surprising, therefore, to find a rising number of scholars—representing not merely history and sociology, but anthropology and some of the area studies as well—beginning to give attention to new ways of exploiting the past. Ancient dogmas of historical uniqueness, of the linear character of time, and of narrative as the only true means of revelation are receding into limbo for at least a few venturesome minds. In their place appear fresh viewpoints: events regarded as neither more nor less unique than, say, contemporary social structures; time envisaged, not as an inalienable attribute, but as a kind of plasma; and the consideration of data in terms of classes or categories rather than in terms of unitary narrative or period vignettes.

Although such viewpoints are assuredly novel when seen against prevailing tendencies of historiography, they are by no means products of the past five or ten years. For at least a half century the comparative study of uniformities in time has had its exponents, including such scholars as Max Weber, F. J. Teggart, A. J. Toynbee, Alfred Kroeber, Pitirim Sorokin, Crane Brinton, Marc Bloch, Howard Becker, and Rushton Coulborn, to name but a few of the more prominent ones. But there are unmistakable evidences of a growing respectability of the enterprise during very recent years, and there is every reason to expect it to widen its ranks during the years immediately ahead. For history such a study promises escape from the Procrustean bed of unitary narrative; for sociology it represents an opportunity to widen and deepen concepts now too often chained either to the static materials of ethnography or to the limited perspective of present-day America.

What are some of the conceptual areas in which work has so far been done in the study of historical uniformities? Three call for at least brief mention: events and processes, social structures, and personal types.

1. *Events and Processes.*   Not all events are easily placed in a conceptual class amenable to comparative treatment and hypothesis. The painting of the *Mona Lisa* was an event, but unless we conceptualize this into something substantially broader, e.g., the creation of masterpieces of painting, we obviously cannot get a class of phenomena for study. To paraphrase George Orwell, all events are unique, but some are more unique than others. Teggart's *Rome and China* is a work concerned with correlations of highly specific, even datable, events—namely, of wars and interruptions of trade routes in the period from 58 B.C. to A.D. 107. In this study, however, it is worth noting that what we are really given is not an abstraction of a class of phenomena

from time and place but a detailed examination of repetitive sequences of events in Eurasia leading in each instance to a specific invasion of the Roman borders. Here the events have a kind of domino-like relation to one another across the Asiatic continent. This is rather a different comparative objective from the one taken by Crane Brinton in his *Anatomy of Revolution,* in which four separated revolutions —the English, French, American and Russian—are studied comparatively in terms of cause, sequence of phases, and results. One thinks also of Kroeber's *Configurations of Culture Growth,* in which the "events" are individual works of art, philosophy, or science appearing, however, in clusters at various times and places, with the clusters themselves developing over a period of time in process-fashion and forming the comparable classes. Weber's studies in the rise of capitalism, Toynbee's comparison of the origins of world religions, and Howard Becker's analyses of secularization in the Hellenic world are all examples of work done with uniformities of event and process in time. Probably Kroeber is correct in his statement that "so far as uniformities lie in events, these will be 'gradual events' in the histories of cultures and their forms rather than immediate acts of individual men or specific groups of men."

2. *Social Structures.* Here I have reference to comparisons of kinship, religious, economic, and stratification systems as they have been manifest in different periods. Undoubtedly, more work in this area has been done than in any of the three I have distinguished. Unfortunately, however, most of it is of a static sort with results resembling nothing so much as snapshots in an album, interesting to contemplate, suggestive for illustrative purposes, but hardly more. Few of these have been concerned with a concrete problem calling for hypothesis and repetitive verification. One of the best and most recent comparative studies of social structure in history is *Feudalism in History* edited, and largely written, by Rushton Coulborn. Behind it is the work of eight experts on feudalism in different ages and places, each scholar being given the opportunity at a special conference to analyze and revise his own contribution in light

of the work done by others in their own areas of the problem. The aim of the study, in Professor Coulborn's words, is "to test feudalism as a developmental uniformity; that is to say, to find out to what extent feudalism has passed through similar stages of development in the different times and places of its occurrence in history, and to what extent it has recurred with similar antecedent, concomitant, and consequent political forms." Professor Coulborn's study, for all the questions of method it raises, can serve as a starting model for the study of uniformities in time; and, at the very least, it stands in refreshing contrast to the so-called comparative studies that turn out to be mere appreciations set side by side and given coherence chiefly by the format of the book. Nor (still thinking of feudalism) would one dare forget the magnificent work of Marc Bloch.

3. *Personal Types.* There are certain repetitive roles in history held by individuals in ways shaped differently by historical climate but possessing, nevertheless, uniformities of sufficient significance to make comparison as feasible as it is among contemporaries of our own age. One thinks of such types as the charismatic leaders, saints, businessmen, artists, poets, founders of religions, and military commanders. The greatest returns would presumably come from studies of those types which, by their very nature, appear infrequently in history—e.g., political leaders of the Caesar type, acknowledged saints, or religious founders. But even with the more commonly repeated types, such as business leaders or artists, there is much to be gained from historical comparison. Here, too, what is wanted is not a collection of biographical studies merely given focus by a scholar's impressionistic insight, but the establishment of a conceptual class of types that draws identity and purpose from a stated problem and to which meaningful hypotheses may be brought. Inadequate as Toynbee's hypothesis of "withdrawal and return" may be in explanation of the dynamics of leadership in history, it must certainly be respected for its relevance to a well-stated problem.

In conclusion I should emphasize that the threefold classification here presented has no methodological significance; it is chiefly descriptive of emphasis in work done. In a study like Coulborn's *Feudalism in History* and in the best sections of Toynbee's work, what we find are event and process, social structure, and personal type conjoined even as they are in human experience.

NOTES

1. *Social Theory and Social Structure* (Glencoe, Ill.: The Free Press, 1949), p. 42.

2. Raymond Firth, *Elements of Social Organization* (London: Watts, 1951), p. 86. George P. Murdock, *Social Structure* (New York: Macmillan, 1949), pp. 199–200.

(6)

The Decline
and Fall of
Social
Class

I

In the vast welter of all that is being written today on social stratification in American society, two themes are outstanding. One is moral and ideological; the other is descriptive and analytical. The first theme declares or implies that social class is bad for society: bad for democracy, for culture, and for personality. The second theme asserts not only that social class is a fundamental part of the American social order but that it is, of all forms of social grouping—kinship, religion, occupation included—the one with the most decisive consequences to political attitudes, economic choices, attitudes toward society, motivation, and life style. Needless to emphasize, the two themes are reciprocally related.

On the first theme I shall be brief. It is enough to say that despite an overwhelming orientation of social philosophers and sociologists for the past century toward the values

This article, in a slightly different version, originally appeared in the *Pacific Sociological Review* (Spring 1959), 11–17.

of equalitarianism, it is far from clear that a classless society would be a good society. It may well be that the ideology of equalitarianism, with its components of ever-ready amiability, other-directedness, celebration of the common man, and gravity toward consensus, has much to do with the rampant invasion of privacy and the erosion of individuality which have so often made it difficult to hold high the banner of intellectualism and cultural standards in our society.

Moreover, on the evidence of history, social class has often been a bulwark against power: power of the kind that erupted when the centralizing monarchs first appeared on the European scene; and power of the kind that the more recent nationalist and collectivist states have represented—in both Western and non-Western countries. Repeatedly in history, from the ancient world down to the modern totalitarianisms, we find that levelling of class is a prelude to seizure and consolidation of power. Pride of social class has been immemorially one of the most effective barriers against the spread of political demagogism, the lure of the charismatic power-seeker, and the inroads of mindless bureaucracy.

It might also be noted that the historical evidence is very clear indeed that the efflorescence of the high periods of culture, the so-called Golden Ages of history—the Athens of Pericles, Augustan Rome, the Florence of the Medicis, Shakespeare's England—have been periods in which the spirit of aristocracy was powerful, preoccupation with inherited rank obsessing.

My chief interest in this essay, however, is not whether a class-based society is good or bad. It is rather whether American society at the present time can reasonably and objectively be described as one in which social class is significantly determinative of human behavior; as determinative, say, as family, religion, ethnic group, occupation, or any of the other major types of grouping that make up our society and which, in the name of simple clarity, must be sharply distinguished from class. Is social class, as an analytical perspective, still relevant to the dominant realities of contemporary American wealth, political power, and distribution of status? This is the essential question.

The answer is that it is not—that however useful social class may be as a concept in the study of the historical past, or of contemporary non-Western societies, particularly undeveloped societies, it has become nearly valueless for the interpretation of American society. A great deal of what is so readily (even compulsively) categorized by sociologists as class behavior in American society is in fact the result of influences which can only with great and sometimes grotesque difficulty be made to fit the Procrustean bed of social class. That political power, wealth, life chances, and social status are unevenly distributed in the American population is not of course in question. What is in question is whether a concept drawn historically from the structure of preindustrial, predemocratic, prerationalized society can be of significant help in the clarification of such a society as ours is today.

It is useful at this point to look at a few clear-cut definitions of social class. We shall take three: by an anthropologist, a social psychologist, and a sociologist.

A class society, the anthropologist Walter Goldschmidt writes, is "one in which the hierarchy of prestige and status is divisible into groups each with its own economic, attitudinal, and cultural characteristics and each having differential degrees of power in community decisions."[1] Richard Centers, writing from a more psychological point of view, has emphasized that "a man's class is a part of his ego, *a feeling on his part of belonging to something*; an identification with something larger than himself."[2] Maurice Halbwachs writes that in a society composed of social classes, "each of these social categories determines the conduct of its members and imposes definite motivations on them; it stamps each category with such a peculiar and distinctive mark, so forcibly, that men of different classes, even though they live amid the same surroundings and are contemporaries, sometimes strike us as belonging to different species of humanity."[3]

All of these descriptions get at the hard core of social class: class, where it exists, is a tangible relationship; it is substantive, functional, and recognizable through ordinary processes of observation. The proof of existence of a social class worthy of the sociological name should not have to depend upon elaborate techniques of multivariate statistical analysis. To prove the existence of social class, surely one should not have to work so strenuously and polemically at it as sociologists so often do.

It is of some value, by way of contrast with present confusion, to look back upon the relatively clear and assured view of social class that existed in this country only a half century ago. Recently I treated myself to a rereading of some of the first-water novels of the turn of the century— by such men as William Howells, David Graham Phillips, Theodore Dreiser, and Robert Herrick. It is an instructive sociological experience, if only for reminding oneself that the idea of social class was then as vivid and widely accepted as is today the idea of status mobility. Such phrases as "clearly a member of the working class," "by habit and bearing of low class origin," "upper class dress," "of low class mentality and deportment," and so on, abound in unambiguous contexts.

Turn to the sociological writings of such men as Cooley, Sumner, and Ross. Here too, along with some penetrating insights into the nature of social stratification, is the unspoken assumption that the reality of class is plain to all, that it needs no substantiation, merely description or analysis. Add to imaginative literature and sociology the lay articles, sermons and orations of the time, and the conclusion is plain that irrespective of the oft-spoken American dream of every man a president, people took class for granted and knew in intimate and daily detail what the content and attributes were of the classes referred to. Despite the ideology of democratic equalitarianism, despite what Tocqueville and Bryce had written about the tenuous character of class lines in the United States, social class, even as recently as 1910, was an understood reality.

How very different is our situation today. So dim and tenuous has class become today that statistical techniques have had to become ever more ingenious to keep the vision of class from fading away altogether from sociologists' eyes.

Were it not for statistical coefficients of status "scores," little would be left of social class. But statistics are not enough. For, as Arnold Anderson has written cogently: "There is a risk that the search for refined techniques may lead to our unconsciously overlooking the original problem. For example, use of multiple techniques for combining scores on different status scales may yield a valid 'status' score. Social class, however, has traditionally implied membership in groups or quasi-groups."[4] To which I would add that some multiple correlations of status attributes have not only produced sociological monstrosities but, more important, have obscured the data and acted to prevent the appearance of new perspectives in stratification.

Consider for a moment a possible analogy to our preoccupation with social class in the United States: the kinship structure known as the kindred. The kindred is an ancient and real form of association. Almost all human society has been at one time or another based upon it. Even today in the United States the kindred demonstrably exists in our nomenclature, not to mention blood and marital relationships. Further, there are even yet small parts of the United States where the kindred has a certain functional importance; is a recognized part of the culture. Now, I do not think I exaggerate when I say that at least as strong a case can be made out for the role of the kindred as for class in the United States and most of Western culture. But who would bother to make it? Who would seriously treat a small Ozarks community with respect to kindred as a "microcosm of American society," as the place where "all Americans live"? How many social scientists would declare that since *kinship* is an unalterable part of human society, the *kindred* is therefore inevitable and that one's failure to know the interests of his kindred is the result of ideological distortion? And, finally, who would suggest seriously that since kinship is inescapable one had best accept his kindred in the interest of peace of mind?

There is no need to belabor the question. The answer is fairly clear and lies, of course, in the realm of political and social values. Unlike other concepts of sociology that of class has had for a long time certain value overtones to which few if any of us could be insensitive. For most social scientists (preponderantly liberal in political matters) any denial of the existence of class seemed tantamount to asserting that all Americans have equal opportunity. Too seldom has it occurred to us that the manifest facts of inequality could be placed in other perspectives of stratification.

A historian of ideas with whom I occasionally discuss sociological perplexities tells me that from his point of view the doctrine of social class would seem to have about the same relation to the data of stratification that the Ptolemaic view once had to celestial phenomena. I judge from my colleague's words that by the end of the fifteenth century the Ptolemaic doctrine was not so much wrong as it was tortuous, inefficient and clumsy. Many of the celestial phenomena which the Copernican hypothesis proved able to absorb easily and economically could actually have been handled by the Ptolemaic doctrine in its later form but only, I am informed, by the most extensive use of epicycles and other assumed patterns which neither observation nor reason could justify independently. In the Ptolemaic theory an immense battery of ever new assumptions and modifications of old concepts was necessary to sustain the fundamental view of the universe on which they rested. The new theory simply swept away the vast structure of assumption and concept that had accumulated and worked directly from the data that were given.

Admittedly, the analogy between the Ptolemaic view and the present theory of class is an imperfect one, if only because we are dealing with a doctrine that must perforce be considered *sub specie aeternitatis*, and in this sense was never correct, whereas in the case of social class we have a concept which is historical in content and which assuredly has relevance to certain ages and areas of civilization.

But so far as contemporary Western society is concerned, there is clarifying pertinence of the analogy. In the same way that the Ptolemaic theory had to depend increasingly upon more refined analyses and upon the use of concepts and subconcepts which removed conclusion ever farther from the data actually given, so, I think, does much of the current literature on stratification in the United States. It is not too strong, I think, to say that the concept of class plagues the study of stratification in about the same measure that social systems research would be if we continued to hold to the old primary group-secondary association dichotomy that early American sociology advanced.

Undeniably, class studies based upon community analysis have produced many essential data and, along with these data, many perceptive and valuable insights into the nature of status behavior, affiliation and prestige. But, for the moment leaving aside my fundamental criticism of the non-historical and noncontextual character of these studies, one is forced to conclude that both data and insights too often suffer from a kind of Procrustean adjustment to a conceptual framework that is at once too short and too narrow. It becomes more and more difficult to suppose that the hypothesis of social class would be invoked at the present time in studies of American stratification and power were it not for the deep roots of this hypothesis in the conceptual memory of sociology.

At its extreme, especially in some of the works of W. Lloyd Warner and his students, the class perspective has the attributes of a Never Never land: observations carefully sterilized of historical considerations, constructed of self-fulfilling interviews and premises, skillfully extrapolated through use of linear scales and multiple correlations; the whole possessing a certain internal consistency, even credibility, but, on overview, possessing about as much relation to national American society as James Branch Cabell's enchanted land of Poictésme does to Times Square.

II

The question is worth interjecting: Why is social class so dominating a theme in interpretative works on American and Western European societies? I ask the question because it seems highly unlikely that intellectuals and social scientists would—were they starting from scratch, empirically, today—seize upon class any more than upon kindred or parish as a crucial variable. Nothing that has to be demonstrated and "proved" so relentlessly and intricately would, on the face of it, be likely to assume such prominence. There has to be something more to it, something that forms a part of preconception and prejudgment, something inherited as a kind of idea-system that for compelling reasons keeps the image of social class a bright one.

The answer is, of course, the extraordinary influence of Karl Marx on late nineteenth and twentieth century social thought. I am not suggesting that the social scientists who are obsessed by social class are Marxists or Neo-Marxists. Not at all. It is a commonplace in the history of thought that ideas reach later generations largely divorced of the contexts and assumptions in which the ideas were first brought into being. In any event, the original rise of the perspective of social class in social thought came as much from conservatives as from radicals. It was in the conservative and radical responses to the two great revolutions— political and economic—at the beginning of the nineteenth century that we first find the modern terminology of class: middle class, lower class, upper class, class conflict, and the like. The conservatives were probably the first to work seriously with these words, for one of the most hated consequences of both the French and industrial revolutions was the sterilization of classes that had been for centuries pillars, along with church and family, of the old order. For Burke, Bonald, Hegel and other conservatives class was an indispensable element in legitimate society.

The conservatives, it is worth emphasizing, prized class but believed it to be undergoing the same ravages and erosions that kinship and religion were suffering under the buffets of modernism.

On the other hand, the radicals, chiefly socialists, saw the matter in reverse terms; prizing equality and the abolition of class, they yet saw the modern order as characterized by class power and class conflict as great as any to be found in premodern society. For socialists—and this is especially true after the publication in 1849 of *The Communist Manifesto*—classes were sovereign realities in the capitalist-democratic world, and class struggle was and would be, as it had been for countless millennia, the indispensable dynamic of social change. For Marxists the major objective of analysis of modern capitalist society was—and remains—that of demonstrating the class base of social organization and culture.

It is for this reason that one must grant Marx the largest share of credit for making the concept of class the dominant one that it is. From about 1870 until a decade or two ago Marxist ideas of stratification in society held undisputed priority in the study of society. Even today in Western Europe—notably in Germany and France but also, to a lesser degree, in England—Marxism or Neo-Marxism is the principal context of thought of those for whom social class is the controlling variable in social analysis. For nearly a century Marx has been, so to speak, the Ptolemy of the study of the universe of social stratification, and if his influence is no longer as resplendent as it once was, no Copernicus has as yet made his appearance.

Marx's influence on the theory of stratification has been in sociology somewhat like Darwin's in the study of biological evolution. In each instance there is to be seen a powerful shoring-up of late eighteenth-century ideas. The manner of original statement in both cases—in the *Manifesto* and in *The Origin of the Species*—has often had the effect of persuading readers of an originality that was not, in fact, there. If Darwin had his Charles Lyell and Thomas R. Malthus, Marx had his Rousseau (I am thinking of Rousseau's *Discourse on the Origin of Inequality*). Whether the special Darwinian theory of progressive, cumulative variation under natural selection rests upon sturdier empirical foundations than the Marxist theory of progressive, cumulative class struggle is not for a nonbiologist to seek to declare.

The essential point here is that social scientists have inherited, largely from Marx, a perspective that has today become generally shorn of Marxist objectives. As I say, this is a not uncommon episode in the history of thought.

One other point should be stressed—the extraordinary influence levied upon both conservative and radical minds in the nineteenth century by the English landed aristocracy. This remarkable structure, it would appear, served as the prototype, the model, of that concept of class that was to be handed down to the twentieth century. It was Burke, under the spur of his hatred of the revolution in France, who first called the world's attention to the class system in England and to the combination of light and leading that it seemed to represent. Europeans were not slow to pick it up. Even in the French conservative tradition from Bonald through Comte, Le Play, Tocqueville and Taine, the model of English class was a luminous one, underlying many penetrating glimpses into the lives of members of this class.

The relevance of the English landed class to both radical and conservative theories lay in its detachment from any formal system of political law and from any apparent external force. In France and on the Continent in general, social classes of the older order had been more nearly of the nature of estates—bounded, reinforced, and maintained by laws of the realm. Not so in England. Despite the powerful role that the landed class played in political affairs, it was not a creature of law and nothing in the English constitution pertained to it.

Space permits only the briefest summary of the characteristics of this class. There was, first, its undifferentiated economic unity founded upon landed property alone. It would be extreme to say that no other forms of property were recognized, but it is fair to note that men who made their fortunes in commerce and business did not usually gain recognition from this class until they had acquired land and based their existence upon it. From generation to generation landed property tended to remain in the same family hands.

Equally notable was the political unity of the class. Economic ownership and political power coalesced almost perfectly. This was to be seen not merely in the overwhelming number of Parliamentary seats that went to members of the landed class and in the astonishing degree of consensus that reigned among them, but in the monopoly they held of administrative functions in local and county government. "The great unpaid," as they were to be called by a later historian, is an apt term. Without formal compensation of any kind, without indeed any position in the law of the land, they performed throughout England the essential tasks of administration including much of the dispensing of justice. It was the generally high sense of responsibility with which the squirearchy operated at local levels—coupled with the absence of the kind of aggressive and independent legal profession that France had produced—that for long restrained a true bureaucracy in England and made of this class a model for all Conservatives.

There was little if any element of caste or even estate. No legal boundaries existed to mark classes and no restrictions of a legal sort prevented others from participating. We know that occasionally men did rise from below to attain influential places in government and society. But they were rare, for although the landed class was not closed, openings were few and could close with extraordinary speed. Overwhelmingly, national politics, local administration, justice and service in the commissioned areas of the armed forces were the functions of this one, socially homogeneous class.

So too was there a high degree of convergence of the various attributes of social status. Except for the handful of intellectuals largely concentrated in London, the only people of education were members of this class, and both the public schools and the two great universities were shaped in purpose and result by landed class needs. The norms of what constituted an educated man were universally understood. Language, including accent, could identify a man in a moment as belonging to this class. All were of the Established Church, most of the higher clergy were themselves products of the landed group, and even when they weren't their loyalties to it were strong.

Over the whole structure towered the governing conception of the gentleman. Hard to define in abstract terms, perhaps, the reality of the gentleman was nevertheless as unmistakable and as universal as that of the land itself. In dress, opinion, taste and conviction the landed gentleman set the life style of all that was invested with prestige and power. It was the pervasive image of the gentleman that had so much to do with maintaining the solidarity of this class, with shoring up its political and economic strength, and with making its behavior and desires so universal in England of that day. All of this we know from the countless letters and diaries of the age. The concept of the gentleman is a norm that has not disappeared altogether even yet in England nor in those older parts of the United States where it was carried.

Finally, we should note that this class was functional in all pertinent respects. Between the social attributes of prestige and the realities of economic and political power there was an almost perfect convergence, leading to a degree of solidarity and self-consciousness that could hardly have been exceeded. Criteria of class were clear, easily identifiable and substantially the same everywhere in England. Knowledge of a family's standing with respect to any one of the criteria was sufficient to place that family accurately with respect to other criteria. Finally, there was stability of this convergence of attributes from one generation to another. In sum, if it was the social norm of the gentleman that surmounted the structure, it was the monopoly of political power and its deep roots in property that provided the foundations.

I have chosen to describe this class for several reasons. In the first place, better than any definition, it provides a guiding conception of class and a picture of a society that is simply incomprehensible apart from class. Second, it was this class that was to provide the model for Socialist predictions of the course that industrialism would take in the development of its own class structure. And, finally, it is the dwindling, ever more attenuated, survival of this class system that forms the essential perspective of those community studies which emphasize class in twentieth-century England and in the United States. For, it must not be forgotten, the massive changes in the nineteenth and early twentieth centuries did not immediately drive out the economic and social characteristics of the older order everywhere. What Schumpeter has called the "precapitalist strata" remained to give stability to the new order and (for a long time) to impose its social and cultural norms upon emerging functions and statuses.

III

It is sometimes said that Marx's emphasis upon the two classes and the directive role they would take in the future of capitalism was the result of a religious turn of mind which simply transmuted the age old theological myth of the war between good and evil into the conflict between proletariat and capitalist. But this is fanciful and overly simple. The truth is, I believe, that Marx, with the vivid model of the landed class and its fusion of power and prestige in front of him, made the understandable assumption that industrial society would follow, *mutatis mutandis*, the same course of class development. And few today would deny that there was much in the character of the industrialism then emerging to give warrant to that assumption. Even Tocqueville, whose larger view of the emerging modern order has proved to be more prescient than Marx's— based as Tocqueville's view is on the disintegration of the historic unity of class, power, and wealth and upon the multiplicity of avenues to status in the modern world, with all the anxiety, as well as mobility that such multiplicity induces—even Tocqueville was willing to grant to the "aristocracy of manufacturers" a power almost as great as that which Marx made central in capitalism.

But however plausible such a view of the emerging capitalist class may have been in the mid-nineteenth century, it has been seriously belied by history. For, the same forces which, as we have no difficulty in seeing today, were dislocating rural village, parish, kindred, and guild were also dislocating that other pillar of traditional society, social class. The same toll that was exacted from village and kindred by powerful forces of administrative centralization, political nationalism, technology and the factory system, mass education, and the whole spirit of what Matthew Arnold epitomized as Philistinism and Max Weber as rationalization, was levied with equal effect upon class—landed upper class and peasantry alike. More to the point, these same forces, in their constantly intensifying and enlarging impact have made steadily more difficult the formation of any new classes—classes, that is, in the sense of the homogeneous, functional, and loyalty-inducing group that the word "class" properly summons up in the mind.

To a large extent, manifestations of social class within national democracy and industrial technology are simply the product of the remaining vestiges of predemocratic, preindustrial society. There are parts of the United States even today, though they are rapidly diminishing in number, in which enclaves of traditional stratification persist; enclaves within which class position is perpetuated from one generation to the next. Here, plainly, class is real and it is important. It is substantive and functional, and it identifies both role and style of life. One finds such enclaves among both rich and poor. But they are all to be found—chiefly in New England, the Atlantic seaboard, the Deep South, parts of the Midwest—in the now fast-shrinking areas of this country where the acids of modernism have not yet corroded the social fabric.

Class is a vivid reality in many underdeveloped areas of the world, and class analysis is essential to an understanding of underdeveloped political and economic systems. Economic and political power are both set in a clear and homogeneous perspective of social stratification. There is a striking convergence of the attributes of wealth, power and status in such areas as the Middle East and Latin America. But, so far as Western Europe and the United States are concerned, this convergence, this assimilation of economic and political influence within differentiated social classes exists scarcely at all except to a small degree in those areas which have been least touched by the processes of modern democratic-industrial society.

In political terms alone it is possible to see why class could never attain the same significance in modern society that it did in the old. In modern democracies ultimate political power is spread in an unstratified way among voters. Parties, pressure groups and other political associations have become decisive and are more and more difficult to stratify on any general scale. Power tends to be plural; elites are, in Raymond Aron's phrase, divided, not unified. Behind the modern state lies the whole development of political, civil and social rights which have made class rule as difficult as local or sectional tyranny. Equally important has been the mass character of the modern state, reflected both in its values and procedures by the use of ever more direct modes of administration. Finally, the sheer accumulation of economic and social functions by the state, discharged by paid and trained bureaucracies of constantly widening scope, has made impossible the development of any group in contemporary society comparable in political terms to the landed aristocracy. To repeat, class, where it exists, is functional or it is nothing.

In economic terms, there is the profoundly altered relation between property and economic power in modern times. A quarter of a century ago Berle and Means called attention to the structural significance of the divorce between property ownership and corporate control in large areas of the economy. This is a tendency that has only increased and it has been deepened and widened by the appearance of labor leaders and governmental officials who demonstrably wield great economic power and who are even more remote from property ownership. This splitting of the atom of property, to use a phrase of Berle's, has inevitably had far reaching implications to the economic foundations of social class. When economic power derives no longer exclusively from the processes of capital accumulation, or even management, when it is a reflection of positions in the economy which arise from and are sustained by labor and government, the relationship between property and class becomes more and more tenuous.

There is also the massive change from an economy based preponderantly upon primary and secondary sectors to one based increasingly upon tertiary occupations. By 1955, as Seymour Lipset has recently emphasized, tertiary employment had more than doubled over the amount in 1919, totaling 30 million workers compared with 28 million workers in the primary and secondary sectors. "Today over 55 per cent of the labor force is engaged in trade, finance, government, transportation, communication, and service." This has an important relation to social mobility, Lipset notes, for throughout American history "the tertiary industries have been the highest paid, followed by the secondary, and finally the primary at the bottom of the scale."[5]

To be sure, quickening social mobility is not inconsistent with the existence of social class, and income differentials among the three sectors do not in themselves negate the possibility of strong class lines. But with a few occupations such as domestic service excepted, it is all too obvious that the majority of jobs falling within the tertiary sector in modern times are not easily subsumed under any class system. Irrespective of high individual mobility in this sector, the job structure itself is too fluctuant, too mobile, to allow classes to form. Finally there is the fact, important to any analysis of class, that the dispersion of productive forces among the three sectors has become more important to the character of our society than the distribution of property.

Equally important has been the deployment of the economy into a large number of functional associations and groups essential to production, distribution and consumption, and which can, only at the risk of fantasy, be arrayed in any unilinear order of hierarchy. For awhile it could be thought that labor unions and consumer-cooperatives were manifestations of lower class position, but anyone who examines carefully the structural position of these, especially the large ones in our economy, not to mention the attitudes of both leadership and rank and file, is increasingly hard put to maintain this position.

As T. H. Marshall has written: "Within the economic structure of society there are many functionally distinct groups, each based on its productive role and the conditions under which it is performed. On some matters the interests of these groups differ; on others they are the same. Associations exist, and spread, for the pursuit of these common interests whenever they arise, and with such degree of combination of groups as they demand. The members of these combining groups differ greatly in social level, and the organizations are for them rationally designed instruments for the achievement of certain specific and limited ends, albeit very important ones . . . And the associations do not necessarily permeate the whole lives of their members, as social classes do, nor are they always in action; and at times the constituent sub-groups may be more important than the largest aggregate."[6]

There is also the striking change in consumption in modern society. It is not so much the fact of relative abundance, an economic condition on which modern states are increasingly dependent for political success, as it is the general elevation of level of consumption and the disappearance of clear and distinct strata of consumption. The difference between the extremes of wealth and poverty is very great, today as always, but the scale is more continuous and, for the bulk of the population, there has been a compression of the scale. Changes in housing patterns, automobile models, clothing styles, and even food preferences all illustrate this. Given both this compression and continuity, it is unlikely that self-conscious and mutually antagonistic groups will arise.

Whether with respect to consumption or production, then, class lines are exceedingly difficult to discover in modern economic society except in the backwater areas. About the most that research comes up with is that wealthy persons spend their money more freely, choose, when possible, better schools for their children, buy clothes at

Brooks or Magnin's, rather than at Penny's, avail themselves of better medical attention, and belong to more clubs. But while all of this is interesting, it says little about anything as substantive as a social class is supposed to be.

The last stand of class as an economic reality appears to be on occupational grounds. If class is linked with production, then occupation must be its chief index. But, to quote again from Marshall,

> "we find that, in study after study, occupation is used only as an index of social status. Or again, if we turn to studies of the influences of social and economic position (including position in the production system) on political attitudes and behavior —an aspect crucial to the Marxist and Weberian concepts of class—we find that class does not emerge as a substantive social group but is little more than a middle term in the chain that links position to opinion. Richard Centers, for example, writes: 'Just as people who differ in socio-economic position differ in class affiliation, so people who differ in class affiliation differ in turn in politico-economic orientation.' But, when one looks closer, it seems that this 'class affiliation' can hardly be said to have any independent existence, and that no concrete social group can be pointed to which is the 'class' toward which this 'affiliation' is felt."[7]

IV

We come, finally, to the social components of class. It is here that sociologists and anthropologists, especially the Warner school, have demonstrated greatest ingenuity in defense of class as a reality in contemporary American life. Through indexes of status characteristics and evaluations of participation in community life, a strong and often imaginative effort has been made to buttress what remains of a perspective that has been declining almost from the time it was first formulated. It is said in effect that even if class conceived as power cannot be demonstrated, life styles and the general preoccupation with social status leave us with self-conscious and culturally implicative classes numbering anywhere from three to ten.

But the evidence here seems to me no more compelling than in the economic and political spheres. I suggest that in the same way that there has been a general disengagement of economic and political power, during the past century and more, from any homogeneous scale of stratification, leaving in its wake plurality and dispersion, so has there been a general disengagement of social status itself from any clearly definable set of ranks. That scales of status exist in our society is incontestable, that they are often of driving concern to individuals is equally incontestable. But social status is at once too continuous within each of the numerous scales of status to make possible any identification of classes that have more than the most restricted or specialized acceptance.

I do not doubt that within a community that is sufficiently isolated from the main currents of national life, sufficiently arrested in terms of historical change, sufficiently homogeneous so far as its economy and government are concerned, a clear and meaningful class system could be discovered. I merely emphasize that to discover such a community today it is necessary to go either to the underdeveloped areas of the world or, in American society, to a few remaining and fast-disappearing pockets of the old order.

It is because social status, like economic and political power, has become disengaged from real class lines in modern society, that such novels as *Point of No Return*, *What Makes Sammy Run?*, and John Braine's recent *Room at the Top* are more illuminating so far as status behavior is concerned than the majority of community studies of social class. These novels are concerned with individuals in a mobile society, preoccupied by status considerations exactly *because* classes have been replaced by impersonal levels connected by ever wider channels of vertical mobility. Perhaps I go too far in the last reference; perhaps studies which are only now really beginning will show that channels of mobility are not as wide and congested as I think they are; but as sociologists we cannot overlook the significance of the almost universal *belief* that they are.

In any event, the crucial point here is not the extent of vertical mobility but rather the fact that we are living in a society governed by status, not class, values, and that class lines recede everywhere in almost exact proportion to the reality and urgency of individual status considerations. As a consequence of its disengagement from class, social status has become simultaneously more individual, more autonomous, and is, on any realistic basis, almost as multiple and diverse as is American culture. If I am wrong on this, will someone please rank for me on any linear *class* scale the following individuals: Ted Williams, Ike Williams, G. Mennen Williams, Esther Williams, Mrs. Harrison Williams, and Robin Williams.

Schumpeter pointed out in his *Imperialism and Social Classes* that "the family, not the individual person, is the true unit of class and class theory." This is correct, and what has happened to kinship in modern society, both to its structure and to its relation to the larger society, has been closely involved in the shift from social class to social status. Social status does not really imply the existence of groups at all; it can be used with reference to a continuous scale of invidiously valued positions, and it is with this in mind that Goldschmidt has insisted that the "proper figure of speech is not that there are rungs of a ladder; it is rather that there is a chromatic scale of status—a glissando."

There may be still a few communities in the United States where a man's professional, marital and associative choices will be, for as long as he lives in the community of his birth, limited by the level of his family of orientation in almost the same way that one's choices are widened or narrowed by the racial or ethnic group he belongs to. Such communities are few. For, generally, family of orientation is regarded as a marker or starting place by which individuals measure the distance they have moved upward or downward, and, on this matter, I repeat, J. P. Marquand

and John Braine have told us more than has Professor Warner.

Admittedly, a status-based society may be as inequalitarian at any given time as one organized in terms of class divisions. Further, it can scarcely be doubted that one's life chances, even his aspirations, will be influenced by the level of his family of orientation. Unquestionably, the sense of personal determination of status will be weaker, on the whole, at the extremes than in middle levels of status, in even the most mobile of societies. Such considerations do not, however, affect the central question of class any more than do the equally vivid facts of inequality of power and wealth in society.

I should say that, nationally, the nearest we come to class consciousness is in what Mozell Hill has called level consciousness. Unlike class consciousness, level consciousness makes for a high degree of individualism with respect to aspirations and life chances; it does not promote feeling of identification or collective involvement. The principal motive of the level conscious individual is to pass up and out of the level in which he finds himself. He is, so to speak, on the make. He lives in an atmosphere of competition that is nourished constantly by education and ideology and by the substantive fact of a shortage of skill in the industrial and professional world. Level consciousness creates awareness of one's differences from others, rather than similarities, and in this respect the individual is constantly moved by distinctions he invents between himself and others, by preoccupation, even anxiety, with these distinctions. As Professor Hill writes, "one by-product of this on the American scene is that people have come to feel that it is not so much a matter of destroying those on a higher level of consumption as it is of acquiring skills, strategies and techniques which will enable one to surmount his level."[8]

It is sometimes said that the failure of individuals to respond accurately to questionnaires which seek to derive a class consciousness corresponding to income level is simply the consequence of "ideological distortion." But, quite apart from the fact that such assertions run the risk of self-sealing and self-fulfilling reasoning, they do not give proper due to the social role of ideology. An ideology is not a shadow or representation. It is as real a part of one's social behavior as job or income. As real, and oftentimes more decisive.

The notable unwillingness of substantial numbers of people to concede the existence of class divisions, despite the bait of forced-choice questionnaires and the heavy pull of terminological tradition, is itself a social fact of the highest order. Granted that some uncomfortable economic realities are often obscured by the ideology of classlessness, whether in suburbia or elsewhere, the fact of this refusal to concede the existence of class is itself a powerful influence in preventing differential social statuses from becoming crystallized into classes.

In sum, the concept of social class has been an important, and probably inevitable, first step in the study of differential power and status in society; admittedly, there are non-Western areas of civilization, as well as ages of the past, where the class concept is indispensable to an understanding of power and status; but so far as the bulk of Western society is concerned, and especially the United States, the concept of class is largely obsolete. Any useful inquiry into the distribution of wealth, power and status, and their interactions, will have to be made, I believe, in terms of concepts that are more representative of the actual history of modern political and economic society.

NOTES

1. "Social Class in America: A Critical Review," *American Anthropologist* 52 (October–December, 1950), p. 492.

2. *The Psychology of Social Classes* (Princeton, N.J.: Princeton University Press, 1949), p. 27.

3. *Psychology of Social Class* (Glencoe, Ill.: The Free Press, 1958), p. 4.

4. "Recent American Research on Social Stratification," Conference on Social Mobility and Social Stratification, Amsterdam, 1954. Published in *Mens en Maatschappij*, 1955, pp. 321–37.

5. Seymour M. Lipset, "Trends in American Society," in Lyman Bryson (ed.), *Outline of Man's Knowledge of the Modern World* (New York: McGraw-Hill, 1960), p. 397.

6. T. H. Marshall, "General Survey of Changes in Social Stratification in the Twentieth Century," in *Transactions of the Third World Congress of Sociology*, International Sociological Association, 1956, pp. 12–13.

7. T. H. Marshall, *op. cit.*, pp. 5–6.

8. Mozell Hill in an unpublished manuscript on class and mobility.

[7]

Moral
Values
and
Community

The relationship between man, the community, and environment is one of the lasting themes to which every generation makes its contribution based upon knowledge and historical circumstances. To a large extent this relationship is dependent upon the system of authority and function which exists in society at large. During the Middle Ages, when centralized authority did not exist, local units tended to be strong and to enlist the loyalties of their members. The downfall of medieval communities came about in very large part as the result of centralization both of political authority and economy during the Renaissance and the Reformation. The basic problem of the community in the Western world is therefore to be seen in terms of what happened historically to the structure of power and function in the larger society. It is very difficult to maintain the eminence of the small, local units when the loyalties and

First published in the *International Review of Community Development* (1960), 77–85.

actions of individuals are consolidated increasingly in the great power units represented by the nation states in the modern world.

But the problem of community is also a problem in values. Because of the widespread emphasis upon technique, mechanism, rationalization of authority, monopoly of economic activity, there has been a general disinclination in the social sciences and in modern planning to remain closely concerned with the problem of human values. Quite apart, however, from the ultimate origin of human values, we know that their nurture and transmission from generation to generation depends upon groups small enough to provide the medium of learning but possessed of sufficient significance to give them a meaningful role so far as the cultivation of values is concerned. Such values as love, honor, and loyalty do not, cannot, thrive in a sociological vacuum.

It is well known in the study of language that the meanings of words and sentences depend upon understandings which exist prior to the utterance of the words themselves. It is equally true that all formal statements of value contain and depend upon certain prejudgments which give formal judgments their roots of meaning and even possibility of communication. Without some kind of agreement upon the unspoken but powerful prejudgments, all efforts to derive meaning from and to reach agreement about the explicit judgments are fruitless. Most of the world's conflicts of faith and action take their departure from lack of agreement about prejudgments rather than from dissension about formal judgments; and these are never within the reach of the language analyst. Finally, it is but an extension of the foregoing to emphasize that the communities of assent on which the spoken word depends, and the silent prejudgments which give meaning and efficacy to formal judgments of value, are themselves reinforced and contained by the more tangible communities of interest and behavior that compose a social organization. No one of these three sets of elements is causative or crucial. They exist as inseparable aspects of the one unified phenomenon. Apart from residual values themselves, human associations can have no more meaning than those which exist in the animal world. But apart from communities of men, the values themselves will not long remain important and meaningful to their human beings.

A wise philosopher, Susanne Langer, has written:

> The mind, like all other organs, can draw its sustenance only from the surrounding world; our metaphysical symbols must spring from reality. Such adaptation always requires time, habit, tradition, and intimate knowledge of a way of life. If, now, the field of our unconscious symbolic orientation is suddenly plowed up by tremendous changes in the external world and in the social order, we lose our hold, our convictions, and therewith our effectual purposes. . . . All old symbols are gone, and thousands of average lives offer no new materials to a creative imagination. This, rather than physical want, is the starvation that threatens the modern worker, the tyranny of the machine. The withdrawal of all natural means for expressing the unity of personal life is the major cause of the distraction, irreligion, and unrest that mark the proletariat of all countries.[1]

It is not strange that in our century we should see so many evidences—in practical behavior and also in philosophy and literature—of the kind of dislocation of moral value to which Dr. Langer refers. The vast changes in government, economy, and technology have had a striking impact upon men's social relationships. In the 18th century the central problem taken by philosophers was the problem of authority, and out of it came the theory and jurisprudence of the modern nation state. In the 19th century the central problem seemed to be economic, and in the works of the great economists of the 19th century we see the outlines created of the industrial world to which all of us, increasingly, belong. In the 20th century it is the moral-social problem that has become uppermost. And it has become uppermost because of the profound changes which have taken place in state and economy.

What are the dislocations and deprivations which have driven so many, in this age of economic abundance and political welfare, to a quest for security and a general concern for community? They lie, I think, in the realm of the small primary personal relationships of society—the relationships that mediate directly between man and his larger world of economic, moral, and political and religious values. Our problem is concerned with all of these values and their greater or lesser acceptability to the individual. It is this that makes our problem also social. It is social in the exact sense that it pertains to the small areas of membership and association in which human values are made meaningful and compelling to human beings.

Behind the spreading sense of insecurity and alienation in western society, behind all of the popular as well as academic preoccupation with the problem of community, there is growing realization that the traditional primary relationships of men have become, in certain areas, functionally irrelevant to the larger institutions of society, and sometimes meaningless to the moral aspirations of individuals.

A great deal of the character of contemporary social action has come from the efforts of men to find in large scale organizations, especially political ones, those values of status and intellectual security which were formally acquired in church, family, and neighborhood. How else can we explain the success of such movements in the modern world as Communism, Nazism except as mass movements designed to confer upon the individual some sense of that community which has been lost under the impact of modern social changes. The horror and tragedy are that such political movements have been based upon, and dedicated to, force and terror.

Too often the problem of modern community is blurred under the phrase, "social disorganization." Such a term is made to cover too great a diversity of conditions. In any society as complex as ours, however, it is unlikely that all aspects are undergoing a similar change. Thus it can scarcely be said that the state, as a distinguishable relationship among human beings, is today undergoing disorganization, for in most countries, including western Europe and the United States the political relationship is being enhanced above all other forms. The contemporary state, with all its apparatus of bureaucracy, has become more powerful, more cohesive, and is endowed with more functions than at any time in its history.

Nor would it be sensible to speak of disorganization of the great impersonal relationships which we find in our society in the form of the large private and semi-public organizations of an educational, economic, and charitable nature. Large-scale labor organizations, political parties, welfare organizations, and business corporations show a continued and even increasing prosperity, at least when measured in terms of institutional significance. It may be true that these organizations do not offer the degree of individual identification that makes for a sense of social belonging but it would hardly be accurate to apply the word disorganization to these immense and influential organizations.

The problem of disorganization, if we are to use the term, must be located more precisely with respect to those types of relationship which have actually undergone dislocation. These, as I have indicated above, are the relationships of the smaller, inter-personal sort. It is worth remembering that when Durkheim first addressed himself to the problem of community in his *Division of Labor*, he did so in the optimistic belief that modern industrialism was creating a new and more viable form of solidarity than had ever been known in the history of the human race. This new form of solidarity, Durkheim said, was organic; organic in the sense it would be based upon division of labor, with each element of the system thereby made the more dependent upon all other elements. Durkheim distinguished this form of solidarity from the old and traditional form which he called mechanical. Mechanical solidarity, Durkheim defined, as that which exists when all human beings are pursuing identical functions.

It was Durkheim's bold argument that such difficulties and maladjustments as we now find in the society around us stem from the fact that organic solidarity has only incompletely and imperfectly come into existence. When the last evidences of mechanical solidarity are erased and when the new system based upon division of labor is functioning perfectly, all such maladjustments will disappear. Men will be drawn to one another not on the basis of ancient traditional interest but on the basis of felt, mutually perceived, functional interdependence.

Such was Durkheim's contention, but, as he himself came to realize after he finished the *Division of Labor* the argument could not really be sustained. Therefore we find Durkheim in his next great work, *Suicide,* proclaiming the need for the re-establishment of forms of association akin to those which existed successfully in the ages characterized by mechanical solidarity. Only these, he was forced to conclude, can rescue modern man from the loneliness and functional inadequacy that he finds in the industrial system around him. Thus, although Durkheim failed in the prime effort of his first great book, he set a problem that he came to answer brilliantly—but very differently, from what he had originally intended—that is, through human communities within industry and the state which would restore once again the sense of solidarity and inspire men with a deep devotion to moral purpose.

The great inadequacy of Durkheim was in failing, however, to search for those natural and autonomous communities of individuals which have developed somehow even within the great impersonal spaces of the modern state. Durkheim accepted the perspective of modern society as being almost unrelievedly impersonal, atomistic, and mechanical. It was for this reason that Durkheim argued the necessity of contriving and establishing from the ground up new forms of community life which would give the individual a sense of identification. This view corresponded, of course, with the view taken by many of the early sociologists in the United States and elsewhere, a view which saw the small primary groups becoming historically archaic and replaced by large "secondary" associations. The argument was that such primary groups as family, neighborhood, and local community are undergoing a process of disappearance, to be replaced by the greater associations of a secondary character based upon economic or educational or religious interest alone. But more careful study in recent decades reveals that even in the largest cities, primary groups of an autonomous and self perpetuating character are to be found.

I should like to refer in this connection to the fine study of the family in London done by Michael Young and Peter Willmott.[2] In this study it was discovered that, contrary to popular sociological belief, the extended family still has great relevance in the lives of many of the people in the lower class areas of London. Furthermore, when thousands of these individuals, under a program of planning, were removed from their slum areas and placed in model housing some distance away from the slums, considerable unhappiness was the consequence. Such unhappiness was the result of small families being separated from relatives on whom they had traditionally depended for a great deal of their human association. In short, well-intended but insufficiently prepared planning had taken modern sociology at its face value and assumed that only the small conjugal family was of any significance in the lives of individuals and that such families could safely thereby be removed.

I think this study of the family could undoubtedly be supplemented and reinforced by other studies of the kinds of small communities which exist, and which are all too frequently neglected by planning which takes the view that cities are merely collections of atomistic individuals.

Much thought is being given these days to the need for community centers, especially in the suburbs and in many of the "model" towns which are coming into existence in so many parts of the world. Such centers are considered as essential to the development of a community spirit. But I do not think there is very much hope for any one of these centers in the instilling of a sense of community purpose so long as they are regarded as mere adornments to the functions and loyalties which actually exist and are related to day to day lives. A community center will be important to individuals only insofar as it adapts itself to the activities and concerns which exist naturally among a people but which need only leadership and guidance to evoke their full manifestation. Such centers can hardly operate successfully in a social desert: that is an area inhabited simply by individuals impersonally united by economic or religious interests but not through the affiliations which actually give life and meaning to one's existence.

The old communities—tribe, clan, joint family, and guild—were held together to a very large extent by sacred, even religious, bonds. The towns of the Middle Ages, which are sometimes, perhaps uncritically, praised as ideal communities, sheltered the lives of their citizens by religious, civic, and economic associations, each of which aspired to be a kind of enlarged family, and was small enough to arouse deep personal loyalty. The reason why religion has figured so prominently in social history is that in any community a feeling of meaning, of shared purpose, is essential to the prosperity of the community. Religion, traditionally, has been the vessel in which most of the shared meanings and purposes of a deeper sort have been carried. But, it must be emphasized, religion is not indispensable so long as there is some other pattern of meanings and purposes which will do the same thing.

It may well be asked: why should we seek communities at all? Is it not sufficient, in an age of the welfare state that we should live simply and solely in terms of the great regulations, laws, and associations which this state provides? It is often said that today, for the first time in human history, the state has become a benevolent and protective association which is able to meet both the social and the physical demands of people formerly met by a plurality of smaller communities. To this we must say firmly, however, that the state which possesses the power to do things *for* people has also the power to do things *to* them. Freedom cannot be maintained in a monolithic society. Pluralism and diversity of experience are the essence of true freedom. Therefore even if the state were able to meet the basic problems of stability and security through its own efforts, we should have to reject it as the solution simply because of our concern for the problem of freedom.

However it is to be noted that the state does not even serve the security need. No large-scale association can really meet the psychic demand of individuals because, by its very nature, it is too large, too complex, too bureaucratized, and altogether too aloof from the residual meanings which human beings live by. The state can enlist popular enthusiasm, can conduct crusades, can mobilize in behalf of great "causes," such as wars, but as a regular and normal means of meeting human needs for recognition, fellowship, security, and membership, it is inadequate. The tragedy is that where the state is most successful in meeting the needs for recognition and security, it is most tyrannical and despotic, as the histories of Communist Russia and Nazi Germany have made clear. The only proper alternative to large-scale, mechanical political society are communities small in scale but solid in structure. They and they alone can be the beginning of social reconstruction because they respond, at the grass roots, to fundamental human desires: living together, working together, experiencing together, being together. Such communities can grow naturally and organically from the most elementary aspirations, they remain continuously flexible, and, by their very nature, they do not insist upon imposing and rigid organizations.

Not only for purposes of viable social planning, as contrasted with the mechanical type of planning, but also for purposes of motivation and general creativity, the contexts of informal association must be understood. These, we have learned full well, are indispensable to the nurture of vigorous and creative personality. They are also crucial to the preservation of political freedom.

When the basic principles of modern liberalism were being formulated by such men as Locke, Adam Smith, and Jefferson, the image of man that existed then in the philosophical mind was one constructed out of such abstract traits as reason, stability, security, and indestructible motivations toward freedom and order. Man alone was deemed to be inherently self-sufficing, equipped by nature with both the instinct and reason that could make him autonomous.

What we can now see with the advantage of hindsight was that the founders of liberalism were unconsciously abstracting certain moral and psychological attributes from a social organization and considering these as the timeless natural qualities of the individual, who was regarded as independent of the influences of any historically developed social organization. Those qualities were qualities actually inhering to a large extent in a set of institutions and groups, all of which were aspects of historical tradition. But, with the model of Newtonian mechanics before them, the moral philosophers insisted on reducing everything to human atoms in motion, to natural individuals driven by impulses and reason deemed to be innate in man.

Given this image of man as inherently self-sufficing, given the view of communities and groups as merely secondary, as shadows of the solid reality of man, it was inevitable that the strategy of freedom should have been based upon objectives of release and the emancipation of man from his fettering institutions.

A creative society would be one in which individuals were "emancipated" from all types of social relationship. A free society would be, similarly, one in which human beings were morally and socially, as well as politically, free from any kind of authorities and institutional functions. The ideal, insensibly, became one of a vast mass of individuals separated from one another in social terms, participating only through the impersonal mechanisms of the market and of the legal state.

Thus, in Bentham's terms the fundamental cement of society would be provided not through groups and close personal relationships, but through certain "natural" identifications of interest rising in almost equal part from man's instinctual nature and from his reason. "It is not strange," George P. Adams has written, "that the self-discovery and self-consciousness of the individual should have steadily mounted higher as the environment of individuals more and more takes on the form of an impersonal, causal, and mechanical structure. For the mobility and freedom of the individual can be won only as he becomes detached from his world; his world becomes separated from him only when organized and defined in objective and impersonal terms."[3]

In strictly sociological terms, what this means is that the

individual's community was becoming an ever more remote thing to him in the 19th century. Because of profound shifts in the structure of authority and functions of society, more and more men were being made small parts in a social machine ever larger, ever more impersonal, ever more regimented. With authority becoming more and more objectified and externalized, the consequences were deleterious to those primary forms of authority with which man had traditionally and subjectively identified himself for ages. These ceased to be important. Their moral virtues were transferred as it were to him, even as their historic authorities were being transferred to the state.

But what we have learned under the guidance of studies in modern social psychology is that the rationalist image of man is theoretically inadequate and practically intolerable. We have learned that man is not self-sufficing in social isolation, that his nature cannot be deduced simply from elements innate in the germ plasm, and that between man and such social groups as the family, local group, and interest associations there is an indispensable connection. No conception of individuality is adequate that does not take into consideration the many ties which normally bind the individual to others from birth to death.

Individuality cannot be understood except as the product of normatively oriented interaction with other persons. Whatever may lie neurologically in the human being, we know that a knowledge of man's actual behavior in society must take into consideration the whole stock of norms and cultural incentives which are the product of social history. The normative order in society is fundamental to all understanding of human nature. We do not see, think, react, or become stimulated except in terms of the socially inherited norms of human culture.

But the normative order is itself inseparable from the associative order. Culture does not exist autonomously; it is always set in the context of social relationships. Only thus do the ends and patterns of culture make themselves vivid and evocative to human beings. And we have learned that with the dislocation of the social relationships which immediately surround the human being there occurs also a disruption of his cultural or moral order. The intensity of personal incentive, whether in the context of therapy or day to day life of the normal human being tends to fluctuate with the intensity of meaningful social relationships. This is what we have learned from studies of motivation in learning, from studies of character formation, and from observation of personal morale in all kinds of stress situations.

John Dewey wrote a generation ago,

> The philosophy of individualism ignores the fact that the mental and moral structure of individuals, the pattern of their desires and purposes, change with every great change in social constitution. Individuals who are not bound together in associations, whether domestic, economic, religious, political, artistic, or educational, are monstrosities. It is absurd to suppose that the ties which hold them together are merely external and do not react into mentality and character, producing the framework of personal disposition.[4]

So too with creativeness. Admittedly, it is the freedom of persons that is crucial. Great works of art or literature or science are not created by anonymous organizations. They are the concrete results of personal performance. But from the obvious centrality of the person in intellectual or cultural achievement it does [not] follow that such achievement is the sole consequence of innate individual forces nor that it is the result simply of processes of separation. To be sure there is in the achievement of any great work, whether it be a painting or a treatise in metaphysics, a relatively high degree of detachment in the minds of the creator. But we are still compelled to regard the important interdependences between the creator and his community.

Creation is individual, or at most the work of a small group, but much creative work would never have been done apart from such communities as the guilds, colleges, philosophical societies, monasteries, and institutes. In such organizations as these the informal, the spontaneous, and the autonomous types of relationship assume great importance. In them the creative process can move freely, tensions can be relaxed and inhibitions overcome. Sparks are thrown off by difference rubbing on difference in small compass. Imaginations are fired. Admittedly small groups can be as deadly as large ones, but the important point is that, unlike more formal types of associations, small and informal groups are not likely to last for long when their purpose is dead and their fellowship flagging. They are not saved by by-laws or dues invested, when their true resources run out.

In conclusion, the search for viable forms of community must be a continuous one. All the resources of knowledge must be brought to bear on the problem. Neither moral values, nor fellowship, nor freedom can easily flourish apart from the existence of diverse communities each capable of enlisting the loyalties of its members.

NOTES

1. *Philosophy in a New Key.* London and New York, 1948, p. 235.

2. *Family and Kinship in East London.* London, 1957.

3. *Idealism and the Modern Age.* New Haven, 1919, p. 35.

4. *Individualism Old and New.* New York, 1930, pp. 81–2.

(8)

Sociology

as an
Art
Form

I

I admit readily that both by temperament and academic background I have always been more interested in the non-uses of our discipline than the uses. I admit further to believing that theories should be tested as much by their reach as their grasp, their importance as their validity, and their elegance as their congruence with such facts as may be at hand. It is my major contention that the science of sociology makes its most significant intellectual advances under the spur of stimuli and through processes that it largely shares with art; that whatever the differences between science and art, it is what they have in common that matters most in discovery and creativeness.

Nothing I say is intended to imply that sociology is not a science. I am quite willing, for present purposes, to put sociology on the same line with physics and biology, applying to each of these the essence of what I say about sociology.

First published in the *Pacific Sociological Review* (Fall 1962), 67–74.

Each is indeed a science, but each is also a form of art, and if we forget this we run the risk of losing the science, finding ourselves with a sandheap empiricism or methodological narcissism, each as far from science as art is from billboard advertisements.

My interest in sociology as an art form was stimulated recently by some reflections on ideas that are by common assent among the most distinctive that sociology has contributed to modern thought. Let me mention these: *mass society, alienation, anomie, rationalization, community, disorganization.* I will have more to say about these ideas and their contexts a little later. Here it suffices to note that all of them have had lasting effect upon both the theoretical and empirical character of sociology. And all have exerted notable influence on other fields of thought, scientific and humanistic.

It occurred to me that not one of these ideas is historically the result of the application of what we are today pleased to call scientific method. If there is evidence that any one of these ideas as first set forth in the writings of such men as Tocqueville, Weber, Simmel, and Durkheim, is the result of problem-solving thought, proceeding rigorously and self-consciously from question to hypothesis to verified conclusion, I have been unable to discover it. On the contrary, each of these profound and seminal ideas would appear to be the consequence of intellectual processes bearing much more relation to the artist than the scientist, as the latter tends to be conceived by most of us. Apart from processes of intuition, impressionism, iconic imagination (the phrase is Sir Herbert Read's), and even objectification, it seems unlikely that any one of these ideas would have come into being to influence generations of subsequent thought and teaching.

For a few, no doubt, this conclusion, if believed at all, may seem like throwing vile suspicion on trusted ancestors: like a child's discovery that his father is a member of the John Birch society or his mother a descendant of the Jukes or Kallikaks. It may smack of an anthropologist's gratuitous demonstration to a pentecostal communicant of the totemistic origins of Christianity. But let us withhold further comment on this aspect of our subject, turning instead for a few moments to a more fundamental and inclusive matter —the habit of treating science as though it were substantively and psychologically different from art.

It is a deeply rooted habit, but by no means universal in the history of modern thought. We need go back no further than the Renaissance to discover a time when art and science were universally regarded as but different manifestations of the same form of creative consciousness. We know that Leonardo da Vinci thought of his paintings and his ingenious works in physiology and mechanics as, equally, art and science. The type of thought and even the outcome in each did not seem significantly different from the other. And, three centuries later, Goethe seems to have felt the same way. He did not suppose that one type of thought operated while he was writing *Faust* and another during his remarkable inquiries in geology and botany. In both the Renaissance and Enlightenment a radical distinction between art and science would have been incomprehensible.

When, then, did the change take place that produced self-consciousness in the scientist and the artist, so like that of Adam and Eve after the Fall? Like a few other things that plague us, it was, I think, in the nineteenth century. Beginning with social movements generated by the French Revolution, and closely connected with processes of division of labor introduced by the industrial revolution, we find a growing tendency in the nineteenth century to assume that the artist and scientist work in ways that are alien, even antagonistic to one another. Gilbert and Sullivan were but giving lyric expression to what everyone knew when they wrote that the scientist is "a matter-of-fact young man, an alphabetical, arithmetical, every-day young man" whereas the artist is "a crotchedy, cracked young man, an ultra-poetical, super-esthetical, out-of-the-ordinary young man."

In art there had developed, by the end of the nineteenth century, the view that creation works through some inscrutable process called genius or inspiration, never through technique and experimental work. We see this vividly in

Romanticism and especially in the *fin de siècle*. Associated with this stereotype was the equally fundamental one that the artist is not concerned with reality or truth, but only beauty—timeless supra-terrestrial beauty. And, forming the context of both of these, was the fateful view of the artist's role in society. Far from admitting any continuity with, or dependence on, society, the Romantic artist emphasized instead the gulf between him and society, seeking in solitary escape the anodyne that his medieval and Renaissance forbears had found in fellowship and social purpose. His rejection of the world that was being created by the industrial revolution was total.

But while art was becoming mythicized in this fashion, science was succumbing to another myth, one of reverse character and of equal influence on the popular mind. This was the myth, not of inspiration, but of method. Here, as in the case of art, we are dealing with something related to the industrial revolution. But, whereas art was generally repelled by the new industrial society, science was virtually absorbed by it. Just as industry began to dominate technology, technology dominated science, making it not what it had been for centuries, primarily a pursuit of the reflective mind, but a profession governed by rules and by criteria of service, all of a piece with law, engineering, and medicine.

The new universities in both Europe and America gave immense impetus to science but, to a very large extent, it was science of the applied type. In the United States the rise of the Land Grant colleges, based in their earliest years on an unrelieved vocationalism, was a major step in the union of science and industry and in the cultivation of the stereotype that science, like industry, is practical, the very opposite of art. The "mechanic arts" became, for several generations, the prime conception of everything scientific, placing their stamp upon the type of science done and respected at large. It was Thomas Edison who became the archetype of the scientist in the United States. A Willard Gibbs was simply overlooked.

Gradually the idea spread that science, unlike art, flows along the same methodical and systematic channels that business or law or medicine does. What is crucial, it was felt, was not free reflection, intuition, and imagination but rigorous adherence to procedure. The machine in the factory was proof that skill could be transferred from man to technology, making human ingenuity an expendable item. Could not method be the analogue of the machine? Several generations of Americans thought that it could, and schools and colleges were filled with students doggedly learning what was thought to be scientific method—not, alas, as an aid to ratiocination but as a substitute for it.

It is little wonder, given the overwhelmingly practical and methodical character of American science that Europeans looked for a long time with scant respect upon American science. It is a safe generalization that had it not been for the European institutes to which Americans in rising number went for advanced work, thus acquiring a truer conception of science, American science would never have burst forth from its shell of useful mediocrity. To be sure there were those of like mind in Europe, especially England; those for whom science was profession, subject to and limited by rules and techniques. But in Europe, where the humanistic tradition was stronger as the result of a much older pre-democratic, pre-industrial past, and where a mind of the stature of Faraday's could reject for himself the title of physicist, preferring that of philosopher, and be understood and honored for it, there was less likelihood of science becoming mired in unrelieved method and technique.

II

The worst result of the nineteenth century separation of art and science is not one of historical interpretation. It is the continuing belief in many classrooms and laboratories that the objectives as well as thought processes are different. At its worst, this view tells us that science alone is concerned with reality; that art's function is simply to titillate the senses in a kind of aimless quest of the decorative and eye-pleasing.

Nothing could be farther from the truth. Any art form that is serious, be it the novel, poem, or painting, is concerned first and foremost with reality. It is interested in throwing light upon reality, and in somehow communicating this light to others. And this, basically, is what science —as contrasted with technology—is concerned with. I venture the judgment that there is more in common between Picasso and Einstein—in objective, in inspiration, and mode of fulfillment—than there is between Picasso and, say, Norman Rockwell or between Einstein and any of the stolid practitioners of what A. N. Whitehead once called "dustbowl empiricism." Both the artist and the scientist are driven by the desire to understand, to interpret, and to communicate their understanding to the rest of the world.

The artist, let it be trumpeted, is *not* interested in decoration, and it is only because Non-Artists have worked as though decoration, fatuous reminiscence, and eye titillation were the highest ends of art that many persons still find themselves accepting or rejecting an artwork largely in terms of whether it is beautiful to the eye. Of course art can be beautiful, but not if it seeks beauty as its chief end. So, let it be remembered, can science be beautiful though no one would suppose that even a mathematician is actuated fundamentally by the goal of beauty.

"The essential nature of art," writes Sir Herbert Read, "will be found neither in the production of objects to satisfy practical needs, nor in the expression of religious or philosophical ideas, but in its capacity to create a synthetic and self-consistent world: a world which is neither the world of practical needs and desires, nor the world of dreams and fantasy, but a world compounded of these contradictions: a convincing representation of the totality of experience: a mode therefore of envisaging the individual's perception of some aspect of universal truth. In all its essential activities art is trying to tell us something: something about the universe, something about nature, about man, or about the artist himself. . . . It is only when we have clearly recognized the function of art as a mode of knowledge parallel to the other modes by which man arrives at an understanding of his environment that we can begin to appreciate its significance in the history of mankind."[1]

The artist's interest in form is the scientist's interest in structure. In each the desire for vision and understanding is dominating. Each works empirically; each strives to communicate what it finds through a pattern or formal structure requiring technique for its mastery. It is worth noting that the word "theory" comes from the same Greek root as the word "theatre." It means, basically, looking fixedly at, contemplation. It is allied with the word imagination—that is, literally, internalizing the outer world to an image that the mind holds tenaciously. Both art and science, in short, depend upon the capacity for detachment and upon the ability to hold back from commitment. The essence of each, wrote Santayana, "is the steady contemplation of things in their order and worth."

In truth, science and art have had a profoundly important cultural relationship for the greater part of the history of man. Eugene Rabinowitch, distinguished chemist and science editor, has recently written some words that might fittingly hang in every hall of learning.

The evolution of the human mind is a single process, revealed with different intensity, different clarity, and different timing—in its various manifestations—in art, science, philosophy, social and political thought. It is like a fugue, or an oratorio, in which different instruments or voices enter in turn. The voice of the artist is often the first to respond. The artist is the most sensitive individual in society. His feeling for change, his apprehension of new things to come, is likely to be more acute than of the slower-moving, rational, scientific thinker. It is in the artistic production of a period, rather than in its thinking, that one should search for shadows cast in advance by coming events, for prophetic anticipation. I do not mean the forecast of future events, but rather the revelation, in the framework of artistic production, of the mental attitudes which only later will become apparent *in other fields of human endeavour. Thus the impending breakdown of the existing order of things, of the generally accepted system of values, should be—and often is—first recognizable in a revolt against the values and canons that had dominated artistic creation; a revolution in art precedes the revolution in society.*[2]

Repeatedly, the history of the West has shown these words to be true. Historians of both ancient and modern European culture have emphasized the directive role played by the artist's mind: how philosophical and scientific images of man were preceded by those to be seen first in the drama, the sonnet, and in painting or sculpture. This first became a vivid truth for me several years ago while going through the great Uffizi gallery in Florence. Here it is possible to trace, in hall after hall, standing for age after age, the historically evolving images of man in Western Europe: from the spiritual, almost mystical and transcendent representations of man to be found in the Italian Primitives, through transitional manifestations that are both divine and human in appearance, to the frankly human, self-contained, and overwhelmingly terrestrial men and women of the Renaissance and Baroque. It is a development that plainly precedes the analogous transitions of image in philosophy and science. It was art with its swift, encompassing, and iconic vision that formed the bridge from medieval asceticism and corporatism to modern humanism; from organism to the obsessing problem of man's relation to society and values.

It was indeed in the Renaissance—and what else was the Renaissance but the conception of man and society as works of art?—that the whole modern view came into existence. This is a view that has since been modified in countless ways—now enhanced, now vulgarized; now made tragic, now trivial; sometimes ennobled, sometimes debased—but never really changed after the late fourteenth century in Italy. Whether the objective was the building of a cathedral or a bridge, the planning of a tapestry or a voyage to the Indies, the forming of a gild or the state itself, Renaissance man saw the world around him from the vantage point of the artist-scientist; not as something to worship or to manipulate but to understand and master even as Michelangelo mastered the marble he worked or Marco Polo the route to Cathay.

The problems and answers that form the core of modern culture are the work, not of the Usefuls in society but of the Visionaries, those who are lost in wonder and who, not knowing where they are going, go therefore the farthest. The same impulse to reality and its communication drove Michelangelo and Machiavelli alike—the one to the majestic David, the other to the Renaissance state—each a product of the artist-scientist.

The basic affinity between the artist and the scientist is, as the mathematician Marston Morse has told us, psychological and spiritual:

> The first essential bond between mathematics and the arts is found in the fact that discovery in mathematics is not a matter of logic. It is rather the result of mysterious powers which no one understands, and in which the unconscious recognition of beauty must play an important part. Out of an infinity of designs a mathematician chooses one pattern for beauty's sake, and pulls it down to earth, no one knows how. Afterwards the logic of words and of forms sets the pattern right. Only then can one tell someone else. The first pattern remains in the shadows of the mind.[3]

These are important words, burning words. They might hang over the entrance to every methodology seminar as a prophylaxis to pedantry. Too many sociologists have assumed that because scientific thought is by definition rational and logical in expression, its psychological roots must therefore be limited to strictly empirical and logical processes. Only that is scientific—so runs the folklore of scientism —that proceeds from an unambiguous and precisely delimited problem, drawn from statistically aseptic data, to a carefully tailored hypothesis. All else is, by definition, art or philosophy. It is hard to think of a better way to apotheosize the routine and insignificant.

Of course science is concerned with problems, with questions rooted in empirical observation as well as reflection. Like the artist, the scientist is interested in understanding the world around him and in discovering significant relationships. But from the large and incontestable truth that scientific thought is ultimately rooted in a preoccupation with the unknown, in a gnawing desire to reduce the tensions of uncertainty, it does not follow that scientific discovery is wholly, or even largely, the simple consequence of problem-defining and problem-solving thought. Such a conclusion has done much to drive sociology into areas of study chosen not because of their intrinsic intellectual importance, but because in them quantitative methodologies can work frictionlessly.

The late Florian Znaniecki foresaw, a generation ago, the trend that things are taking. He was referring to the already manifest influence of methodology courses:

> This influence consists in substituting tabulating technique for intellectual methods, and thus eliminating theoretical thinking from the process of scientific research . . . A condition can be foreseen—indeed, it has almost been reached —when anybody who has learned by heart the various technical rules and formulae of statistics, with no other education whatsoever and no more intelligence than a moron, will be able to draw from a given material all the conclusions which statistical problematization makes possible . . . The role of creative thinking in science, according to this conception, will be reduced to the function of formulating hypotheses which are to be tested by technical means. But we have seen that the only hypotheses statisticians ever have formulated, and ever can formulate, in view of the unavoidable limitations of their method, are no more than superficial generalizations of common-sense practical reflection. There is little place for creative thought and even less for scientific progress in this kind of problematization.[4]

Despite the candor of many distinguished scientists in telling about their work, and despite what we are on the way to learning about processes of creativity in general, there is still a great deal that we do not know about how scientists arrive at their problems, do the really crucial work on them, and draw their basic insights. But this much is clear. Such problems and ideas, from all that we can presently learn, seem to come as often from the unconscious as the conscious mind; from wide and extraneous reading, or from buried experience, as from the data immediately in view; from the "left handed" processes of feeling and intuition as from "the right handed" imperatives of logic and reason. Therefore, may we not draw this conclusion?: Anything that shrinks the field of experience and imagination, that in any way diminishes the sources of inspiration, that routinizes the workings of the intelligent mind, is to be regarded with suspicion.

III

It is time to return to the ideas in sociology I referred to at the outset of my paper. Let me describe them briefly again, for they are indubitably the most distinctive and illuminating contributions of sociology to the study of culture and society. There is, first, the view of human association as containing endemic processes of disorganization, dysfunction, call them what we will. Second, there is the view of the individual as alienated and anomic. Third, there is the perspective of community—in contrast to rationalistic and contractual forms of relationship—involving the key concepts of hierarchy and status. Fourth, we have the great theme of rationalization as a process in history and in the whole structure of modern society.

We know where these ideas came from: from the writings of four or five remarkable minds in the late nineteenth century: Tocqueville, Weber, Simmel, Tönnies, and Durkheim. I need not enlarge upon their formulations of the ideas. I am more interested in the processes by which the ideas came into being: that is, the contexts in which the ideas were uttered, the traditions they came out of, and, if it were possible, the mental states behind the ideas. Obviously, we are limited in what we can say positively, but I believe certain points are clear.

There is, first, the manifest discontinuity of these ideas in the history of modern social thought. Not one of them could have been deduced from the propositions of rationalism on human behavior that flourished in the Enlightenment. The true heritage of the Enlightenment is to be found, not in sociology, but in classical economics, individual psychology, and utilitarian political science. What we find in sociology—that is, in its distinctive currents—is a revolt against the rationalist view of man and society.

The second point is this. Not only are the key ideas of sociology unrelated to prior "scientific" ideas; they have their closest affinity with an art movement, Romanticism. In the same way that the Renaissance image of man proceeded from prior currents in art, so, I argue, the sociological image arises in the first instance from visions which had their earliest and most far reaching appeal in Romantic art.[5]

Weber has somewhere likened his own concept of rationalization to the poet Schiller's earlier view of the "disenchantment of the world." He was candid and accurate. Tocqueville, Simmel, and Durkheim might well have done likewise. From the first burst of the Romantic spirit in the late eighteenth century—rising to do battle with the classicist-rationalist view—we find luminously revealed two central visions: (1) the estrangement of the individual from a growingly impersonal and disorganized society (and the consequent spiritual inaccessibility of modern institutions—city, factory, mass society); (2) a celebration of status and community—whether rural, religious, or moral—in contrast to the individualistic and contractual society of the *philosophes*.

Third, and most important, even if most elusive, are the psychological affinities between the Romantic artists and the sociologists. It is impossible, as I have already suggested, to entertain seriously the thought that these major ideas were arrived at in a manner comparable to what we think of as scientific methodology. Can you imagine what would have happened had any one of them been subjected, at the moment following its inception, to a rigorous design analysis? Can anyone believe that Weber's vision of rationalization in history, Simmel's vision of metropolis, or Durkheim's vision of *anomie,* came from logico-empirical analysis as this is understood today? Merely to ask the question is to know the answer. Plainly, these men were not working with finite and ordered problems in front of them. They were not problem-solving at all. Each was, with deep intuition, with profound imaginative grasp, reacting to the world around him, even as does the artist, and, also like the artist, objectifying internal and only partly conscious, states of mind.

Consider one example: the view of society and man that underlies Durkheim's great study of suicide. Basically, it is the view of the artist as much as that of the scientist. Background, detail, and characterization blend into something that is iconic in its grasp of an entire social order. How did Durkheim get his controlling idea? We may be sure of one thing: he did not get it, as the stork story of science might have it, from a preliminary examination of the vital registers of Europe, any more than Darwin got the idea of natural selection from his observations during the voyage of the *Beagle.* The idea, the plot, and the conclusion of *Suicide* were well in his mind before he examined the registers. Where, then, did he get the idea? We can only speculate. He might have got it from reading Tocqueville who could certainly have got it from Lamennais who could have got it from Bonald or Chateaubriand. Or, it could have come from personal experience—from a remembered fragment of the Talmud, from an intuition born of personal loneliness and marginality, a scrap of experience in Paris. Who can be sure? But one thing is certain. The creative blend of ideas behind *Suicide*—a blend from which we still draw in our scientific labors—was reached in ways more akin to those of the artist than to those of the data processor, the logician, or the technologist.

It is not different with the ideas and perspectives of Simmel—in many ways the most imaginative and intuitive of all the great sociologists. His treatment of fear, love, conventionality, power, and friendship show the mind of the artist-essayist, and it is no distortion of values to place him with such masters as Montaigne and Bacon. Remove the artist's vision from the treatments of the stranger, the dyad, and the role of secrecy, and you have removed all that gives life. In Simmel there is that wonderful tension between the esthetically concrete and the philosophically general that always lies in greatness. It is the esthetic element in Simmel's work that makes impossible the full absorption of his sociological substance by anonymous, systematic theory. One must go back to Simmel himself for the real insight. As with Darwin and Freud, it will always be possible to derive something of importance from the man directly that cannot be gleaned from impersonal statements in social theory.

This leads to another important fact. Our dependence upon these ideas and their makers is akin to the artist's dependence upon the artists who precede him. In the same way that the novelist will always be able to learn from a study and re-study of Dostoevski or James—to learn a sense of development and form, as well as to draw inspiration from the creative source—so the sociologist can forever learn from a re-reading of such men as Weber and Simmel.

It is this element that separates sociology from some of the physical sciences. There is, after all, a limit to what the young physicist can learn from even a Newton. Having once grasped the fundamental points of the *Principia*, he is not likely to draw very much as a physicist from re-readings (though he could as a historian of science). How different is the relation of the sociologist to a Simmel or Durkheim. Always there will be something to be gained from a direct reading; something that is informative, enlarging, and creative. This is precisely like the contemporary artist's return to the study of medieval architecture, the Elizabethan sonnet, or the paintings of Matisse. This is the essence of the history of art, and why the history of sociology is so different from the history of science.

IV

That such men as Weber, Durkheim, and Simmel fall in the scientific tradition is unquestioned. Their works, for all the deep artistic sensitivity and intuition, no more belong in the history of art than the works of Balzac or Dickens do in the history of social science. The conclusion we draw is not that science and art are without differences. There are real differences, as there are among the arts and among the sciences.[6] No one asks a Picasso to verify one of his visions by repeating the process; and, conversely, we properly give short shrift to ideas in science that no one but the author can find supported by experience. The ideas of Durkheim may, as I have suggested, be dependent upon thought-processes like those of the artist, but none of them would have survived in sociology or become fruitful for others were it not for criteria and modes of communication that differ from those in art.

The conclusion, then, is not that science and art are, or should be, alike. It is the simpler but more fundamental conclusion that in both art and science the same type of creative imagination works. And everything that impedes or frustrates this imagination strikes at the source of the discipline itself. This unhappily is what is happening today in large areas of sociological instruction and research. It is a recurrent phenomenon in philosophy and science.

All too often in the history of thought we find techniques, methods, and doctrines becoming puny earthworks, hiding the view of the Olympian heights. How many mute, inglorious Simmels, how many village Cooleys lie today buried in required sequences of curriculum and in the computer rooms, their talents occupied not by development of ideas and insights but the adaptation of trivial or well worn ideas to the language of the machine or the endless replication of studies that often shouldn't have been done in the first place? Such servitude is justified on the false and appalling ground that the student can thus be taught the "method" of science. One may observe cynically that he sees no Simmels and Durkheim's walking the campus today. I venture the statement that there would have been none in their day had certain curricular requirements and terminological fashions been then in existence.

Which leads me to my final observations. I have stressed the art element in sociology not because I think the villain is the machine—any more than it is the machine tender who occasionally walks like a social scientist. The danger, if I may indulge myself in the presidential prerogative of the sermon, is not technological; it is sociological; it is the systematics and the dogmatics that always threaten to seep into the cellars of intellectual disciplines, thus driving out the art elements. For art's war is with system building, not science. I know of no better way of expressing this than in the form that Francis Bacon chose three centuries ago. That is, in the form of the Idols of the Mind. Let us call them the Idols of the Profession.

There are, first, you will remember, the Idols of the Tribe. These are the inclinations, perspectives, and modes of perception that are common to all; they are unavoidable, but must nevertheless be allowed for. The mere fact that we are sociologists—instead of biologists or economists—means that there are certain endemic, uniting ways of seeing the world around us. They are valuable and unavoidable, but not final.

Second, there are the Idols of the Cave—those that come, not from the character of the profession as a whole, but of that small part of the profession each of us lives in. Here we have the idols of specialization; the human but nevertheless dangerous tendency to reduce the richness and variety of the whole to the specialized perspectives and techniques that each of us operates with and that always threaten to become as rigid and fixed as the skills of technicians.

Third, we have the Idols of the Market Place—words phrases, and neologisms that become substitutes for ideas. Who among us has not learned to his advantage or disadvantage of the hypnotic fascination that is exerted upon foundations, research committees, and certain editors, by phraseology? And who does not know of the ease with which the words conveying the concept become the thing itself—with resulting inability to go beyond the words?

But, the greatest and most formidable of the Idols are those of the Theatre. Here Bacon had reference to systems of thought, systems which become, like bureaucracies, their own reason for being; where original goals have become displaced, leaving only the goals of systematic survival and self-maintenance. It seems to be the mark of all systems that their very degree of initial success leads before long to an almost ritualistic conclusion. We have all laughed at the teacher of classics who saw in the *Antigone* "a veritable treasure house of grammatical peculiarities." And for this teacher's students the classics were indeed killed. But why do we not laugh also at the teacher of sociology who introduces his students not to the rich and endlessly diversified field of social and cultural experience but to dull and potentially alienating analyses of fashionable systems and methodologies. Is not at least part of the attraction today of the natural sciences for the gifted student the assurance that he will be introduced immediately to the materials and problems of science and not to the locutions of systems? Systems so easily become bureaucracies of the spirit, subject to the same pettifogging rules and regulations.

Art abhors systems, and so does all creativity. History is the graveyard of systems, and this is precisely why Simmel and Cooley and Sumner remain fresh and valuable for us today and why few read Spencer or Ward. How often do system-builders produce students who are themselves creative and viable? The system killeth, the insight giveth life. What remains today of nominalism, realism, sensationalism, pragmatism, and all the other systems that once paraded over the landscape of Europe? Dead, all dead. God lives, Blake wrote, in the details. I amend this to say he lives in the insights, the intuitions, the imaginations of the artist. I cannot better conclude than with one final excerpt from Marston Morse.

The creative scientist lives in "the wildness of logic" where reason is the handmaiden and not the master. I shun all

monuments that are coldly legible. I prefer the world where
the images turn their faces in every direction, like the masks
of Picasso. It is the hour before the break of day when
science turns in the womb, and, waiting, I am sorry that
there is between us no sign and no language except by
mirrors of necessity. I am grateful for the poets who suspect
the twilight zone.

The more I study the interrelations of the arts the more
I am convinced that every man is in part an artist. Certainly
as an artist he shapes his own life, and moves and touches
other lives. I believe that it is only as an artist that man
knows reality. Reality is what he loves, and if his love is lost
it is his sorrow.[7]

NOTES

1. Sir Herbert E. Read, *Art and Society*, London: W.
Heinemann, 1937, pp. x–xii.

2. Eugene Rabinowitch, "Integral Science and Atomized
Art," *Bulletin of the Atomic Scientists*, 15 (February, 1959),
p. 64. The entire issue is organized around the theme, science
and art, and contains a number of highly perceptive pieces by
both scientists and artists. Particularly valuable are those by
Rabinowitch, Marston Morse, Carl Holty, and Martin Kamen
and Beka Doherty.

Some prolonged, if unsystematic, personal questioning of
scientists suggests to me that there is a stratification of acceptance of the art element in creative science. Mathematicians
and theoretical physicists, currently high in the status system of
modern science, are prone to accept immediately the reality of
intuitive and non-logical elements in scientific discovery. So, for
the most part, are those working in such relatively new and
highly creative areas as biophysics and biochemistry. Geologists,
today low in the pecking order of science, appear least likely to
accept or understand the art element in science, although they
have much company in the more established and formalized
areas of other disciplines, including biology and physics and
chemistry. In the behavioral sciences generally there is a greater
insistence upon rigor and logic of method—and preoccupation
with method itself—than is true of the physical sciences. There

are differences, of course, by field. Thus the educationists are more likely to fluff their scientific feathers than are the anthropologists in whose number unabashed artists have always flourished and who have, on the whole, spent least time on matters of abstract methodology. Similarly, my experience indicates, acceptance of the art element in science seems to follow the curve of personal distinction. I am told that one Nobel laureate, a chemist, dismissing method, describes scientific discovery as "rape followed by seduction."

3. Marston Morse, "Mathematics and the Arts," *Bulletin of the Atomic Scientists, op. cit.,* pp. 56–57. Two recent literary studies have shown, with impressive imagination and learning, how unreason and reason, unconscious and conscious, hunch and hypothesis, have worked together historically. See Wayne Shumaker, *Literature and the Irrational,* New Jersey: Prentice-Hall, 1960, and Ernest Tuveson, *Imagination as a Means of Grace; Locke and the Aesthetics of Romanticism,* Berkeley: University of California Press, 1960.

4. Florian Znaniecki, *The Method of Sociology,* New York: Farrar and Rinehart, 1934, pp. 234–235.

5. I have discussed this at greater length in my "Conservatism and Sociology," pp. 73–89. See also Leon Bramson's interesting discussion in his *The Political Context of Sociology,* Princeton: Princeton University Press, 1961, Chapter 1.

6. Charles Morris, the philosopher, has suggested that the major difference is this: although both science and art communicate by the use of ideas and representations not completely describable in terms of sense experience, science typically seeks to make its communications capable of identification or verification by the largest number of individuals, whereas art tends to insist that each individual translate the original vision into something peculiarly his own creation.
There are probably also interesting role differences between artists and scientists, though this is, so far as I can discover, a relatively unexplored area of study. Martyl Lansdorf, an artist, and Cyril S. Smyth, a scientist, in a joint article in the *Bulletin of the Atomic Scientists* already cited, say: "In many contacts with humanist and scientific friends we have noticed only one consistent difference of professional attitudes—the scientists are jealous of their ideas; the humanists do not seem to mind if someone appropriates their ideas but are outraged by a plagiarism of form." This is an important insight, but I judge that it has more relevance to painters and sculptors, and possibly poets, than to novelists and playwrights who are certainly as jealous

of ideas, and as secretive, as are the scientists. Legal battles over plots are not unknown.

One commonly alleged difference between scientists and artists deserves critical comment. It is an old stereotype of the scientist, sedulously cultivated in many a seminar, that the scientist, simply because he is scientist and not artist, is pre-conditioned to a willingness, even a desire, to be displaced by the work of students and others. But this stereotype says more about the ideal world of science than it does about actual scientists. The desire for self-preservation is surely as strong among scientists as among artists, and the evidence suggests that in such matters as protection of personal theories, hoarding of data, and secretiveness of intent, there may not be very significant role differences.

Passion for self-preservation may be more functional in scientific thought than is commonly supposed. Marston Morse, in the article referred to above, is of this view so far as mathematics is concerned. He cites the famous feud between Poincaré and his young colleague Lebesque, suggesting the similarity of conflict and outcome to the revolt of Philipp Emanuel Bach against the work of his father, Johann Sebastian. In each case the reactions were dictated by instincts of self-preservation which, as Professor Morse points out, were clearly to the advantage of posterity.

On one point the evidence is clear. Scientists have a far higher sense of priority—though not of competitiveness—than artists. This would seem to follow from the broad differences of context. It is highly unlikely that anything in the history of art resembles what Robert Merton has emphasized in his studies of priority in science or what Frederick Reif has described as prevailing practice among physicists in an article, "The Competitive World of the Pure Scientist," *Science*, 134 (December 15, 1961), pp. 1957–1962.

7. Morse, *op. cit.*, p. 58.

(9)

Power
and the
Intellectual

Today politics has the prestige and enchantment that religion had in Western thought until the end of the seventeenth century and that economics acquired after Marxism began to spread in the late nineteenth century. To go to the root of a thing today is to go to its politics. Everything—business, science, race, the arts, even states of mind like hope and despair—must be placed in the category of politics. The word itself is talismanic. A publisher friend tells me that it is a rare book indeed whose appeal to readers cannot be increased by adding, however irrelevantly, to the title the words "the politics of. . . ." What is business but the politics of production; education but the politics of teaching and research; religion but the politics of grace? Politics, in short, is not today what it was for the American intellectual for so many decades: a separate realm of values, a highly specialized and limited activity. It is total process, unique perspective, even redemptive vision.

Yet it is often said that political thought has lost its historic sense of value commitment, of engagement in hu-

This article, in a slightly different version, originally appeared in *The Yale Review* (March 1964), 321–341.

man history. Two social scientists, Stephen Rousseas and James Farganis, in a recent article in *The Nation* entitled "Retreat of the Idealists," are representative of this view. "American political thought," they write, "has been leached of all its passion for meaningful social reform and has degenerated into the apotheosis of a non-committed scientism." They lament the passing of the ideologue "who is committed to the consequences of ideas and is governed by passion" and the coming of the nonideological liberal who "is uncommitted and free of any chiliastic vision of the transforming moment."

Few would deny that there is an emphasis today upon politics as a technical activity and a field for empirical research that was lacking when politics was conceived as a branch of moral philosophy. But, having said this, I have to dissent strongly from the view that current political thought is leached of commitment. All that has happened, it seems to me, is that the perspective of commitment has changed from economic and social values to more strictly political values. In this respect the present age has more in common with the eighteenth century than with the nineteenth and early twentieth.

In an arresting article in *The American Scholar* (Summer 1962) titled "The Modern Liberal's Casebook," K. R. Minogue has noted the historic affinity between the liberal intellectual and "suffering-situations." It is useful to quote a few lines: "Suffering is a subjective thing depending on individual susceptibility; politically, it can only be standardized. And it has been standardized, over a long period of time, by an intellectual device which we may perhaps call a suffering-situation. . . . The point of suffering-situations is that they convert politics into a crudely conceived moral battleground. On the one side we find oppressors and on the other a class of victims. Once the emotional disposition to see politics in this way is established, then we find people groping around to make the evidence fit."

As Mr. Minogue points out, in the nineteenth and early twentieth centuries the suffering-situations that gave impetus to liberalism were slavery, poverty, class oppression, child labor, working-class rights, and social security, among others. These were the issues which provided the successive moral battlegrounds of the age. They were drawn from Capitalism.

What is the "suffering-situation," the moral battleground, that has succeeded capitalism in the mind and heart of today's liberal? It follows directly, I suggest, from the prevailing orientation toward politics and power. Specifically, it is the existence of what is widely called "private powers" in American society—the quasi-autonomous authority exercised by business corporations, independent professions, cooperatives, and labor unions. Such powers, by the challenge they seem to pose to "public power" (that is, to the state), loom up in liberal-radical writing today with all the evil countenance that capitalism once did. By the diversity of these private powers, by their lack of coordination in national purpose, and, above all, by the hold they so often have over allegiances of their millions of members, they appear distractive and sometimes subversive.

There is, it should be noted well, a major advantage that the issue of power has over the older issue of capitalism. It permits an exciting combination of idealism and empirical realism. There is an uncomfortably utopian element in hostility to the capitalist order. It is difficult to combine the ethic of socialism with the desire for hard-core empiricism and *wertfrei* theory that began to seize social science a couple of decades ago. No such difficulty inheres in the power issue. Preoccupation with political power allows the intellectual to indulge idealistic passions in terms which also satisfy the passion for empiricism and objectivity. What could be more hard-headedly realistic than recognition of the vast and penetrating system of public power that has evolved in this country, and what, conversely, could be more idealistic than the rationalization and extension of this power?

Public power is endowed by the liberal-rationalist today with a natural superiority, with an immaculateness that no private power can claim, not even those private powers—such as the universities and foundations—that a special case must be made for. Labor unions, so long the bearers of grace in the liberal mind, have lost their dispensation in this regard, and one finds more and more liberals today putting labor unions in the same lumber room that business has long been consigned to. Private power carries much the same odium today for the liberal that persisting feudal enclaves of privilege carried for the eighteenth-century *philosophe*. Such power seems against nature and contrary to reason.

The key word in this crucial distinction between public and private power is *legitimacy*. I know of no satisfactory definition of this word, at least in contemporary usage, but this does not prevent its almost unlimited use by contemporary liberals in discussions of power. What gives public power its incomparable moral superiority to all private powers is its claimed legitimacy, by which is meant presumably that its roots lie ultimately in the people taken as a corporate whole—that is, in mass electorates—rather than in the people taken as diversified in their ordinary economic, social, and cultural activities—as society, if we may use this word as a term of contrast to the political state.

To do the modern liberal justice, he does not think there is boundless magic in public authority, and he may admit uneasily, if vaguely, that public control should not be unlimited. He is least enthusiastic about that part of the public power wielded by Congress; most enthusiastic about the Presidency which has gradually come to take on some of the charm once exercised by the Napoleonic idea. He can be made bitter and disillusioned by any given bureaucracy at any given time—Federal Housing Authority, ICC, State Department, etc. But in general, as against the mortal dangers to individual freedom and initiative that lurk in the private sectors of society, those inhering in public power seem venial and remote.

In the nineteenth century, the liberal tradition—the tradition of Lamennais, Tocqueville, Mill, Acton, and Max Weber—saw in the existence of private powers a valuable check on the centralization of the state and on the spread of an atomized mass society. Such powers, it was held, constituted a necessary structure of intermediate authority in society, acting as a buffer for the individual against a powerful state. Rarely is this value seen today by the American liberal who has become, in ever larger numbers, oriented to the more radical tradition of unitary political rationalism. Today's liberal is more likely to see private powers in society as Rousseau saw them, as Hobbes had seen them a century earlier in England, and as Plato had seen them more than two thousand years ago: as distractive to common purpose, inimical to common welfare, and potentially subversive to common government.

A number of recent works, all highly regarded by liberals, give substance to what I am saying. Consider first *The Paper Economy* by David T. Bazelon, a lawyer. At first glance this book might be thought to be merely a latter-day addition to the tractarian literature of the New Deal 'thirties. There is the familiar hostility to the large business enterprise, the monetary and profit system, and to all the irrationalities of competition and oligopoly. There is the equally familiar earnestness about total national planning which, having been proved in Mr. Bazelon's judgment to be technically feasible by two world wars, should now be restored on a permanent basis for use in the "social war."

But there is a political cast to Mr. Bazelon's thinking that was never present in New Deal writings, which typically saw the enemy in the economic terms of private property and competition. In Mr. Bazelon's view, such terms are today obsolete. "The term for understanding an organization is hierarchical power, not ownership; exit the sway of property insofar as property remains private." While the intellectuals were debating capitalism and socialism, the organizational revolution passed them by, leaving them categories without substance. Today "the categories of appropriate comprehension are—technology, organization, power, politics." Business is simply the politics of production.

Characteristically, Mr. Bazelon finds two governments operating in society: public and private. Of these only the first is clearly democratic, resting as it does in the will of the political electorate. The second, private government, "governs mostly by denying its own existence—which requires immense ideological distortion—and by additional domination and perversion of the entire national culture, which it finances. It attacks directly and covertly undermines its weak sister, the official government, on a continuing basis. It lives not by the sword, but by perfidy. If the traditional state exists by virtue of a domestic monopoly of armed force, then our second form of government exists through the exercise of a monopoly of effective fabrication."

Here, I suggest, is the prevailing liberal image of the structure of American political power at the present time. In the public sphere, in Mr. Bazelon's words, "non-rule by non-leaders"; in the private, "autocratic baronies." The whole, vast system of Federal legislative, executive, and administrative power—vaster, probably, than history reveals anywhere save in the totalitarianisms—can be thought of as a "weak sister," the helpless prey of private governments. For Mr. Bazelon, private government may be likened indeed to "voluntary totalitarianism," and he finds "scores of extremely effective measures to ensure the dominance of private autocratic government which have been incorporated into our political system," thus providing, it would appear, a kind of built-in subversion of democracy. The people, it follows from this whole analysis, are deceived and yearning for leadership and release from uncertainty.

Mr. Bazelon proposes the establishment of what he calls a Power Review Commission. This body "should undertake to identify existing power centers wheresoever throughout American society, and then periodically to review the exercise of these powers by the stewards thereof." Even if the truth does not make us free, it can make us more noble in our degradation, and it may "finally disgust us with the garish irresponsibility of our institutional elites." Beyond this truth-telling function, the Power Commission "could lead attacks on *unnecessary* power, on administrators who *misuse* their power, and all in all it could help individuals to feel like individuals." It could also examine "the rigid assumption" that industry must be autocratic.

Clearly, Mr. Bazelon stands in the tradition of political rationalism. His Commission is far more modest in its initial scope than Plato's class of guardians or the French Revolution's Committee of Public Safety, but, given the sheer extent and depth of evils in American society that, according to Mr. Bazelon, flow from the existence of private government, it may be assumed that the role of such a Commission would be an expanding one. Central to political rationalism, from Plato on, is the gigantic assumption that the truth is simple and need only be broadcast for men of good heart to understand. Complexity, intermediation, indirection—these are manifestations of non-truth, of evil. There is the added note of populism in Mr. Bazelon's words: "I think we will be amazed at the wonders that can be accomplished by simple, direct, honest intelligence applied to national problems, even if only descriptively."

At one point the author refers to "the beauty of the Simple Truth." For the political rationalist truth is always upper-case, and its beauty lies in its simplicity. It is not wholly clear what the Simple Truth is in Mr. Bazelon's mind. That it is radical and total is implied by his view that all existing economic, political, and legal theory is bankrupt. That it is perhaps Brahmanical is suggested by his appeal to class and elite leadership ("The lack of respectable class and elite leadership is the important factor, the truly shameful factor, the ultimate American tragedy"). That the Simple Truth may have even more exciting possibilities is to be inferred from his typically rationalist impatience with Congress and his celebration of the Presidency.

We are in a deep crisis—this is the theme of Mr. Bazelon's book, as it is of virtually every work ever written in his tradition—and "it must be presented to the people by a responsible element of our class and elite leadership. . . . There is no time for anything else." There never is time for anything else in the mind of the earnest political rationalist. Hence the attraction to the Lawgiver, the Statesman, to the enlightened despot, to the super-individual who can work his way relentlessly and messianically through complexity and corruption until he reaches the masses with the Simple Truth.

One of the things that gave sophistication as well as humanity to the liberal-pluralist tradition in the nineteenth century was its distrust of Rousseauian simplicity imposed upon large aggregates, and this is why Burckhardt could refer to *les simplificateurs terribles*, why Tocqueville could see totalitarian seeds in democracy's union of Cartesian rationalism and populism, and why Max Weber foresaw "not summer's bloom . . . but rather a polar night of icy darkness and hardness," the consequence of rationalization carried to the nth degree. But today's political intellectual is not likely to be put off by the moralizings of nineteenth-century liberals.

.   .   .

The degree to which a moral concern with private and public power has replaced a concern with capitalism and socialism in the liberal mind is nowhere better illustrated than in Henry Kariel's *The Decline of American Pluralism*. It is industrialism above all else that the author fears—its discipline, its ends, its modes of association—but what we have in this book is no old-fashioned labor-versus-capitalist morality treatise. There is no evidence that Professor Kariel likes labor organizations any better than he does business corporations, or, for that matter, workers better than managers. He sees, to be sure, repression and exploitation everywhere in American society, but it is put characteristically in the political terms of private government—and this includes the Teamsters' Union, the Farm Bureau, and the American Medical Association as well as General Motors.

The tyranny and regimentation embodied in the present system can be ended, and true freedom established, only by action of the public power. Because "the individual is encroached upon by large-scale organizations . . . it remains necessary to keep him, by state action if need be, as unattached to the economic and technological order as possible. If his autonomy and essential equality are to be respected, he must be made as free as possible from the hierarchy imposed by modern industrialism."

Measures taken by the state must, Professor Kariel insists, stop short of establishing an illiberal government, but when one scans the frank and explicit agenda that Mr. Kariel presents for the state in the accomplishment of individualism, one cannot help wondering how a certain illiberality will be escaped. For the government must, among other things, keep in check whatever forces threaten to subvert the esthetic, intellectual, moral, or spiritual goods of the individual; the government must steel the individual to dissent within groups; government officials must see themselves as authorized to liberate human energies by reducing man's preoccupation with making a livelihood; government must check the enervating routines which tend to standardize life and frustrate those private arrangements which, masquerading as healthy pluralism, tend to stratify and congeal society. Lest any voluntary associative or local tendencies threaten to express themselves in social security matters, it is imperative that the state keep old-age, unemployment, and sickness benefits from being localized; above all, the state must detach educational, recreational, and cultural opportunities from both parochial organization and the industrial order lest the educational curriculum as well as leisure-time activities respond to overspecialized needs.

Some readers, on concluding Mr. Kariel's detailed agenda for Americans, might wonder with Tocqueville, "what remains but to spare them all the care of thinking and all the trouble of living?" But Mr. Kariel knows Tocqueville well, and he has explicitly thrown in his lot with Rousseau. "I would have us move, if this still be possible, from the much celebrated ideal of Tocqueville toward the still unfashionable one of Rousseau, from a hierarchical public order toward an equalitarian one."

This, it seems to me, is the single most striking aspect of current liberal ideology—its virtual abandonment of the pluralist perspective of freedom, and its growing commitment to the unitary political idealism of Rousseau. There is the same envisagement of the existing social scene (Professor Kariel specifically likens ours to the *Ancien Régime*) as one of irrational confusion and hypocrisy; the same yearning for a Legislator who will, instead of patching-up, clear the scene of its wreckage and spoilage; the same dislike of associations, especially large ones, that do not derive specifically from the state; the same trust in an immaculate and legitimate public power that requires nothing else for its actualization but the extirpation of the private powers which now corrupt it; and, finally, and perhaps most important, the same obsession with an abstract individualism that is held up as the timeless norm of human society. We must expand on this last point, for it is crucial to the whole liberal thesis of private power.

Nearly all contemporary studies of power (and also of social stratification) are based on the supposition of an overwhelmingly individualistic past in America. In the same way that the eighteenth-century liberal used a conceptualized natural order as the premise of his attacks on traditional society—a natural order in which individuals were seen as free, requiring only the power of the rational state to make this order actual—so contemporary liberals are prone to appeal to a conceptualized past in which individualism flourished, largely unimpeded by institutions and other concentrations of collective power.

This retrospective individualism goes somewhat as follows: economically, America was composed of small entrepreneurs, tradesmen, and farmers, no one of them of sufficient influence to affect others except through the more or less free workings of the market. Socially, the dominant characteristic was an absence of class. A constantly open frontier, together with the ethos of individual achievement, kept class ties weak and tenuous; mobility was universal and commonplace. One man was as good as another and even a little better, as the homely phrase has it. Politically, America was made up of individual citizens, expressing themselves unrestrictedly through the ballot box. No "private governments" clouded the political atmosphere.

It is against the background of this idyll, if I may use the word, that most liberals today cast their proposals for the intensification of central political power. A conceptualized and even romanticized past becomes, so to speak, the natural order, and all that is manifestly in opposition to this natural order is suspect. Hence the familiar attack upon the private collectivisms which, it is assumed, are of recent

origin, which represent a betrayal of the American individualist heritage, and which, as we have seen, are likened
to a new feudalism in America. Hence too the argument
that only by the force of the federal government can the
lost liberties and equalities of the American people be restored. Exactly like his forebears in the eighteenth century,
the liberal today looks to the emancipative mission of the
state. The enemy is the same, the underlying premise is the
same; it is only the statement of the premise that has
changed, a conceptualized past replacing the eighteenth-
century natural order.

How correct is this individualist view of the American
past? I confess that I am as skeptical of it as I am of analytical individualism in general. It reveals a woefully under-
nourished view of society and history.

There was, let us be clear, a powerful and formidable
body of institutional authority in early America that limited
individualism. We sometimes write of American immigrants,
beginning with the Pilgrims, as though, in leaving Europe,
they left behind all institutionalized life and tradition. This,
of course, is absurd, for Europeans brought with them European ways—habits of authority, stratification, and respect
for privilege—that were adapted to the new environment but
not abolished. The fact that laws of primogeniture and en-
tail were rarely enacted in this country, that no gilds, walled
towns, or titled nobility came into being should not be
taken naïvely as an indication of total absence of pre-Cal-
vinist, pre-capitalist, and pre-democratic traits in early
America.

Any real picture of early American society must include
a social class system that was in many parts of the country
as striking as anything to be found in England. Classes were
substantive entities, allegiances to them were strong, and
with classes went sizable differences in power and prestige.
The symbol of the gentleman which crowned the English
class system was hardly less potent here. In a host of ways,
the class one was born in followed him through life—
affecting life chances in a way hardly known today, by contrast. Anyone who thinks such a class system was confined to

cities like Philadelphia and Charleston does not know what
it was like to live in many a Western town even in the early
years of the present century. Given the strong coalescence of
family and land (or other hard property), the enormous
differentials in education, and the ease with which governmental agencies, from legislatures down to city councils,
could be approached by those with money and social influence, class power was a vivid reality.

There was also the authority exerted over individual lives
by great landed estates in almost all parts of the country, in
contradistinction to Jefferson's ideal of a society of small
freeholders. From the great plantations of the South to the
vast cattle and sheep ranches of the West, land holdings
existed that could sometimes more nearly be likened to
feudal estates than to anything encompassed by the individualist myth. In trade there were the powerful mercan-
tile and shipping companies in the East. Collusion was
certainly not unknown, and competition among the largest
ones could be devastating to individuals who got in the way.
Even that alleged Eden of individualism, the Rockies, was
conquered during the great fur trade days not by individuals
or tiny volunteer groups but by some of the most regimented
business organizations of America—organizations that paid
wages to gangs of trappers and traders, bossed them in ways
that might have shocked Judge Gary, and ruthlessly restrained competition.

There were also powerful families—kindreds would be
the more apt term—in literally all sections of the country;
great families that could wield extraordinary economic and
social power over the lives of people in communities and
whole regions. What the Kennedy or Rockefeller kindred
stands for today in its union of kinship and economic and
political power was once commonplace. This was as true in
the nineteenth-century West of the Huntingtons, Crockers,
and Stanfords as it was in the East and South all the way
back to the colonial days.

Add to these the perhaps subtler but not less impressive
powers of the local community and the church in the

eighteenth and nineteenth centuries. It is mere fancy to suppose that these were not profoundly limiting upon the mental impulses, esthetic sensibilities, moral freedoms, and mobilities of individuals. Rural communities could be tyrannous; more so, I suspect, than contemporary corporations in moral and intellectual matters. The phrase religious individualism is a good one, if you can actually find it in practice. But it would be hard to conceive groups and associations more tightly disciplined, resting as they did upon perpetual assent, and more corporate in spiritual and moral matters than those of many of the early Protestants.

The point I am making is that it won't do to take the contemporary corporation, profession, and labor union, and set them against a past assumed for analytical or strategic purposes to be largely devoid of private powers. From a sociological and historical point of view, it is important to see the social powers in any age in terms not of what authority may be presumed to have been taken away from abstract individuals in a state of grace, but rather from other and earlier powers. This is obvious in the whole history of Western civilization, the state having grown to a very large extent on what it has taken from competing institutions— rather than from individuals—but it seems to me to be equally applicable to the dominant private powers of our own age, such as the corporation, labor union, and profession.

Are private governments in America today more authoritarian, more enveloping of individual human values and thought than they were a century ago? Is their authority less legitimate, less subject to due process, as these terms are commonly understood? Is there less moral and intellectual individualism, more conformity in culture as a result of these private governments? Are barriers between the constituted will of the people and achievement of democratic purposes more formidable? Liberals, one must infer from their books and articles, answer these questions affirmatively. But leaving ideology aside, I think it would be extremely difficult to prove the case either on present evidence or by historical argument.

That organizations like General Motors, the American Medical Association, and the United Auto Workers are powerful and exert great and sometimes highly undesirable influence on their members is plain enough. That the power, potential or actual, of all such organizations makes them quasi-public bodies and hence properly subject to some form of public control is equally plain. But is it true, as so many today seem to think, that it is the size and relative autonomy of these private governments that is the real evil, making other evils the inevitable consequence? I think only incurable populism could conclude this. Given the present character of the American market, the radically transformed life styles, allegiances, and mobility patterns, given the size and scope of public government in America today, it is inconceivable that any but very large and powerful private organizations could meet the test either of a viable economy or that of the countervailing power properly required for an enormous Federal bureaucracy.

To think in terms today of a nation of small businesses, small and independent medical or other professional units, and small labor unions is hardly realistic. I hold no brief for any specific corporation or union, and I do not question the perpetual necessity of scrutinizing and, where necessary, limiting their operations by law. But, forgetting for the moment any actual economic and professional organizations, if one were to be given the theoretical problem of devising units in modern society that were functional to the demands of economic viability and political freedom—given the nature of the national and world-wide economic market and the sheer vastness of the Federal government—I am inclined to think he would come out with units substantially like those to be found at the present time.

Admittedly, where there is a strong realm of private government in a social order there is the ever-present possibility of conflict. But limited conflict among institutions, especially on matters of power and loyalty, has been a continuous tendency of Western society, and there is every reason for regarding conflict as actually functional to the distinctive nature of the Western political community. The extraordinary reciprocality of power and liberation that has made the state, ever since Marsiglio of Padua, the special vision of the political intellectuals—who compare remarkably as a corps with that marshaled by the Church in the Middle Ages—would not be possible, it seems to me, apart from the solid background of institutional authority that the state's power and liberating force could be directed against. The generally creative tendencies of rationalization and generalization of power, and of individualization of membership, that are to be seen in the history of the Western state have required the continuing and stimulating context of other institutions—that is, of private governments.

Conflict among private powers, and between private powers and the public power, has been a persisting aspect of history since the Middle Ages. First the state had to cope with a powerful church and kinship system; then the gild, commune, feudal association, and the university. All of these represented formidable structures of authority, function, and allegiance. In the nineteenth century, after the older private governments had been brought, for the most part, to terms with the state, new ones arose: professions, labor unions, and business corporations, as well as a profusion of other associations based on interest and value. Throughout the long historic process, human freedom and creativity have been based on divided allegiances, on what A. N. Whitehead so well calls "many intersecting institutions pursuing diverse ends."

To be sure, there is always the problem of balance of power in society. Power has been out of balance before, and conceivably could be today. But it requires evidence—comparative and historical—and not ideology to prove that this is the case. Alan F. Westin has recently edited a volume, *The Uses of Power*, that offers an unusually enlightening insight into the ways that public and private power collide today on major issues. Seven able political scientists, in as many individual case histories ranging from President Kennedy's Aid to Education bill to the bitter fight in Pennsylvania between the trucking interests and the railroads, have described the ways by which decisions are reached. The editor and authors carefully eschew ideology and generalization about the total picture in America, and what I draw from their book in the way of conclusion cannot be charged to them. It is this. Despite an occasionally sordid, sometimes brutal, and frequently messy picture, their data suggest to me that no generalized, chronic imbalance between public and private power exists. Tensions and conflicts of authority do not seem different, except in pattern, from those of other ages. And it is difficult for me to see any underlying pattern of monopolization of decision-making implied by those who see the nation in the grip of the "private authoritarianisms," the "absolute archonries," or "anonymous managerial groups," that are cited by the writers I have mentioned, or the management-labor-government elite that C. Wright Mills sought to establish in his *The Power Elite*.

It can be said, of course, that decision-making in our system of mixed public and private power is wasteful, time-consuming, and disorderly. This is one reason why the American system of government has always been the despair of rationalists. But I would like to quote here some words of a wise young political scientist, Aaron Wildavsky, whose recent *Dixon-Yates: A Study in Power Politics* is a model of what is required in the study of collision of public and private governments. Following several hundred pages of detailed analysis of the Dixon-Yates episode (for all the detail, it makes exciting reading), Mr. Wildavsky concludes:

The absence of a single, visible guiding hand makes it easy to underestimate the creative role of conflict among independent political forces, and to neglect entirely the heroic feats of rational calculation performed through the interplay of interests within the American political system. To postulate goals for others, to discover what they will give and take, to determine the intensity with which they will pursue interest, to predict the consequences of available alternatives, *constitutes an enormous task. Yet all these calculations were made by the affected parties as they pursued their interests and subjected their desires to the acid test of what others would accept. Viewed in its entirety the TVA experience reinforces the conclusion that if the desired goal is the determination of policy outcomes most satisfactory to the widest range of interested parties, then the clash of interests may well be a more efficient process for achieving this end than calculation by any single hierarchy.*

Despite the common liberal fear of private governments, I wonder if there is not good ground for considering the reverse of the asserted threat: that is, whether, certain present tendencies continuing, private governments will be strong enough. There is, for example, the future role of labor unions. The political importance of these organizations is already beginning to suffer as the result of undermining by automation and the perhaps human tendency of this generation of workers to think of high wages and good working conditions as now a part of the universe. Equally serious may prove to be the apparent determination of some high Federal officials to challenge the historic independence of labor-management negotiations and to bring these ever more closely into the regularized processes of governmental decision. For obvious reasons, labor leaders like this no more than management, a situation that could draw labor and management into an unwontedly close ideological position.

More to the point is the growing alienation of many liberal intellectuals from organized labor. The loss of ideological commitment by most labor leaders and their tendency to look and talk like business executives rather than idealists at the barricades have not endeared them to most intellectuals. The labor union is coming to look to liberals more and more as the gild looked to the *philosophes* in the Enlightenment: contrary to reason and a corruption of the general will. The feeling is strong that whatever may have been the historic contributions of the unions to worker benefits, the state can now be expected to handle these more surely and more democratically. Edward Ziegler probably does not exaggerate the liberal position greatly when, after noting the virtual disappearance of lofty motivation in union leaders, he suggests that before long the labor union will be a historic relic, much like the Vatican's Swiss Guard, performing ceremonial functions, vaguely remembering that once there were great battles requiring zeal, selfless devotion, and great courage. A possibly shrewd, if cynical judgment—but, what becomes of the political function they have performed?

That private governments are frequently guilty of unjustifiable invasions of private right and security is not in question. Neither is the fact that large, oligopolistic organizations require a contemplation by law and the courts different from small groups and enterprises. Human beings are entitled, surely, to the same protections from arbitrary and crippling actions by large labor unions and corporations that common law and equity give them from similar actions by public agencies. Why should not arbitrary exclusion of a worker by a labor union or peremptory treatment of a dealer by a national corporation be regarded as actionable within the same courts that deal with long accepted torts?

What is required, however, is an approach that stems from experience and jurisprudence rather than ideology. I am inclined to think that it is fantasy to try to deal with the problem of organization and freedom today in Rousseauian or Populist terms, sniffing irresponsibility, illegitimacy, and even subversion whenever private organizations become large and powerful. And it is fantasy also to deal with the problem of power against a conceptualized background of an individualism and a general will that never existed.

The rationalist perspective, based simultaneously on individualism and the general will, never has been analytically relevant to the social order, and it has ceased to be valuable even as an ideal. It is this perspective, not pluralism and federalism, that has become obsolete. For, unlike the eighteenth-century world, ours is not surfeited by private governments and ancient institutions that dwarf the state.

Ours is a world, plainly, that calls for reinforcement of social and economic diversity, of legitimate hierarchy, of institutional balance of power. On evidence, it is the lack or weakening of these that attends the only kind of substantial tyrannies that the twentieth century has known.

(10)

The Impact
of Technology
on Ethical
Decision-Making

Technology, like any other force, has moral consequences only when it becomes a part of the effective normative environment. Considered solely in its mechanical aspects, technology is no more capable than the raw, physical environment of directly affecting cultural and moral consciousness. It may have a broadening or limiting effect on economic and social possibilities—and therewith on ethical alternatives—but it will not become a significant ethical force until it is involved in a pattern of social meanings central to society.

This is, I think, the basic and lasting point that Max Weber made in his critique of Marx's account of the origins of capitalism in the West. Despite certain inadequacies in Weber's application of the point to the causal relation between puritanism and capitalism, the essence of his value theory, applied to historical change, can scarcely be chal-

First published in *Religion and Social Conflict*, Robert Lee and Martin E. Marty, eds. (New York: Oxford University Press, 1964).

lenged. Only when technology becomes institutionalized, only when technology becomes itself a social system, subject to processes common to all social systems, can we discover its impact on ethical decisions.

I

THE PLACE OF TECHNOLOGY IN CONTEMPORARY LIFE

There has never been a time since man emerged from the higher primates when he has not been in possession of at least a minimal degree of technology, and so were created the first earthen pot, the spear, and the mortar. Behind the appearance of each of these lay some extraordinary mind, restless and dissatisfied, working in terms of its own and other observations, striving to bring environment within control, to facilitate the business of living. In our own overwhelmingly technological age there is often a danger that we will underestimate the role of technology in other ages. We must not, for it has always been present in one degree or another in human history.

So much is true, yet it must be emphasized that in no other age of history has technology held the central and determining role that it does in our own. Never have so many persons been involved so directly in technological pursuits. At no time in the human past has the technologist-scientist held the crucial role that he does today. Marvel though we may at the ingenious accomplishments of Hellenistic Greece, Imperial Rome, the late Middle Ages, and the Renaissance, they are small indeed by comparison with the works of the modern age.

What philosophy, theology, and art have been in other periods—the major contexts of human creativity—technology is today. Each age produces its own type of hero: soldier, diplomat, theologian, scholar, statesman, or businessman. Today, who would deny that the technologist occupies the hero's niche? Nobel laureates, National Academy members, scientist-administrators, all possess a prestige that makes front page news and carries them to the highest councils of government and society. The time has passed when technology needs to justify itself by its contributions to other spheres of society. Today the ends of technology are sufficient and autonomous.

More important is the fact that in the modern West, for the first time in history, technology has become institutionalized. An institution is a way of behavior, common to a large number of persons in a society. Handed down from generation to generation, it is a generally recognized solution to a recognized problem. In every relevant respect, technology today is as fully and distinguishably an institution as law, religion, or kinship. It is neither more nor less "material" than other institutions. There is no more reason for limiting technology, as a concept, to the machines and tools it employs than there is for limiting the family to housing, law to court rooms, or religion to church buildings.

What is central to technology is the application of rational principles to the control or re-ordering of space, matter, and human beings. We are prone to think of technology in its physical manifestations—skyscrapers, lawn mowers, nuclear bombs—but technology represents social things as well—organizations and processes concerned with human ends. There is as much technology in a school of business administration or education as there is in a school of engineering. The one is as concerned as the other with the rational and calculated achievement of ends which, more and more in our society, are autonomous and self-justifying ends.

This last point may require brief justification. Surely, it will be said, the ends of technology are subordinate to those of economy, religion, politics, and war—all older and more accepted areas of human purpose. This was true, once, but it is no longer true. The conquest of space, the control of physical environment, the mastery of organization, are objectives today fully as distinct as any to be found in the classic areas of statecraft, war, and business.

Innumerable foundations, institutes, vast research and

development laboratories, not to mention huge budgets for technological development, all attest to the autonomy as well as prestige of technology. Admittedly, military defense is the context of a great deal of present-day technology, but I would argue that technological imperatives have attained a degree of primacy not likely to be offset by any changes in the international scene.

Modern technology has its own characteristic structures, its built-in drives, its moral codes, its dedicated servants (as hierarchically ordered and motivated as any to be found in church or state), even its own mystique. Because technology serves an autonomous set of values in our society, and because it is itself a clear pattern of functions and authorities, it inevitably comes into moral conflict with other institutions in society. The tension that Thorstein Veblen was able to discern a half-century ago between the engineer and the price system has become a not uncommon tension between technology and other areas of society—political, esthetic, religious, as well as economic.

Until perhaps a century ago, technology was only an instrumental value. Its significance came from the institution it served. Throughout much of the modern era, especially in the nineteenth century, this significance was economic. Hence the still almost synonymous use of the words "industrial" and "technological."

But before industry, technology served the needs of war. The word engineer was indeed so closely identified with military activities from the fifteenth century on that it became necessary in the late eighteenth century to prefix it by the word "civil" in order to specify a non-military orientation. But quite apart from its earlier ancillary function in society, technology is today an autonomous pattern of ends, functions, authorities, and allegiances.

From the point of view of the history of social institutions, there is nothing extraordinary in this process of "autonomization." We can see it in the histories of religion, politics, and education. In the early Roman Republic, religion, far from being a separate institution, was simply one function of the family. The chief end of religion under the *patria potestas* was that of welding the family into a unity, not merely in space but in time. But as we know, religion became, at a later period in Rome, a separate and autonomous institution; and in its Christian form, a powerful rival to both family and state.

The same transition may be seen in economic processes. In many cultures, economics is subordinate to some other institution: family, religion, or community. It is ethnocentric to assume, as did the classical economists in the nineteenth century, that economic ends and processes are everywhere sovereign and independent. In the West, since approximately the Enlightenment, economic institutions have been autonomous, though this situation shows signs in our own age of undergoing significant change.

As an institution, technology has today, then, its own function: the rational control of man, space, and matter— and its own governing values. It is no stretch of meaning, I suggest, to hold that technology has sacred overtones in the minds of many. To contravene the values of technology in favor of, say, nationalism or economic profits can seem as impious to a scientist today as contravention of religious ends, in the name of economic gain, seemed to a medieval theologian.

II

ETHICS AND SOCIAL CONFLICT

Because technology in our society is an institution and because ethical decisions are closely related to what happens to institutions, it is important at this point to examine briefly the character of institutional change. It is my contention that conflict is the essence of such change. And it is in circumstances of institutional change that ethical values become most luminous.

Too often institutions are conceived as structures endowed with immanent tendencies toward change. They are regarded much as the biologist regards organic life—as something inherent in growth and development, with new phases arising directly and inexorably out of the old. For a long time this organic analogy has plagued Western social thought and confused the study of change in society.

Institutions are complexes of functions, authorities, and values, and apart from their interaction with other institutions—competitive and conflicting interaction—there is no reason to suppose that significant change in any one of them takes place.

In all institutional behavior there is a powerful tendency toward integration and conformity, resulting from the implicit striving of each institution for the total allegiance of its members. What Frank Tannenbaum has written along this line is instructive:

> Each institution in its own inner logic tends to be all-embracing, laying claim to the entire man, and showing an impelling tendency to assume all responsibility in society . . . Institutional friction and instability are, therefore, the normal state of society, and the hope of peace and quietude is an idle dream. Competition, imbalance, and friction are not merely continuous phenomena in society, but in fact, are evidences of vitality and "normality."[1]

Conflict and competition in the institutional scene are inevitably reflected in the minds and moral aspirations of the persons concerned. Institutional conflict is matched by the conflict of human loyalties. Conflict of this type can sometimes be drastic and difficult, as we know from the frequently agonizing experiences of immigrants involved in the transplanting of mores and life-patterns from one culture to another. Much of American social history is made up of this transplanting and with it there has been frequent conflict of institutional and moral loyalties. Out of such conflicts, to be sure, have come some of the great intellectual and moral achievements of American civilization, but out of them have also come some of our bitterest social and moral problems.

In the orthodox, rationalist tradition, little attention was paid to change considered as crisis and to the persisting conflicts of values among institutions of the same society. The gospel of homogeneity and adjustment held the field. That a plurality of institutions could exert powerful and possibly irreconcilable conflicts of allegiance upon individuals was not often envisaged by those who saw change as a smooth and orderly process.

Nevertheless the conflict is there, and it is a fact of the highest significance in history. Sometimes this conflict is passive, awakening only vague sensations of tension. Elements of persistence and conformity in the individual may reduce the effects of conflict on his allegiances. At other times it may be fierce and overt, reflected in widespread mass upheaval and in the central problems of moral philosophies.

Such conflicts, small and large, do not, as the progressive rationalist has thought, resolve themselves inevitably into systems of new coherence and order—either in the individual consciousness or in the overt relationships of major institutions. Where they are matters of crucial allegiance—as with respect to family, church, ethnic group, and state—they may remain for centuries, now relatively passive, now evocative and fiercely antagonistic.[2]

Ethical history is fundamentally a history of the conflict of social loyalties. How else do we account for the history of moral values in ancient Athens except in terms of the struggle between the ancient kinship group and the new city-state? The fifth century B.C. was a time of the breaking up of ancient kinship structures and the gradual emergence of the individual as ethical man, as political man. The reforms of Cleisthenes a century earlier had led to the reduced political position of tribe and clan, but the moral appeal of these groups and their implicit and ancient norms remained binding for the Athenian.

It was in the gradual diminution of kinship norms and the simultaneous rise of the free individual and the popular state that the great moral issues of the age found their setting. Of all ethical problems the greatest was individual responsibility. This is the recurrent theme of the dramas of

Aeschylus, Sophocles, and Euripides. How is guilt to be assigned? To the individual, as the new legal polity suggested? Or collectively—to family and clan—as ancient tradition had it? This was the great conflict in the fifth century, and it would be difficult to understand either the moral philosophers or the dramatists apart from it.[3]

In Roman civilization we see the conflict between the family and the military power, between *patria potestas* and *imperium*. In political terms it is a conflict for power over individuals and property. In social terms it is a conflict of statuses—the status of the son under kinship authority and the status of the son as soldier under the *imperium*.

Ethically, the conflict is to be seen in the problem of both where guilt lies—in family or in the individual—and where the sanctions for violation of norms lie—in the family or in the state. The conflict reached its zenith in the final century of the Republic, a period of pandemic disorganization, and was resolved, legally at least, by Augustus' far-reaching decrees on morals which for once and all, put moral sanctions in the hands of the state.

But the diminution of the moral authority of the family was one of the factors leading to the attractiveness of Christianity to Roman masses. By the second century, the struggle between church and state characterized the ethical history of Rome, which was not moderated until Constantine's conversion.[4]

In various ways the conflict of institutions continued in the periods that followed in the West. In the early Middle Ages, at a time when the church sought to Christianize the Teutons, the struggle was between church and clan. It was a conflict between two inner ethical orders—the moral order of the family and the moral order of the church.

Expressed most concretely in such matters as rights over baptism, marriage, and disposition of the dead, the struggle manifested itself in a host of ways, all related to functions and authority within each institution, and to the loyalties which these two institutions were able to attract. In the process of its eventual victory over kinship, the church took on many of the attributes of an enlarged family.[5]

The triumph of the church in matters of individual conduct was short-lived, for, as we know, by the thirteenth century political power began to challenge religious power. Here was perhaps the most fundamental and implicative conflict in the whole history of the West. At first it looked as though the church would win—consider the monumental significance of Canossa. In the long run, however, the centralizing, nationalizing tendencies of the state could not be stayed. Again we see, as we did in Athens, the simultaneous emergence of the individual and the state, each freed, increasingly, from the legal and moral bonds of medieval traditionalism.

In the twentieth century such conflicts continue, and are to be seen in court cases involving the competing claims of church or family against state in such matters as flag observances in the schools, released time for worship, military service, and other matters. On a vaster and profounder scale they are to be seen in countries where totalitarianism has taken command; here the old conflict between the state and social groups is converted from something latent or intermittent to something that is at the very heart of freedom and morality. The struggle between family and state, between church and state, between trade union and state was vivid in the early days of National Socialism in Germany. It was only when the Nazi state destroyed or completely fettered these competing groups that its own power could be called totalitarian.

So, too, in the non-Western societies throughout the twentieth century, do we see institutional conflict that is deeply moral and spiritual in result. Sidney Nettleton Fisher has concretely expressed this conflict as it appears in the Near East:

At the heart of the tension is the clash of family and national loyalties. The family or the clan has been the basic unit of Near Eastern society for millennia: The ecumenical context in which these units have been more or less loosely welded together has been the religious commune to which they gave allegiance and in which they cooperated for larger *ends. Yet today the nation state and militant nationalism are thrust between these two, claiming to overarch, if not indeed to supersede them. There emerge tensions and fears, hesitation and irresolution on the part of individuals and groups who suspect, generally unconsciously, their ancient values are threatened, and therefore they draw back from wholehearted allegiance to the nation, at least to the nation's claimant representative. Just when the state or government wishes and needs to prevent a strong front against some opposition or threat, so often a politician's or statesman's family and communal ties will interfere and hopelessly tangle the web of decision.*[6]

The conflict between Western and non-Western cultures is, as A. J. Toynbee has written, the single most important fact of the twentieth century. In whatever form it first expresses itself, political, economic, or technological, it becomes inevitably moral and spiritual: it becomes a tension of ethical norms and judgments.

Normative loyalties tend to become directed toward the spheres which have the greatest significance in maintaining life and integrative social meanings. Although never a crude relationship, there is a close relationship between the spiritual appeal of symbols and the extent to which symbols are rooted in the effective social community.

As Susanne Langer has written:

The mind, like other organs, can draw its sustenance only from the surrounding world; our metaphysical symbols must spring from reality. Such adaptation always requires time, habit, tradition, and an intimate knowledge of a way of life. If now the field of our unconscious symbolic orientation is suddenly plowed up by tremendous changes in the external world and in the social order, we lose our hold, our convictions, and therewith our effectual purposes.[7]

This plainly is what is happening to large parts of the non-Western world at the present time, and the results are frequently to be seen in cultural disorganization and moral confusion. The wresting of economic significance from clans or social classes; the withdrawal of political power from the tribe; the introduction of a new administrative or technological system in a native area; all of this can have deep moral consequences.

III

TECHNOLOGICAL PROCESSES AND ETHICAL DECISION-MAKING

Let us return to technology and to some of the specific forms of its impact on society and ethics. In the foregoing pages I have emphasized two major points: 1. Technology will significantly affect human behavior only as it ceases to be something external and becomes internalized in a culture, a recognized part of norms and institutions. 2. Conflict, in one degree or another, is the essence of social change, and ethical conflicts are themselves manifestations of institutional struggle for functional dominance and superiority.

There is an abundant literature in history, anthropology, and sociology documenting the impact of technology on culture and social institutions. As one surveys this literature, there are four distinguishable processes, it seems to me, which represent the common and even predictable effects of technology. Naturally, they do not work alone. Technology never enters a culture, or makes its rise within a culture, apart from political and economic currents which provide contexts. Nevertheless, the technological processes are distinguishable and important. They are: abstraction, generalization, individuation, and rationalization.

1. The first of these I choose to call *abstraction*. I mean by this the separation of moral values from the contexts of immediacy and concreteness that they tend to have in traditional, pre-technological society. The norms of science and technology are abstract and impersonal, and their net effect, over a period of time, can be to make other values seem less urgent, less sacred in character, and more like propositions of utility. Moral behavior is concrete and per-

sonal; it is tied to sharply defined symbols in the community which draw their own efficacy from essentially non-rational sources. The more abstract and remote, the more impersonal and utilitarian these symbols become, the less urgency they have to individuals.

There is also the key role in traditional society of *social membership*. Norms arise from and are inseparable from the close groups in which individuals have membership. It is never man as man, but man as member of clan, tribe, guild, or class that is important. The ethical values are properties of these close and influential groups.

In the kind of society that technology helps create, however, human identity does not rest exclusively on the small and personal type of association. It tends increasingly to come from qualities which the individual holds in common with large numbers of other persons whom he never sees or knows, persons who fall into abstract categories.

Ostrogorski has described this vividly in his treatment of the impact of technology on modern Europe.

> In proportion as the new conditions of existence enlarged the social horizon in the sphere of life, just as it expanded by means of thought, the process of abstraction extended to all social relations. The rapid growth of large towns destroyed the old neighborly intercourse, or at all events, its intimate character. The extension of markets stripped buyers and sellers of their concrete individuality, and resolved them into the general categories of tradesmen and customers. Railways, by bringing together for half an hour men who saw each other for the first and perhaps the last time, reduced them to the general notion of travelers, all placed on an equal footing by uniform tickets, a piece of pasteboard printed wholesale for all present and future travelers. In great industrial enterprises creative energy and active will associated in the form of shares, negotiable securities, transferable to an infinite series of potential entities existing only as shareholders. Even the feelings which take their rise in the depths of the soul, such as the love of one's neighbor and pity, were obliged, when projected over a larger area to conform to abstract notions; the familiar picture of the wretched Jim or Tom

who had been the regular recipient of relief, gave place to the idea of the poor man, the poorer classes.[8]

The Hammonds, writing with particular reference to the impact of technology on England in the nineteenth century, could see the machine in the guise of a new rhythm and tempo of life. Gone was the rhythm of the rural countryside, based upon the direct experience of the passing of the seasons, the rising and setting of the sun, the planting and harvesting of the crops. In its place now was the rhythm of the machine, the never-ending turning of the wheels and gears. Behind the rhythm represented by the factory bell and the overseer, the precise division of the day into units of wages-time, and the machine itself, there lay, as the Hammonds emphasized, the great, impersonal system within which human beings congregated not as members of a moral community but as so many abstract units of energy and production, rationally organized for specific, mechanical purposes.[9]

2. Closely related to abstraction is a second process, *generalization*. Again it is illuminating to quote Ostrogorski.

Confined hitherto to the narrow range of his social circle, it (the moral sentiment) now spread further and further beyond these limits; the tribunal of public opinion sat in judgment wherever cognizance could be taken of the individual's conduct; at the bar of his conscience man became responsible not only to his own society in the restricted sense of the word, but to society in general, to his country, to the nation, even to humanity. Thus a readjustment of forces took place in man's social existence between the particular which constituted nearly all his being and the general which occupied but a small portion of it. Destined as he is by his finite and limited frame to cling to the concrete and the particular as his starting point and strongest support, man nevertheless launched on all sides into the general, with the result that henceforth his social relations were bound to be guided not so much by sentiment, which expresses the perception of the particular, as by general principles, less intense in their nature perhaps, but sufficiently comprehensive to

*take in the shifting multitudes of which the abstract social
groups were henceforth composed, groups continually subject to expansion by reason of their continual motion.*[10]

In one of the most illuminating chapters of his *Democracy in America*, Tocqueville has shown how the concept
of honor, beginning as a fundamental value of one class
alone, the nobility, and drawing its sustenance from feudal
contexts of authority, becomes steadily more general in
modern times. Tocqueville concludes:

> When ranks are comingled and privileges abolished, the
> men of whom a nation is composed being once more equal
> and alike, their interests and wants become identical, and
> all the peculiar notions which each caste styled honor suc-
> cessively disappear. The notion of honor no longer proceeds
> from any other source than the wants peculiar to the nation
> at large, and it denotes the individual character of that na-
> tion to the world . . . As honor among democratic nations
> is imperfectly defined, its influence is of course less power-
> ful; for it is difficult to apply with certainty and firmness a
> law that is not distinctly known.[11]

What Tocqueville writes of honor is not less true of a
large number of other values—loyalty, integrity, guilt and
innocence, patriotism, piety. In each instance we are dealing
with a norm that arose in the first instance within clear and
decisive contexts. Generally, they were the contexts of small
association. Morality, as we have noted, was indistinguishable from the inner order of clan, village, or class. It was
as concrete as it was associative, and because it was concrete
it had meaning in the daily lives of individuals.

In the same way that the development of the political
community has meant the generalization and abstraction of
all the local and particularized authorities which traditional
society abounded in, so the spread of technology has meant
the generalization and abstraction of the various norms
which, in earlier times, had been limited to small communities. The same technology which made possible mass

society made possible mass norms—another way of referring to generalization and abstraction.

3. A third process to be noted is *individuation*. Technology is one of the modern forces that have had a frequently fragmenting and dissolving effect upon traditional communities. Because technology is itself a social system, with a place in it for the individual conceived in a new status, it has an individualizing effect upon the older communities. By virtue of the abstract and impersonal character of the technological system, the individual is able to perceive himself more vividly as a separate being rather than as an organic member of a community. The late G. P. Adams wrote:

> It is not strange that the self discovery and self consciousness of the individual should have steadily mounted higher as the environment of the individuals more and more takes on the form of an impersonal, causal, and mechanical structure. For the mobility and freedom of the individual can be won only as he becomes detached from his world; his world becomes separated from him only when organized and defined in objective and impersonal terms.[12]

Such sociologists as Tönnies, Simmel, Durkheim, and Weber have all emphasized the processes of modern history that have led to a mechanization and atomization of the primary social relationships. No doubt it is easy to exaggerate this, and we cannot forget that technology has synthesized even as it has fragmented, but it remains true that the very impersonality and abstractness of technology formed a background against which the individual could seem more real than the primary and communal ties from which he was being separated.

The rationalist image of society in this age powerfully supported the individualizing tendencies of the new technology. In man alone were now placed virtues and stabilities that had earlier developed within associations. How else, rationalists asked, could the moral imperatives of emancipation be fulfilled except by the premise of man's separateness and his autonomy? The demands of freedom appeared to be in the direction of the release of large numbers of individuals from the statuses and identities that had been created for them by history. A free society would be one in which individuals were morally and socially as well as politically free, free from ancient traditions and corporate groups. Order in society would be the product of a natural equilibrium of economic and political forces, just as order in technology itself is the result of an equilibrium of levers and gears.

4. To these three processes I would add one more that seems to me deeply embedded in the impact of technology on society: *rationalization*.[13] Here I am referring to the widespread tendency throughout modern society to bring under the formal rules of hierarchical administration areas of thought and behavior which have been traditionally areas of informal and individual decision-making. Rationalization of decision-making is plainly a deep tendency in education and religion as well as in industry and the state.

The very progress of modern administrative techniques has created a problem in the maintenance and nurture of individual thought and action. In the same way that the technological revolution reduced man's significance through the transfer of, first, strength, then skill, and finally thought itself, to the machine, it now appears to have a fourth phase: one in which individual decision is being transferred to the machine—conceived as scientific and channeled organization. By its very triumph of rationality, scientific administration has reduced much of the elbow room, much of the intellectual and moral friction which ethical individuality must have if it is to flourish.

In one of his essays, the distinguished physicist, P. W. Bridgman, now retired, tells us that it becomes steadily more difficult for him to conceive the emergence of great *individual* physicists in our age of science, simply because of the increasing involvement of so much scientific research in the costly and elaborate machinery of administrative organization. Such administration, and all that it implies, can too often take away the informal and challenging atmosphere that creative people need.

Ethical decision-making is, from one point of view, a form of creativity, and it is no exaggeration to suggest that it may suffer in related ways. Quite apart from the time-consuming complexity of much administration, it can contain a kind of tyranny. The tyranny consists of tiny rules governing action and decision; of innumerable channels and levels; of committees and all the other types of rational administration which, however effective they may be from a purely technical point of view, powerfully affect the ethical role of the individual. Ethical decision-making, like leadership, requires a certain degree of autonomy from the rules, an opportunity for occasional error and an understanding that the individual himself, not the organization, bears responsibility.

Decision-making, as Robert Presthus has recently written, becomes vague and impersonal in the big organization, the instrument of an anonymous, fragmented intelligence.

> Each decision is the result of various technical and personal considerations, the sum of the contributions of the sum of everyone involved in the deciding process. This diffusion means that "everyone" (i.e., no one) is responsible. In extreme cases the condition may lead to arbitrary and immoral behavior, particularly when compounded by intense personal identification with the state, the party, the church, or the "organization." In every case, the probabilities that the organization may act unjustly are increased by the weakening of individual responsibility. Only "the system" is responsible.[14]

In a brilliant article, Harold Rosenberg has recently dealt with the Eichmann trial in these terms. Mr. Rosenberg points out that Eichmann's defense was based almost entirely on a proposition that he knew could not help but have appeal to large numbers of persons in our society. Basically, this defense rested on his transference of guilt from himself, as an individual, to a soulless, impersonal organization within which he was but a simple cog. Guilt, as we have known the concept throughout most of history, is individual, and thereby requires a sense of the self. But if the self is obliterated, if the organization takes command, reducing individuals to roles without responsibility, how can there be guilt? The very essence of the Nazi system was the blurring and extinguishing of the sense of the self. And as Eichmann shrewdly realized, this has become a pervading characteristic of the modern technological world.

Eichmann's defense was designed to appeal to the universal appreciation of the plight of the organization man. Who cannot grasp that one in the middle of a chain of command—a link in the sausage—simply passes down orders he receives from above, without having the power to alter their content or to influence their ultimate effects? Everyone in an organization is in a sense nothing but a traffic officer while the directors at the top reach decisions that reflect a collective mind separate from that of each . . . It is not thinkable to be the dispatcher of human shipments to death factories but by analogy with the clean hands of the office man in charge of shipping fertilizer or veal carcasses, it is thinkable.[15]

VI

CONCLUSION

We conclude where we began. Technology viewed simply as the machine is powerless to affect human culture or ethics. Only as it becomes institutionalized, only as its ends conflict with and override established norms, does technology become a dislocating and moulding force in society. Technology need not weaken individuality in society—not any more than physical landscape need weaken it. But when its institutionalization reaches the point of reducing the normal conflict of institutions through techniques of abstraction, generalization, and rationalization, it may be regarded as posing a threat to individuality and to ethical decision-making. Technology becomes one of the forces in society whereby the individuality and concreteness of ethical norms—such norms as honor, guilt, loyalty—become tenuous and indistinct.

The making of ethical decisions is always related to conflict of one kind or another: there is a conflict of *institutions* in society or a conflict of *ends* in the individual consciousness. It is unlikely that without the large institutional conflict, any significant inner conflict of ends and meanings could occur. Within the very circumstances which helped liberate individuality from the older traditional types of community, the key problem of the present age, I believe, is that of maintaining individuality of ethical decision-making.

NOTES

1. Frank Tannenbaum, "The Balance of Power in Society," *Political Science Quarterly* (December 1946).

2. See my *The Quest for Community* (New York: Oxford University Press, 1953), Chapter 4.

3. The best treatments of this are Gustave Glotz, *La Solidarité de la famille dans le droit criminel en Grèce* (Paris: A. Fontemoing, 1904) and Louis Gernet, *Droit et société dans la Grèce ancienne* (Paris: Sirey, 1955).

4. I have dealt with this at greater length in my "Kinship and Political Power in First Century Rome," pp. 203–224.

5. The best of all treatments of medieval institutions and the conflicts among them is Edward Jenks, *Law and Politics in the Middle Ages* (New York: Henry Holt, 1898).

6. S. N. Fisher, *Social Forces in the Middle East* (Ithaca: Cornell University Press, 1955), p. 258.

7. Susanne Langer, *Philosophy in a New Key, A Study in the Symbolism of Reason, Rite, and Art* (New York: New American Library, 1948), p. 237.

8. M. Ostrogorski, *Democracy and the Organization of*

Political Parties (New York: Macmillan, 1902), Vol. 1, pp. 45 ff.

9. J. L. and Barbara Hammond. See esp. *The Town Laborer* (London: Longmans, Green, 1917), *passim.*

10. Ostrogorski, *op cit.,* pp. 49–50.

11. Alexis de Tocqueville, *Democracy in America* (New York: Knopf, 1945), Vol. 2, bk. 3, ch. 18.

12. G. P. Adams, *Idealism and the Modern Age* (New Haven: Yale University Press, 1919), p. 35.

13. It was, of course, Max Weber whose writings first identified and documented this process in modern European history.

14. Robert Presthus, *The Organizational Society* (New York: Knopf, 1962), pp. 53–54.

15. Harold Rosenberg, "The Eichmann Trial," *Commentary* (November 1961).

[11]

Kinship
and
Political Power
in First Century
Rome

I

My subject in this essay is a problem that has long been of interest to historians and sociologists of legal institutions: kinship authority (*patria potestas*) and its decline in ancient Rome. Quite apart from the intrinsic interest of the subject, we can learn much from it, I believe, of what is more generally involved in the shift of authority from one institution to another, in the rise of legal individualism, and in the dislocation of important social groups from functional significance in a social order.

Exactly a century ago, Sir Henry Maine gave brief but striking attention to the problem, and his own statement is

Reprinted with permission of The Macmillan Company from *Sociology and History*, edited by Werner Cahnman and Alvin Boskoff. Copyright © 1964 The Free Press of Glencoe, a Division of The Macmillan Company.

worth repeating. Whereas, Maine pointed out, we find the house father possessing in early Rome the *jus vitae necisque*, the power of life and death, over his children and others under his power, along with comparable authority in other spheres—economic, religious, and educational—the Imperial Age reveals the decline of the *patria potestas* to a level scarcely greater than that to be found in the modern family.

> The unqualified right of domestic chastisement has become a right of bringing domestic offenses under the cognizance of the civil magistrates; the privilege of marriage has declined into a conditional veto; the liberty of selling has been virtually abolished, and adoption itself, destined to lose almost all its ancient importance . . . can no longer be effected without the assent of the children . . . in short we are brought very close to the ideas which have at length prevailed in the modern world.[1]

It would be difficult to state the problem more concisely, and, as we shall see, Maine has some penetrating observations to make on the factors involved in the decline. The principal objections to Maine's presentation—apart from a lack of data that more recent scholarship has supplied—are, first, the view he takes of the general nature of change and, second, the strict and uncompromising legalism of his treatment.

Like most of his contemporaries, Maine wrote under the spell of the evolutionary perspective. He regarded change in an institution as endogenous, proceeding as does growth in an organism, in a slow, gradual, and continuous manner. Past phases of any social institution are deemed to be immature or imperfect, mere steps in a development whose true and proper nature lies ahead. Thus, Maine tells us, the *patria potestas* could not have been a durable institution; it was inherently unstable and imperfect. The essential problem of change is not that of accounting for actual transformation in the *patria potestas* but rather "to guess at the causes which permitted the *patria potestas* to last as long as it did by rendering it more tolerable than it appears."[2]

This leads to the second difficulty of Maine's approach—

that of dealing with his subject in an exclusively legal manner. Writing as a lawyer—albeit a broadly educated one —Maine chose to regard the *patria potestas* as a power much like sovereignty in the modern state—abstract, impersonal, and remote—rather than as an institution embedded in religion, morality, and economics. It was because Maine fixed his attention almost strictly on the power aspects that the problem of the *patria potestas* could appear as one of accounting for the length of time it was able to maintain itself, rather than that of uncovering the historical forces which were in fact necessary for the dislocation of one of the most durable institutions in all Roman history.

Most subsequent students of the Roman family have dealt with the subject in substantially the same terms. Sociologists, in particular, have done so in the same way that they have handled social change in general—as the consequence of internal forces and tensions, only moderately and perhaps catalytically affected by external factors.[3]

Major social change is not, however, the consequence of internal tensions, nor of immanent variations and mutations proceeding in ways best known to biologists. It is, on the contrary, the result of intrusion, external impact, or conflict.

It will be the primary purpose of this paper to show that the *patria potestas*, far from being unstable and driven to its decline by innate difficulties, was in fact a powerful and tenacious institution, one that did not change in any important respect until it was subjected to the force of another—and eventually greater—authority, the military *imperium*. It was the unequal conflict between these two forces, as we shall see, that transformed the kinship system in Rome and, with it, the basis of the larger society.

II

We have no difficulty in describing the nature and significance of the *patria potestas* in the Republic—that is, the period down to approximately the end of the first century

B.C. An imposing body of scholarship gives us a clear and detailed view of our subject. What has too often been overlooked or underemphasized, however, is the key role of the *patria potestas* in the larger structure of power in the total society of the Republic. As we shall see, the fateful change in kinship authority came only where there began to take place a massive rearrangement of this larger structure of power.

To properly see the picture of early Roman society, [Strachan-Davidson writes]

> we must imagine a number of households, each united under its own paterfamilias. Inside the household the father is the sole judge, beholden to no one for his actions and performances. . . . No Roman writer ever attributed the patria potestas either to the magistrate, whether king or consul, or to the sovereign people itself, and there is no trace of the power exercised by the state authorities developing out of those exercised by the head of the family.[4]

Strachan-Davidson's last point is an important one to our problem. So many anthropologists and historical jurists in the modern world have treated political sovereignty as if it were the simple outgrowth of family authority that the essential separateness of the two has been minimized or overlooked. In the final section of this paper, I will expand upon the significance of this separateness to the problem of change. Here it suffices to emphasize that the *patria potestas* was an original and autonomous power within Roman society, drawing its vast authority over individual behavior from immemorial tradition, not from any higher agency within the Roman state.

Strictly speaking, the *patria potestas* was much more than power. It stood for the unity of the family, its continuity in time, and as the irreducible atom of society as a whole. The word for father, *pater*, did not connote generation, but authority and protection. The basis of the Roman family, Fowler has emphasized, was the right of ownership, inseparable "from the idea of land settlement and therefore essentially *das Hauswesen*, the house itself, with persons living in it, free or servile, with their land and all their property, all governed and administered by the *paterfamilias*, the master of the household."[5]

The centrality of the family in law was reinforced by its agnatic character. The framework of the Roman family was not common birth; blood brothers were not *ipso facto* members of the same family. Two people were related agnatically if they were in the *patria potestas* of the same man, or if there was some common ancestor in whose power they would both have been were he still alive. Thus, given Roman male succession, a father and his brother were agnates; so were a father and his son. But a Roman male and his married daughter or sister were not agnatically related. For there was only cognatic relationship, and to this the Romans, in the Republic, attached little importance of any kind, and no legal importance whatsoever.

The reason for strict insistence upon the agnatic tie in all matters of law, property, and religion is not far to seek. The organization of Roman society would have been disrupted if men had claimed relationship to their mother's blood relatives. For then a person would have fallen under more than one *patria potestas*, with all the related confusion that would prevail in a society that did not possess a centralized political power over persons. "As long as the family was an *imperium in imperio*, a community within a commonwealth, governed by its own institutions of which the parent was the source, the limitation of relationship to the agnates was a necessary security against a conflict of laws in the domestic forum."[6] It was only after the public power penetrated and became eventually sovereign in private matters that the principle of agnation could be safely abandoned. And, as history records, by the second century of the Empire, the agnatic relationship meant little more than it does in modern society. It had ceased to be the center of gravity of Roman society.[7]

Individualism did not exist in the Republic—legally, economically, morally, or socially. Tradition united with overt authority in making each Roman feel, first, a member of a group, with duties, and, only second, an individual with rights. Until very late in the Republic the family bore responsibility for most individual offenses, and it was the prime agency of retribution for injuries suffered by one of its members. Not until 149 B.C. did true criminal law make its appearance, in the statute known as the *Lex Calpurnia de Repetundis*, resulting in the establishment of the first *Quaestio Perpetua*—that is, a permanent commission for consideration of public crimes. Prior to this date such offenses were dealt with by the Senate as a whole, much as they did with any other public responsibility.[8] In the execution of criminals, even when the offense was against the whole state (treason, for example), it was the family itself that served as the vehicle.

> Over and over we find the actual execution of punishment, capital or otherwise, committed to the relatives of the culprits instead of being carried out by servants of the state. The noticeable point is that this occurred not only with those who were under the potestas of father or husband . . . but with women who were sui juris, but who were nevertheless put to death or banished by propinqui or cognati.[9]

Repeatedly we are struck by the autonomy of the family in the law and custom of the Republic. Magistrates and censors could exhort, but little more.

> The officers of the commonwealth, the consuls and other magistrates, did not dare cross the threshold of a father's house; they assumed no power to interfere within his doors. The head of the family was its sole representative; he alone had locus standi in the tribunals of the state. If a wrong was done by or to any member of his family, he and not they must answer for it or demand compensation.[10]

The legal majesty of the *patria potestas* could not have endured as long as it did, and been as difficult to dislodge in the end, had it not been for roots in the religious, economic, and social life of Rome. This is the point that has been too often overlooked by historians and jurists. And when the *patria potestas* did come to an end as a major part of Roman society, it did so, as we shall see, within a larger context of change that included religious and economic, as well as political dislocations.

Thus, religion, throughout most of the Republic was hardly more than a spiritualization of family life, reaching back to earliest ancestors and forward to the unborn. Public pontiffs had few and limited rights of supervision. The *Lares* and *Penates*, being gods of the household were private; ceremonies were secret. Nothing violated the priestly authority of the father over his hearth, and religion was deemed as inextinguishably a function of kinship as was life itself. Birth, marriage, and death were the ceremonial high points, and in each ritual the authority and unity of the family were, in effect, reaffirmed. No child was born into the family; he had to be accepted. What else were death rites but the means whereby one left the earthly members of the family to join the departed—who were deemed not the less living for their eternal stay elsewhere? To allow others—strangers—into the religion of the hearth was to risk alienation of the departed; and for a family to fail to make food offerings at each meal to the gods of the household, or, most direly, to permit the sacred flame to go out, was to risk extinction of the departed souls. Similarly, marriage, far from creating a new family, was the ceremony (purely private) whereby the young woman, the intended wife of a son under power, was, in effect, cleansed of the worship under which she had previously lived, and made the subject of a new religion, that of her husband.[11]

Finally, and equally crucially, property and wealth were regarded as possessions of the family, never of individuals. At no time in the Republic could a son under power, however important he might be in military or public affairs, or whatever his age, legally own property. Nor could he even retain income personally earned, unless with the consent of the father. Beyond this, there was the strict limitation of rights of inheritance. Property could not easily be alienated from the agnatic family. Law and custom joined in stress upon the corporate, kinship character of property.[12]

Let us summarize briefly the character of the society within which the *patria potestas* flourished. (1) It was the very opposite of an individualistic society, for the family was the irreducible unit in law, economics, religion, as well as other functional areas. (2) It was a society strong in descriptive law—tradition, convention, custom—rather than prescriptive law. (3) Pluralism, rather than monism, was the essence of the social system, although we should not underestimate the ease and effectiveness with which the early Romans could mobilize into military unity. (4) It was a society based upon legal decentralization rather than centralization, a condition emanating naturally from its pluralism. For the *patria potestas* could hardly have flourished in a society where the power of the state directly impinged upon each individual.

III

So much for the background of the problem. We must turn now to the events and changes which specifically and decisively changed the character of the *patria potestas* in Rome and, with it, the foundations of order in Rome. Our subject is intimately involved in the social transformation which characterized the end of the Republic and the rise of the Empire at the very end of the first century B.C.

We can do no better than quote some words of the Roman historian, Dio Cassius, as the means of introducing this section. "So it was," he wrote of the fateful accession of Augustus in 27 B.C., "that all the power of the people and the Senate passed over to Augustus, and from that day pure monarchy was established."[13] Monarchy is perhaps not the word we would apply to a personal absolutism founded, not upon tradition or right of succession, but rather upon military power united with popular appeal to the masses that is best known as Caesarism. Julius Caesar had offered the vision, and, for a moment, the actuality of absolutism founded upon mass appeal; Augustus Caesar now supplied both the blueprint and the implementation of a form of totalitarian power that was to survive in one form or another for half a millennium.

The façade of the Republic was maintained in the form of the Senate, but after 27 B.C., as Rostovtzeff, among others, has emphasized, the crucial elements were "the now permanent army and its commander-in-chief, the Emperor Augustus, *Imperator Caesar divi filius Augustus.* . . . The army was the master of the State, and, in the restored Roman republic, the Emperor ruled wholly through the army and for so long as the army was willing to keep him and obey."[14] There was, to be sure, much to recommend the new form of government. A century of bitter, destructive civil wars among the rival military commanders—based, as Rostovtzeff has pointed out, upon no social programs or objectives; merely the struggle for absolute supremacy in the state— had so thoroughly weakened the traditional foundations of the commonweal that effective rule by the Senate was impossible. It is, of course, tribute to the majesty of the idea of the Senate that Augustus strove to make his government at all times seem to rest upon the Senate. But every Roman historian who touched upon the matter makes clear that, in fact, Augustus was the unrivalled and absolute ruler of Rome. All else was convenient fiction.

Time does not permit an examination of all the changes which were the consequence of the penetration of Augustan political power into the recesses of the social structure in Rome. Our specific concern here is the *patria potestas* and the role of the family in the new order. It is enlightening, however, to note by way of preface that changes in the *patria potestas* were themselves parts of a larger program that involved also the reconstitution of social classes in Rome, new foundations of property and wealth, the character of religion, and even the social origin of members of the Senate. As Pelham has written, legislation on the family "formed an integral part of the general policy of social and administrative reconstruction in Rome and Italy which Augustus kept steadily before him from the beginning to the end of his long reign, and it is only in connection with that policy that it can be properly studied and understood."[15]

I will merely summarize the consequences of this broad program. There was, first, the centralization of political power. No longer would Rome be, in political terms, a decentralized and cellular society as it had been for centuries in the Republic. In the same way that the Senate had been supplanted by the Emperor as the effective source of public power, so would all other social bodies that lay intermediate to the individual and the government: social classes, gilds, and the family itself. Gradually there took form the doctrine that was, within a century, to become the basis of the texts of Roman jurists (the texts which, after their codification in the age of Justinian, were to comprise the powerful and historically significant code of Roman law). The essence of this doctrine was the axiom that law—in contrast to mere custom or tradition—flows from the sovereign alone, who must be, by definition, above the law.

Second, and functionally related to the doctrine of centralized sovereignty, was the rise of legal individualism. A century of social atomization caused by civil war and political turmoil greatly facilitated this, but the theoretical essence of legal individualism lay in the idea, closely related to the idea of sovereignty, that individuals alone are the true units of the state, not social units; and such individuals, and all the relations among them, exist under the contemplation of the legal sovereign. Everything between the state and the individual inevitably had, now, an insecure existence, for it was the state alone that could give sanction to a corporate unity. From this fateful perspective of legal individualism arose, within a century, the important doctrines of legal fiction and legal concession. By legal fiction was meant the proposition that no social group, however old and embedded in tradition, has true or real character. It is a concept in the contemplation of the sovereign— nothing more, so far as law is concerned. Reality lies in individuals, not groups. More important was the related but distinguishable idea of concession. Those groups and only those groups may legally exist whose foundations have been created, so to speak, by specific concession of the sovereign.

This is, stated simply and baldly, the Roman doctrine of corporations, and it means, in the words of the great Maitland, that "all that stands between the individual and the state has but a derivative and precarious existence." I do not suggest that this momentous doctrine, which was to aid the transformation of Europe a thousand years later with the revival of Roman Law, took its full shape in the Age of Augustus. We must wait a century for this. But there can be no doubt that the specific measures of centralization and individualization that took place in Roman polity under Augustus, at the end of the first century B.C., were the true source of later legal formulations.[16]

What happened to the *patria potestas* in 18 B.C. is of a piece with the other measures which were being taken to bring power firmly into the central government over associations and classes throughout society. If public order was to be restored and Rome's greatness secured in the world, there must be no *imperium in imperio,* no social allegiance, not even the agnatic family, which could detract from necessary political centralization.

The professed object of the famous *Leges Juliae* in 18 B.C.—and in particular the two laws *de adulteriis* and *de maritandis ordinibus*—was moral: to clean up the moral delinquencies and to restore marriage to its once proud estate. We need not question motive. The austerity of Augustus' personal life—unchallenged by contemporaries—is perhaps sufficient proof of this. But neither can we overlook the fact that in the establishment of these laws on morality and marriage, we are dealing with the first *official* limitations in Roman history of the historic authority of the *patria potestas* over these matters. It must further be kept in mind that the new laws, far from being isolated manifestations of moral reform, constitute an integral part of that larger reconstruction of Rome which, whether dealing with water supply, fire control, education, religion, or corn dole, was to lead to complete centralization. As Pelham has written:

When we turn to the measures of reform adopted by Augustus it becomes clear that his efforts were by no means limited to the removal of the obstacles which impeded the growth of material prosperity or the repression of the vices which disgraced society. Great statesman as he was, he realized from the first the necessity, if either the political system which he had established was to stand or his other reforms were to have any lasting effect, of creating in a people demoralized by faction and civil war a healthy and vigorous public feeling.[17]

For centuries, however imperfectly at times, the sole authority over adultery and other moral matters had been the power of the corporate family. Exile for personal delinquencies was not uncommon, but it was a power wielded under the authority of the *patria potestas*, not by a public magistrate nor even by the Senate unless damage to the commonweal had been done. Similarly, responsibility for marriage, for its motivation as well as for its operation, was, as we have also seen, a sacred function of the family. No public officer intruded into the decisions and ceremonies involved.

Now, at a stroke, these matters are brought within public jurisdiction. In the case of adultery, the nature of the offense was defined, the procedure fixed which was to be followed when a case arose, and the penalty laid down.

For the primitive and probably decaying jurisdiction of the pater familias [writes Pelham] and the equally primitive right of private vengeance where the guilty parties were caught in the act, the Lex Julia aimed at substituting the more regular procedure of the law.[18]

So it did, but it also, as Pelham himself points out, suggests, as do Augustus' other social and moral reforms, his anxiety not merely to restore social order by assigning to each class an appropriate career, a definite status, and definite privileges, but to connect each class with himself and his rule by special ties.

So far as we know, the first object of the new law was

Augustus' own daughter, a young woman who, apparently, deserved exile for the reasons given. But the genius of the punishment lay in the fact that, having just established a public law which for the first time in history arrogated such punishment to the public agency, any possible sting in its first application was taken away by the familiar spectacle of a father exiling his own daughter. Further genius was shown when, for a time, he showed considerable mercy in dealing with others guilty of adultery, turning them over to their own families. But the all important precedent had been set, and under the head of *de pudicitia* in the law, various other regulations governing public decency—behavior at public games and shows, women's attendance at athletic contests, extravagances in dress, and undue expenditures on banquets —were passed under the authority of the *Leges Juliae*.[19]

The same kind of transfer of authority is to be seen in the sections on marriages. Here too the ostensible aim is the encouragement of marriage and the production of children, an aim on which Augustus could indeed claim the sanction of ancient custom and opinion. The aim had more than once, in earlier times, been made the subject of exhortation by various censors. But there is more in the Augustan decree. For the first time in history marriage becomes a matter of state concern and supervision. Marriage is made obligatory upon all men between the ages of twenty and sixty and upon all women between twenty and fifty. Childlessness in men over twenty-five and in women over twenty was made punishable. Widows and divorced women were also ordered to remarry within a specified time. "To enforce these regulations a system of penalties and rewards was devised. The unmarried were declared incapable of inheriting property or accepting legacies; the childless were mulcted of half the amount of such bequests."[20]

Perhaps even more significant was the limitation placed upon the right of marriage among certain classes, specifically with persons who were not freeborn. Marriage between the freeborn and those who were not—the freedmen were a large and growing class—was forbidden to patricians. Marriages to freedmen were forbidden not only to senators but to their children, grandchildren, and great-grandchildren. Here too it might be said that the aim was moral—the reduction of the license that had grown up, often leading to the exploitation of the lower class member as well as to dilution of ancient families. But, from our point of view the result is the same: for the first time the state intervened in a matter that had been traditionally private, reserved to the *patria potestas*.

The penalty forbidding the unmarried from inheriting property was, of course, an invasion of what we have seen to be the autonomy of the family in matters connected with its own property and income, and it is closely related to a separate act of Augustus during this period. This was the *peculium castrense*, which permitted the sons under power to retain all booty, income, and property they had acquired during military service. It will be remembered that at the basis of the *patria potestas* was its economic solidarity, the corporate possession of property by the family alone, not its individual members. In this decree, plainly, lie the beginnings of economic individualism and, with it, of contractualism, a concept that was also to become primary in later Roman law codes. Later emperors, beginning with Hadrian, were to extend this right of individual ownership to all public employees and civil servants, eventually to all citizens. Not unrelated to Augustan decrees on property and family were those touching on membership in the Senate. Senatorial status was no longer inherited through family lines; it was to be conferred by the Emperor.[21]

There was, finally, the religious aspect of the *patria potestas*. As we have seen, family authority was deeply rooted in the religion of the *Lares* and *Penates*. Privacy of the corporate religion of the family was one of the very pillars of the *patria potestas*. This, too, was radically modified. In 12 B.C. Augustus became Pontifex Maximus, thus uniting the political and religious life of the commonweal. But far more important from our point of view is the political penetration of the family hearth. Images of Augustus began to make their appearance within family domiciles, thus giving root to the novel and exotic efflorescence of emperor worship, a form of religion in the East that had aroused the revulsion of Romans a century or two before.

> Along with the image of the Lares and Penates was placed that of Augustus. So this "genius" shared with the Lares the libations poured in their honor and the offerings placed for their acceptance. The worship which thus established Augustus as a household god in the homes of the people and gave him a place in one of their oldest worships was admirably fitted to serve his interests and those of the empire on a larger scale.[22]

Thus, in three decisive ways, the *patria potestas* was challenged by the military *imperium*—in control of marriage and descent of family property; in the fragmentation of economic ownership; and, finally, in the invasion of the religious sphere. All of these momentous changes took place in the decade, 18 to 8 B.C., and they are at the heart of that simultaneous rise of individualism and political centralization in the Empire.

> Relations between the state and the individual became ever more direct. The various situations in which the juridical person found himself affected him alone, and there was no more need to break or form any bond with a jealous and exclusive family group. Being no longer the foundation of the Republic, the paterfamilias ceased to interpose between the individual and the state. . . .[23]

IV

Let us turn, finally, to the question of what social forces, over a considerable period of time, had combined to form the effective bases of the Augustan decrees? Obviously these decrees did not take effect in a society totally unprepared for them. Change in an institution or concept may be the consequence of impact and intrusion from external forces, but conditions for the assimilation of this intrusion must be present—as studies of diffusion have made clear.

Here it is tempting to take refuge in such abstractions as secularism, commercialism, and religious skepticism in Rome during the century or two leading up to Augustus. These, it is said rightly enough, formed the context that alone permitted acceptance of the radical Augustan inroads on the family and other forms of association. No one familiar with the history of Rome in this period would doubt that such generalized forces were indeed involved.

Without pretending to exclude these forces, I would like, however, to put the matter in somewhat different terms— terms that are at once more precise and more sociological. I shall illustrate this in a context that had been potentially present in Roman society from earliest days. This is the conflict between the *patria potestas*—the ancient authority of the family, and the *imperium militiae*—the authority over soldiers that came into being at the outbreak of any war.

The *imperium militiae* was not, strictly speaking, military power alone. "The Romans," writes Strachan-Davidson, "knew no such thing as a severance between supreme military and supreme civil authority. They merely distinguished between the space inside the walls (*domi*) and the rest of the world which was comprehended in the locative case by the word *militiae* 'on service.' This full imperium, then, governs all the world, less the city of Rome."[24] So much is true, but the fact remains, and it is crucial, that it was in a military context that "the rest of the world" became of significance to the Romans, and, more important, it was in its intrinsic military role that the *imperium militiae* first conflicted with the *patria potestas*.

I stressed earlier the fact that the public power did not and could not deal with the multitude of private and social matters that came under the *patria potestas*. The opposite, however, is also true, and here I present a brilliant clarifying insight from Maine:

> In every relation of life in which the corrective community might have occasion to avail itself of his wisdom and

strength, for all purposes of counsel and war, the filius familias, the son under power was as free as his father. It was maxim of Roman jurdisprudence that the patria potestas did not extend to the jus publicum. Father and son voted together in the city, and fought side by side in the field; indeed, the son, as general, might command the father, or, as magistrate, decide on his contracts and punish his delinquencies.[25]

Here, I suggest, is a potential conflict of roles, a tension, that lies at the heart of our subject. So long as the public role of the *filius familias*, the son under power, was minimal, just so long was the claim of the *patria potestas* upon his allegiance an unqualified and undistracted one. There could be little conflict of authority and role. On the other hand, all that tended to maximize the son's public role—either in quality or extent—tended equally to weaken the prestige and moral authority of the *patria potestas* if only because of the greater relative sphere of matters in the son's life over which the *patria potestas* had no influence.

We are justified in assuming from the evidence that it was in times of war that the maximization of a son's public role—and, correspondingly, his sporadic releases from the *patria potestas*—was heightened. Historically, as we know, war puts a premium upon the services of the young, not the old. Ordinary civil affairs in Rome, like ordinary business affairs, could be, and were, handled by those who were *sui juris*, those who held the *patria potestas* and were not under it. The most honored title indeed of the members of the Senate was the *Patres Conscripti*. But in war, different requirements prevail, and when warfare is extended and intensified, as it became in the later Republic, these requirements can become decisive.

The conflict between kinship society and the military is, as Jenks has brilliantly emphasized, one of the key conflicts of history.[26] Kinship society is inherently cellular—composed of compact and largely autonomous groups, families, clans, and *gentes*—whereas the military, as we find it in its earliest form is, by comparison, individualistic. Between the power of the commander and the individual soldier there is no intermediate authority, for such authority would weaken both the unity and the necessary directness of command. The very directness of the military *imperium* therefore induces a kind of potential individualism in social relations if only because of its corroding effects upon intermediate groups. In the second place, military society operates primarily in terms of command—not custom, tradition, and the *mores*. In the interstices of command, accordingly, there is a degree of moral freedom unknown in kinship society, which is governed not by prescriptive law, but by the less specific and infinitely more inclusive ties of custom which, by its nature, fills in every possible crevice. In short, there is a kind of secularizing and individualizing quality in military life.

In the third place, military society, unlike kinship, is, or by its nature aspires to be, rational in its distribution of function and authority; that is, whether explicitly or implicitly, both authority and function tend to fall into hands that are most competent, irrespective of considerations of age or social prestige. It does this, that is, if it is to be successful. Kinship society, on the other hand, tends, as we have seen, to accept seniority and age as the crucial qualities of leadership, with such matters as descent and inherited prestige close in importance. We may summarize the difference between the two societies by saying that in the first —kinship—it is ascribed status that counts, whereas in the second—the military—it is achieved status that is alone significant, if victory is the prime consideration.

We know that the Romans were well aware of the differences between the two types of society and the potential consequences of military service to kinship and ordinary civil authority. An ingenious variety of checks existed to prevent possible thrusts to ascendancy of victory-intoxicated returning soldiers. For centuries there was the custom by which no militia could form within the walls and no returning militia could enter the city gates until it had disbanded outside. When the individuals reentered the city, they were thus symbolically, as well as actually, freed from the *im-*

perium and once again under normal civil authority, and especially the *patria potestas*.[27] Such checks, however, whether customary or constitutional, could not forever withstand the growing number of wars, the increasing size of the forces themselves, and, perhaps most important, the constantly growing pressure for a regular standing army with continuous command.

One by one, from the end of the second century on, the old checks upon the military ceased to function. There began that fateful affinity between military service and popular following, between military triumph and political success, that, in Rome, as in many another society, was to have a transforming effect upon government and society. The key personage, undoubtedly, was the powerful and ruthless Marius at the beginning of the first century B.C. "Marius was not content to supplement his army by drawing upon the 'bravest men of Latium' and recalling to the colors *evocati* or discharged veterans known to him by reputation. He employed another method of enlistment. The proletariat . . . now legally qualified for enrollment, were signed on for a definite period of service, in all probability for twenty years."[28] The soldier might be a citizen when he joined up, he might be uncomplainingly under civil and paternal power, but the mere length of service that he among tens of thousands of young Roman males was now to look forward to—making him in effect a mercenary, knowing little and caring less about traditional matters—would make him restive, to say the least, when he returned on furlough or following separation.

> The army strongly detached from civil institutions, had chiefs who were absolute chiefs. Soldiers entered the service because they liked it; they hoped for loot and allotments of land. Who could give them this privilege? The General. So there grew up between the general and his men a closer association based not on the old discipline, nor even on the religion of the standard, but on mutual interest and greed.[29]

It is therefore, I suggest, in the rising incidence of war in Roman history, especially from the second century B.C. on, that we find the setting for the tensions that were eventually to reduce the *patria potestas* to innocuousness. For it was in the circumstances of increasing warfare that more and more sons under paternal power found themselves for lengthening periods of time under the *imperium militiae*, a form of authority that differed vastly from the *patria potestas* and provided, for all its own stringency, the essential conditions of that special type of individualism that was to sap the foundations of kinship society.

As Maine has reminded us,

> the military tribune and the private soldier who were in the field three-quarters of a year during the earlier contests and, at a later period the proconsul in charge of a province and the legionaries who occupied it, cannot have had practical reason to regard themselves as the slaves of a despotic master; and all these avenues of escape tended constantly to multiply themselves . . . We may infer, I think, that a strong sentiment in favor of the relaxation of the patria potestas had become fixed by the time that the pacification of the world commenced on the establishment of the Empire.[30]

NOTES

1. Sir Henry Maine, *Ancient Law*. First published in London, 1861. Everyman edition, pp. 81–82.

2. Maine, *Ancient Law*, p. 82.

3. This is, of course, one of the consequences of the continuous influence exerted upon European thought by the Greek concept of organism; from Aristotle down to contemporary functionalists in the social sciences, there is scarcely an exception to the view that change is inherent in the institution or culture.

4. James L. Strachan-Davidson, *Problems of the Roman Criminal Law* (Oxford University Press, 1912), Vol. 2, pp. 28–29, 38.

5. W. W. Fowler, *The Religious Experience of the Roman People* (London: Macmillan, 1911), p. 70.

6. Maine, *Ancient Law*, p. 88.

7. See Henry J. Roby, *Roman Private Law in the Times of Cicero and the Antonines* (Cambridge: University Press, 1902). See Bk. 2, Ch. 7 *et seq.*

8. See Pandias M. Schisas, *Offences Against the State in Roman Law* (London: University Press, 1926), pp. 125–129. See also Maine, *Ancient Law*, p. 227.

9. Strachan-Davidson, *Problems of the Roman Criminal Law*. Vol. 1, p. 32. Poste writes (p. 402): "Injuries which in modern law are punished exclusively as crimes could throughout the history of Roman law be vindicated by the private party as private wrongs."

10. William A. Hunter, *Introduction to Roman Law* (9th Ed., London, 1934), p. 14.

11. By all odds the finest and most beautiful account of the religious basis of the Roman family may be found in Fustel de Coulanges' *The Ancient City*. See especially Bk. 2, Ch. 2.

12. See especially J. Declareuil, *Rome The Law-Giver*, translated by E. A. Parker (London: K. Paul, Trench, Trubner & Co., 1927), pp. 156 ff.; French ed. J. Declareuil, *Rome et l'organisation du droit* (Paris: La Renaissance du livre, 1924).

13. Dio Cassius, Liii, 17. Dio together with Tacitus and Suetonius form the basic source of all that we know of this fateful period.

14. M. I. Rostovtzeff, *The Social and Economic History of the Roman Empire* (Oxford: Clarendon Press, 1926), pp. 39–40, 41.

15. Henry F. Pelham, *Essays on Roman History* (Oxford: Clarendon Press, 1911), p. 94. The entire essay on the domestic policy of Augustus (pp. 89–151) is a brilliant sociological analysis of one of the greatest ages of change in Roman history.

16. See especially, Declareuil, pp. 152–54 and 354–55. Also P. Willems, *Le droit public romain* (Paris, 1888), p. 611 f. F. W. Maitland dealt with the centralizing and the individualizing characteristics of Roman imperial law as profound forces of change in the rise of modern Europe. See *Collected Papers* (Cambridge University Press, 1911), Vol. 3, p. 309.

17. Pelham, "Domestic Policy of Augustus," pp. 95–96.

18. Pelham, p. 115.

19. See E. H. Haight, "Reconstruction in the Augustan Age," *Classical Journal*, Vol. XVII, pp. 335–376.

20. Pelham, p. 120.

21. On this momentous economic invasion of the *Patria Potestas* see James Hadley, *Introduction to Roman Law* (New Haven: Yale University Press, 1931), p. 213; also Declareuil, pp. 159–60.

22. Pelham, p. 109.

23. Declareuil, p. 314.

24. Strachan-Davidson, p. 100.

25. Maine, *Ancient Law*, p. 81. It is this kind of insight that makes Maine one of the great sociological minds of his age.

26. Edward Jenks, *Law and Politics in the Middle Ages* (New York: Henry Holt, 1908), p. 308 f. My comparison of the two types of society here is greatly indebted to Jenks' work.

27. See Mommsen's treatment of this in his *History of Rome*, W. P. Dickson translation (New York: 1895), Vol. 1, p. 335.

28. H. M. D. Parker, *The Roman Legions* (Oxford: University Press, 1928), p. 24.

29. Leon Homo, *Roman Political Institutions* (New York: 1930), p. 164.

30. Maine, *Ancient Law*, p. 82.

[12]

The
Permanent
Professors:
A Modest
Proposal

I

Although tenure is widely regarded as essential to the idea of the university, I would like to suggest it is far from certain that such is the case. Tenure differs sharply from academic freedom in this respect. A university worthy of the name is simply unimaginable apart from a broad and fully protected policy of freedom for each faculty member (tenure and non-tenure alike) to teach, write, and advise without interference from within or outside the university in all matters germane to his academic competence. Whatever qualifications of this right may exist, they are established by the corporate faculty itself, not by the administration or the public. More, it is, today at least, the very essence of academic freedom that a faculty member's views

This article, in a slightly different version, originally appeared in *The Public Interest* (Fall 1965), 37–50.

on matters outside his stated professional competence—
however shocking these views may be, however suggestive
prima facie of want of ordinary intelligence or moral responsibility—shall not be held against him when he is being
considered for retention or promotion.

Academic freedom, so conceived, justifies itself not by
what it grants the individual but by what it does for the
university. We have learned that it is absolutely necessary to
the search for, and the communication of, knowledge. It is
an essential attribute of the university; not a special privilege of the individual.

Can the same be said for academic tenure? If the university is to be regarded as a center within which the governing criteria are those of intellect, given visible sign by
continuing creativeness in study or classroom, should there
be any limitation on these criteria, even those provided by a
man's age, rank, or length of service?

The case for tenure, if there is one, must be made to rest
upon what it does for the university, not upon a claim of
special privilege for a class of individuals who form today
but one part of the larger corps of the creative and intellectually productive in society. Tenure must be divorced
from mere gratitude for prior services rendered. Such gratitude can be expressed in other ways—by honorary degrees,
plaques, professorships named after the meritorious, even
money payments. Tenure must also be divorced from need
by the individual and his family for financial security, for
this is a universal need in society, not one confined to professors. It could be met precisely as it is met in other areas
of the economy—by unemployment insurance, by severance
pay, by more liberal pension provisions, and by the varied
modes of job security which exist in law offices, newspapers, the theatre, industry, and other parts of our diverse
and creative society.

It is surely possible to reward the professor, to honor
him, and to reinforce his security without, however, committing the university to his permanent tenure, thereby
crippling departmental teaching and research programs, and
stupefying generations of students, which is what happens

all too often today. If academic tenure is to be justified, it must be done in terms that relate to some unique role occupied by academic man in society; a role demonstrably different from the roles held by all the non-academic professionals and intellectuals who also serve the cause of knowledge and culture but are denied anything resembling tenure. Once, such justification would have been easy. Today, frankly, it is not.

II

Few outside the academy are likely to appreciate what is fully involved today in academic tenure as it exists in practice. They may suppose it is simply the academic equivalent of the type of job security that exists in, say, General Motors, the Bureau of the Budget, or the Los Angeles Dodgers. (I deliberately select three organizations that the contemporary university, in one or other of its phases, comes more and more to resemble. The first two require no explanation, but the last-named may. I am referring to the now common quest in professional sports and the university for stars and superstars whose names and salaries are the source of as much pride and publicity to faculties as to trustees and club owners.) In each of these a man is guaranteed his job so long as he competently fulfills its specification, whether this be installing carburetors, performing an audit, or playing second base, and he is not likely to be dismissed or demoted on grounds extraneous to his competence except possibly for commission of felony or flagrant insubordination.

Any supposition that this describes academic tenure is, however, pure illusion. Tenure as we find it in the university today is as nearly impregnable a form of differential privilege as the mind of man has ever devised. Once attained by an individual, it is, on the evidence, proof against virtually any degree of moral obliquity, mental deterioration, or academic torpor. Tenure in the academy is more than economic security. It cannot even be understood in economic terms. One would have to go to the realm of religion for its exact counterpart in its blend of mystique and the sacred.

Most of us on university faculties rationalize the guilt that occasionally assails our consciences—as we look at our friends who do not possess tenure but who also contribute to scholarship, culture, and creative imagination—by our imagining of the dread spectacle of Administration ever ready to fire amiable, elderly scholars, each cast in the role of Mr. Chips, deeply devoted to, and loved by, his students, unworldly in manner, probably a utopian socialist in politics, unfitted for any other type of occupation, long sworn to the scholar's role and poverty, and therefore utterly helpless, were he to be dismissed.

This individual, as I shall emphasize later, hasn't existed on a major university campus for at least two decades, but he is, so to speak, our Folk Hero. It is his abiding reality in our minds that gives us the strength to insist upon tenure for ourselves when our friends in the theatre, in journalism, in the foundations, and in industrial or government laboratories do not have it. I will come back to this lovely ghost later. For the moment, I want only to emphasize that did our Folk Hero in fact exist on the campus today, administrators and trustees would surround him in near rapture—socialist convictions and all—for he makes *them* no trouble and he would represent the embodiment or fulfillment of an old image of teaching and scholarship that they like to discuss nostalgically in their offices and clubs. Moreover he would be immobile; hence not a replacement problem. The real enemies that this departed Hero would face, were he to be resurrected, would be not administrators but colleagues. The Grand Inquisitor would be, not a dean or president, but a faculty associate, ferociously productive and unable to suffer amiable age and socialist dreams gladly—not when their presence threatens to cut off a million dollar grant from the National Institute of Mental Health.

But let us return to the reality of tenure. What is it? To begin with, it is granted to an academic person when he reaches a certain rank (usually associate professor, irrespective of age) or has served a certain number of years in the institution (ranging across the country from three to eight). Far from fearing a man's acquisition of tenure, administrations and faculties today grant it ever more freely as bait for appointment or retention. What a tenure code or tradition says (on the evidence, *unwritten* tenure systems are stouter than those written—for here, as elsewhere in life, words can be hostages) is innocuous enough. Once granted, tenure shall not be abrogated except on good cause and after equitable and duly prescribed hearing by the man's colleagues. There is surely nothing wrong with this. One's only thought, viewing it abstractly, is: why not the same for *all* members of the faculty? On what basis other than "good cause" and with the assent of those faculty qualified to judge, would even a first-year instructor be dismissed?

"Good cause" is today more and more often left undefined, and this, it must be emphasized, is at the behest of faculties themselves. Historically it meant—and in some places is still specified as—"moral turpitude," "gross insubordination" and "mental or academic incompetence." The first two have a quaint sound today and their decreasing appearance in published statements is testimony to the increasing embarrassment most of us feel in trying to imagine, much less define, them in a degree that would today warrant dismissal of even *non*-tenure faculty.

Some years ago an able faculty member, who held tenure rank, was dismissed by his university when he confessed to, and was found guilty by the Superior Court of, a felony—repeated thefts over a period of years of substantial amounts of property from nearby wealthy homes. His dismissal produced no outcry from the faculty. From the Court he received a ten year suspended sentence—which could easily have been synchronized to the demands of his professorship. Today we would ask: why, therefore, was he dismissed? He had been found guilty of no *academic* wrong. He was a fine teacher, good scholar, and impeccable in moral behavior on the campus. I venture the guess that, in many institutions today, given the same circumstances, the outcry from students and faculty would be immediate, and that under the charge of "double jeopardy" the institution would be hard put to dismiss a man on whom neither the label of intellectual incompetence nor insubordination or *academic* moral turpitude could be accurately placed. And I am inclined to think such a position would be, today, defensible.

Once, many years ago, the university stood *in loco parentis* (whatever that really meant) to its students, and moral probity could therefore be made a binding requirement of continuing faculty appointment. But today, by common assent of students, faculty, and, more slowly but surely, parents, it does not stand in this role, and it may therefore be properly asked: what does a man's status before the law or his extra-mural morality have to do with his eligibility to teach? Homosexuality is the commonest basis today of dismissal on the ground of moral turpitude, but even here (and especially in light of the ever-rising status that modern literature has given the homosexual) it is hard to suppose that, except in circumstances of extreme repugnance to academic sensibility—involving, I should guess, chronic forays on unwilling students—an otherwise acceptable faculty member (*with or without tenure*) would be dismissed on this count. Not, certainly, without strong opposition of the faculty. For, again, the question could be asked: what, precisely, in an institution devoted strictly to the discovery and teaching of *ideas*, does a man's "moral turpitude" have to do with his appointment?

If moral turpitude has become a virtually extinct ground of dismissal in the university, what about that other hoary ground, "insubordination"? It is hard to know what this word means in practice. The university, as President Robert Gordon Sproul of the University of California used to say, differs from all other corporate institutions in that no one, not even the president, ever actually gives orders. For the university does not have a very clear-cut chain of command. Sound academic tradition, with large grants of autonomy to faculty committees, insures this. It is impossible for me to imagine any act of "insubordination" by an individual at the present time, against *either* faculty or administration, where dismissal would not predictably be followed by powerful dissent. Admittedly, ways can be, and usually are, found, most often by professors themselves, whereby, through processes of harassment, ostracism, repeated recommendations against salary increases, extra-microscopic scrutiny of academic record, etc., life for the insubordinate or fractious faculty member can be made so unattractive that he tends to leave—with warm recommendations, naturally, from his colleagues—for another job. The point is, however, that "insubordination" like "moral turpitude" is a vanishing concept in tenure codes. For quite apart from the antique flavor of each, nothing is said that is not today equally relevant to the status of the non-tenured. There is, after all, no more legitimacy to a dismissal of the non-tenured on these grounds than there is of the tenured. Or, putting it in reverse, if we are justified in dismissing the instructor or assistant professor for these offenses, then we are equally justified in dismissing the full professor.

Today the only ground of dismissal of the tenured that has ready and instantaneous acquiescence from the faculty is that of mental or academic incompetence. Never, in a quarter of a century of university teaching, have I ever heard dissent from a faculty member from this proposition: no man's job, however securely rooted in past achievement or glory, or in whatever number of years of service, should be proof against manifest intellectual incompetence. *But neither, in the same quarter of a century, involving association with literally thousands of faculty members, have I ever seen a single case in which a tenure faculty member was in fact dismissed or demoted on grounds of academic incompetence or mental deterioration.* The nearest to an instance in my own experience is that of a physical scientist in a distinguished department some twenty years ago, whose academic incompetence and mental frivolity had become so appallingly evident, so embarrassing and crippling to colleagues and students, that the trustees bought up the ten-year remainder of the man's tenure (involving a very sub-stantial sum of money, for he was a fairly high-salaried full professor), thus permitting him, with his own signed con-currence, to resign.

Perhaps this was indeed the best way. As I said earlier, the least important aspect of the consequence of tenure is financial. Its crime is not what it costs in dollars but in creativeness. How often does not one hear anguished reports from friends in adjacent departments, or in other colleges or universities, of the intellectual blight caused by a single man, year after year, in his association with students and faculty? But only the naive or non-academic would ask the obvious question.

III

Although the rise of tenure is to be seen, historically, as a part of the wider movement of worker security that began in the United States in the early part of the century, its justification, both then and since, has been largely built around the claimed uniqueness of the academic function. So unique is the university, the argument goes, that the person who makes it his career—who deliberately consecrates himself to it in preference to other, better paid and more prestigious opportunities for self and family—is stuck with it. His commitment—like that of the clergyman—has made him immobile. Once, there was a great deal of truth in this statement.

Down until about the end of the Second World War, the university had two central functions: teaching and scholarship. A gulf existed between the university and the rest of society that was seldom crossed, occupationally, by academic man. He had, as it were, a trained incapacity for performing any of society's other jobs, whether in industry or government.

Scholarship and teaching were the professor's functions

and in each lay a fragility that required special protection. A work of scholarship, typically, required years of preparation, resulting from the need for bibliographic research, thoroughness, and specialized depth of inquiry. The product did not often become visible through publication. "Productivity" indeed, as a word, was still confined to the assembly lines of factories. It was not brilliance that was sought after in scholarship, but thoroughness, soundness, and mastery. I do not wish to glorify. A great deal of this scholarship was dull, unimaginative, and, in the long run, useless even to scholars. The case might even be made that it sank eventually from its own leaden weight. None of this, however, is to the point. What is to the point is that, good or bad, scholarship was academic man's unique mode of expressing himself in print; it was not something that non-scholars could, or were expected to, appreciate; it required years of preparation and, by any assessment, demanded the security of tenure for the man willing to undertake it. The wall then between what professors wrote and what non-academic intellectuals wrote was very nearly an impenetrable one.

Equally fragile was the teaching role, which, even in the great universities was regarded, down until a decade or two ago, as more fundamental, more truly identifying of academic man than even scholarship. Teaching was fragile for a number of reasons. First, there was the deep-seated conviction in this country, largely as the result of the American system of lay boards of trustees, that the professor was an employee, literally a hireling, and hence as subject to the wishes of his "employers" as anyone who worked for a railroad or department store. It is not easy today to summon up an accurate vision of how powerful trustees, individually and severally, once were in the minute decisions of colleges and universities—or how fundamentally indifferent they were to those values of teaching and scholarship that had come to this country at the end of the nineteenth century from Europe.

In addition, there was the fragility of academic role that came from a professor's commitment to *campus*. The academic world was composed exclusively of "locals" in contrast to "cosmopolitans." Characteristically, a man's status and his advancement depended far more upon what he was in the eyes of those immediately around him—colleagues, administration, and students—than upon whatever reputation he may have acquired in national or professional terms. Transfers were, to be sure, not unknown, but even through the nineteen thirties, so vivid was a professor's "local" identity in contrast to his "professional," that such transfers, once a man became established, occasioned surprise. There may have been some virtue in this localism, but it contained also the insecurity that is always the price of immobility.

Even less was the likelihood of a professor shifting to a non-academic occupation, even temporarily. To suppose that an academic man—whether scientist, social scientist, or humanist—might be able to shift from academy to corporation, government, or agriculture, as he so plainly does today, would have been to suppose the impossible. Did anyone imagine that practical men of business or government could conceivably profit from academic advice? Consulting, even for the physical scientist, was negligible as a source of income and altogether absent in the other disciplines.

Finally, the very image of academic man in the public mind contributed to his immobility and his utter dependence upon the academic institution. This image was for the most part that of an unworldly, impractical, idealistic individual, lost when it came to the responsibilities of administration, budgets, and management of affairs outside classroom or study. Contributing to the uniqueness of the image was the fact that, although the professor's income was small, his social status was vaguely that of the gentleman of leisure. To conceive of him as a man of affairs, as consultant and advisor to corporations, professional associations, and departments of government was fanciful. It is nearly as easy to imagine, today, a clergyman taking appointment in State or Defense, in General Electric or the Auto Workers Union, as it once was to imagine an academic man shifting regularly to these and many other non-academic pursuits. And with the possible exception of the clergyman—with whom on so many counts the professor was once comparable—no social type was so immobile and hence occupationally dependent as was academic man until a couple of decades ago in this country.

V

But this picture has changed substantially. There is no longer uniqueness, only moderate and diminishing differentness, in the role of the academic man. Through vast changes in the nature of the university and in what the academic man typically and actually does today—paralleled by the immense changes that have taken place in the non-academic culture of the United States, witnessed (for our purposes) by the extraordinary proliferation of research, consultative, and intellectually and artistically creative jobs in all parts of the economy—academic man has become ever more like, at the one extreme, businessmen and administrators and, at the other, the non-academic intellectuals.

Consider the latter. Nothing is more striking than the narrowing of the gulf that once existed between writers, artists, and journalists outside the academy and those today working within it. I think it would be difficult at the present time, in looking through *Commentary, Partisan Review,* the *New York Review of Books, The Hudson Review,* and other prestige-journals to decide, simply on the basis of subject and style, which were the academic and which the non-academic writers. The decision would once have been simple. In such journals, had they existed at the beginning of the century, there would have been few, if any, academic contributors. In the first place academic thought and style would not often have passed muster (one recalls here the experiences of editors like Albert Jay Nock and H. L. Mencken with academics in the twenties). The few who could have passed muster would then have had the frightful experience of justifying their divagations to shocked department chairmen and colleagues.

Admittedly, non-academic literary intellectuals today are still less likely to author substantial, deeply researched volumes on minor poets or major influences; they require the income and nourishment of prestige that more frequent publication insures. But the difference is offset, I should say, by the fact that fewer academics are writing those either; for academic intellectuals also increasingly require the reinforcement to ego and competitive position that frequent publication insures, and, beyond this, academic humanists draw a larger measure of prestige from publishing in, say, *Partisan Review* than in *PMLA*.

There is the further fact that the context of the humanities in the universities is rapidly changing. It is becoming more like the sciences. Within the past ten years it, too, has become institute-infested, center-grown, and the not very secret dream of most humanists of becoming the director of a Center for Renaissance Studies is nearly as widespread as its counterpart in other areas. Once a Federal foundation for the humanities appears—and it is as certain as anything I can think of, if only to allay restlessness in this final fastness of academic individualism—the conversion will have become as complete as in the sciences. Institutes and centers, to receive huge Federal grants, will mushroom.

Consider now today's ever more typical scientist. He is engaged in large-scale research, working on an around-the-calendar basis, housed in special institute or center, equipped with staffs of secretaries formidable enough to frighten away all but foundation executives, with budgets to prepare constantly, grants to apply for, payroll sheets to fill out. Is it not easier to conceive of him as corporate executive or civil servant rather than professor? Add to this his governmental, professional, and industrial consultantships, his membership on national and international committees, his almost ceaseless travel to meetings and conferences, and the traditional image of academic man seems almost as archaic as that of guildsman or cavalryman.

Once the distinction of type between the academic scientist and his industrial or governmental counterpart was striking. Today, changes in all three areas have reduced this to near nullity. For just as business and government have, on the whole, come to grant a larger measure of individual autonomy to scientists working in their laboratories, so academic scientists have voluntarily committed themselves to forms of contract research that sometimes threaten to bring them closer to the norm of their professional colleagues in General Electric or the Department of Agriculture.

What is so evident in the humanities and natural sciences is equally evident in the social sciences. Scholarship, in the old sense of this word, is fast disappearing from what is today known as "the behavioral sciences," leaving in the wake of this disappearance, at one extreme, minds primarily interested in impressionistic analysis or criticism of the social order and, at the other, those engaged in the preparation of reports and surveys in closely-administered centers and institutes or in professional consultantship. At each extreme it becomes ever more difficult to distinguish the academic from the non-academic. Today a Distinguished Service Research Professor in Political Science at a major university can, in subject as well as style, compete (and month after month does compete) with a Walter Lippmann or even a Joseph Alsop or James Reston. And at the other extreme one finds it ever harder to distinguish between what comes out of non-academic centers for the analysis of public opinion, attitudes, purchasing habits, religion, education, government, and what comes from the universities. At social science association meetings, the papers presented by academic and non-academic technicians have become the same —a fact which says as much for the rise in level of the latter as for what has happened to the former.

Why, we are thus led to ask again, should one part of the intellectual corps in modern society be granted the privilege of absolute tenure when, by no stretch of vision or imagination, can it be found in the other, the non-academic, part? Except in the rarest instance, we can no longer claim the kind of precariousness of status that once lay in our uniqueness of type, and the evidence shows we are hardly blind to the near infinity of jobs that today have opened up in all sectors of the economy for the intellectual-technician, whether he be chemist or economist, biologist or sociologist, or even historian or philologist. Non-academic intellectuals and professionals live by fee, royalty, salary, and wage, and I assume that there are varying degrees of security attached to income, once a name for excellence has been acquired. But they do not live by tenure.

V

Despite the gradual disappearance of academic man and the conversion of universities into institutions more and more like corporations or government bureaus, there are two possible defenses of tenure, either of which, if valid, would justify continuation of the system.

First, it is said—though not as often as it once was—that tenure has been responsible for the gradual rise in salary levels for university professors over the past half century. This is historically dubious. What is certain is that tenure could be abolished tomorrow, and, given the critical shortage of academic talent—a *persisting* shortage—and the ever greater dependence of society upon the skills and knowledge of our academic technicians and professionals, there would be not the slightest effect registered upon salary scale.

The second, and much more common, assertion has to do with the relation between tenure and academic freedom.

Tenure, we read in countless declarations, is the steel frame of freedom of teaching in the classroom, the solid base of the scholar's exemption from erosive fears of status and livelihood that would otherwise attend his teaching and publication of truths distasteful to dean or president, government or public. "If I didn't have tenure," one hears in familiar refrain, "I wouldn't be free to teach as I want to teach." If this is true, it alone offers all the justification necessary. But is it true? Let us pass over the tens of thousands of public school teachers—at elementary and secondary levels—who assuredly have tenure but who equally assuredly do not have freedom in the classroom. Let us confine ourselves to the university. Several points suggest themselves.

Academic freedom—the freedom of the teacher to teach, the scholar to write—is supported today by a number of forces that did not exist a generation ago. First, and most important, it is supported by the mobility that the competent teacher-scholar has, given the huge increase in job opportunities, academic and non-academic. Second, there is the enhanced respect in which university professors are today held by business and government and, providing the solid base of this respect, the indispensable position that the modern university holds with respect to industrial, military, and national welfare. Indeed, the forces that have made a privileged aristocracy of the professoriat have made for a degree of autonomy, boldness, aggressiveness and occasional arrogance and bad manners that have ever been attributes of recognized aristocracies. Once a Northwestern University trustee could say: "As to what should be taught in political science and social science, they [the professors] should promptly and gracefully submit to the determination of the trustees when the latter find it necessary to act. . . . If the trustees err it is for the patrons and proprietors, not for the employees, to change either the policy or the personnel of the board." Such a statement made today would embarrass fellow trustees and shock editors, civic officials, and the industrial elite. But it would not shock or shame academics; it would merely break them up in hilarity. It is a mark of where we are at the present time that such a statement would not even be dignified by a student revolt!

The rise in real academic freedom—defined in the terms with which I began this article—has been among the more notable aspects of the history of American culture during the past fifty years. It has been part of, and has drawn its essential support from, external currents of rising tolerance and sophistication that flow from an ever more educated citizenry. However, I will not press that point too hard. It may well be that the threats to academic freedom are today as great as they ever were in this country. Even if they are not, I am inclined to think that, for tactical purposes, it is always well to assume that they are and, accordingly, remain vigilant. The central point here pertains, in any event, to the role of tenure. Is it indeed a bastion of academic freedom?

I see little evidence that it is, or that it should be so regarded, *for the proper sway of academic freedom is faculty-wide, not merely for those holding tenure.* In point of fact, where academic freedom has been abrogated in recent years, as it was at the time the University of California imposed its loyalty oath, the tenure of nearly half the non-signers was no safeguard. And when, after court action, the non-signing faculty members were restored to appointment, those without tenure were restored along with their tenure colleagues. And during an earlier period, when American Legion squads were committing their nuisances upon universities, I recall no instance in my own university —which suffered its due share of the nuisances—in which there was discrimination between tenured and non-tenured in what the University was willing to do to protect its faculty. In one outburst, the American Legion called for the dismissal at Berkeley of an eminent tenured scholar in law and, at the same time, a teaching assistant in economics. Each, I recall, received the same assurance of protection from President Sproul.

Quite apart from the university's changed relation to state and society in these matters, there has been a substantial expansion of academic freedom by faculty members themselves. A half a century ago, the beginning instructor or assistant professor generally had no more freedom than tenure—measured by contemporary standards. Freedom—of teaching, research, and extra-mural utterance—was a state to which he could only aspire; one that would come with seniority. The situation is dramatically different today. We divide a faculty between the tenured and the non-tenured, but we certainly do not divide it—not in any first-rate university—between the academically free and unfree. The chemist, sociologist, or philosopher has as much academic freedom, both in principle and in practice, at the beginning of his career as at its zenith. He may, as a tyro, be given more chores and fewer plums, larger teaching loads, scanter office space, smaller research funds, etc., but his academic freedom could hardly be greater than when he takes appointment. Despite a popular supposition that the assistant professor is more likely to be timorous or discreet than his tenured brethren, little that I have seen in a quarter of a century within the University of California, or witnessed from afar in the academic world, suggests that this is the case. Indeed if sheer volubility and intensity of attack upon "the Establishment" be taken as the true measure of academic freedom prevailing in an institution, one could make out a stronger case for the non-tenured—who are younger, and have given fewer hostages to fortune—than the tenured.

VI

We have gradually banished from the academic world, over a period of many years, the criteria of ethnicity, political membership, and religious belief, each of which once held all-too-substantial a place in the appointment and retention of faculty members in American universities. On what logical grounds, then, do we claim exemption for age and rank, in certain respects the most feudal of all feudal qualities? We pride ourselves, as professors, upon inhabiting a shining fastness of meritocracy in a society that still bears too many elements of traditional privilege. How, then, do we legitimately rationalize a system of privilege which can, and frequently does today, exempt a person of thirty or thirty-five years of age (the lowest age at which I have seen life tenure granted is twenty-seven, to a mathematician) for the rest of his life from the competitive pressures and insecurities to which the rest of the intellectual world is subject?

It is hardly conceivable that the senior university professor would be jobless if let out by his university for reason of loss of the brilliance that had led to his initial appointment. To begin with, there are hundreds of administrative jobs open in the university world. To say that these men are for the most part unsuited to administration, by reason of temperamental disinclination, belies everything I have seen over a period of twenty-five years in teaching and administration. "Scratch a faculty member and you find an administrator" is an aphorism the truth of which has, with only the rarest of exceptions, been made steadily more emphatic in my experience. Administration is (or at least is commonly regarded as being) power; and there is nothing the intellectual, academic or nonacademic, craves more.

Administrative jobs in the universities are, however, only the beginning. There is, as I have before suggested, the whole burgeoning area of industry and government, in each of which there is almost child-like pride today in taking onto its public roster university faculty members. In government, one need but think of the voracious needs in the years immediately ahead of the Department of Health, Education, and Welfare. In the multitude and layers of command posts that this single Federal department represents, there must be opportunity for all of the academics who would be dismissed, were tenure to be denied them as further support. And we have said nothing about the other departments and divisions of government—local, state, and federal. Of how many professors might it not be said that, by leaving their university and joining the government, they raised the intellectual level of each?

But to return to the matter of tenure: how, it will be asked, can equitable and accurate decision be made as to the relatively small number of senior members of the academic meritocracy who are to be let out annually in favor of those more brilliant, more productive, non-tenured faculty members who are ever ready to move into the places of their seniors?

Andrew Dickson White, notable early president of Cornell, once proposed, we are told, annual scrutiny of each faculty member by the trustees, with dismissal to follow upon a certain number of negative ballots. Balloting by trustees on a matter in which they could not possibly have informed judgment is certainly a grotesque and repugnant thought. But what about balloting by a man's colleagues? I do not mean balloting in any literal sense, of course, but simply in that of continuing scrutiny by those of his peers who are plainly qualified to judge—those within his institution and those in other institutions who might be engaged as confidential consultants. We do this now for those under consideration for promotion to a tenure position or for initial appointment at highest rank in an institution. And we do this, even with those who possess tenure, when it comes to such matters as promotion from associate to full professor, salary increase, nomination of a colleague to an endowed chair, or to academic-administrative positions such as chairman or dean. Why not also for decisions as to continuation?

We are in part victims of the system of academic promotion that prevails almost universally in this country. When a faculty committee and dean consider the promotion of a man from one rank to another, the question that is now asked is: has this man *earned* it? This is unfortunate, for experience shows that the advance set of mind of both committee and administration tends to be favorable. After all, what person has not done *something* that cannot be said to qualify him for promotion? How much better it would be if we asked the altogether different question: Is there at this time, available in the profession, someone who is superior to the individual under review and who may therefore be appointed to the position for which this individual, through promotion, is being considered? If there is, we appoint; if not, we promote. In a genuine intellectual meritocracy, this would be the criterion in promotion, and it could be equally the criterion of *retention* of faculty— of all faculty.

A distinguished colleague of mine, who will himself never

need the support of tenure and who shares many of my convictions about the evil of the matter, proposes a fundamental modification of the present system. Let us, he says, reaffirm tenure but reverse its application. Grant beginning instructors (who, of all faculty, plainly most need it) tenure of perhaps fifteen years. When, however, they receive promotion to assistant professor, tenure will be reduced to ten years; with advancement to the associate professorship, it will drop to five years. But with the full professorship all tenure ceases, for, by very proof of his right to this exalted rank, he has proved also his capacity, through teaching and scholarship, for retaining it on merit.

There is much to recommend this, but I think the tensions under it would be horrifying. For the stablest element in the academic community—that is, in terms of guarantees of position—would be the instructors and assistant professors. The ferocity with which they now view their elders would be intensified by the feel of power. Possessing tenure, they might well wish to do what tenure faculty now do; decide the fate of the non-tenured. No, it is far better to abolish tenure outright.

The abolition of tenure, it goes without saying, will not be initiated by trustees or administration in this country. The mere prospect would shrivel these bodies, leaving them in helpless panic at the thought of the consequences that would be visited upon them. Nor can it be done by government action, which is normally the liberal and progressive way of attacking privilege in our country. The academic community has become much too powerful for even the Federal government to risk its alienation.

From the faculty alone can action properly come, and it is in this light that I propose leadership by the American Association of University Professors. This is the proper body; it is national, it has a distinguished history, and, in past decades, has been the chief lobby *for* tenure. Such leadership could give new vitality to the Association itself and free it for its central function, that of acting as watchdog of academic freedom. I think it would be impossible to exaggerate the tonic effect that such action, coming from the united faculty itself, would have upon the morale of the rest of the intellectual community in the United States, and upon the vitality and effectiveness of the university.

Need I also say that I think it impossible to exaggerate the unlikelihood of the A.A.U.P. doing any such thing?

(13)

Project
Camelot and
the
Science of Man

I

Project Camelot may well have been the worst single scientific project since King Canute dealt with the tides: the worst conceived, worst advised, worst designed, and worst executed. But this much has to be said for it. Never has one project in the social sciences aroused interest so broad, so diverse, and in such high places of the national government. More important, never has one project produced, or at least stimulated, results so momentous (and possibly beneficial) in the long run to government policy with respect to the social sciences.

What was Project Camelot, and why the fuss?[1] Reading through the multitude of reactions and comments aroused by Project Camelot one is reminded irresistibly of the ancient tale of the three blind men and their individual descriptions of an elephant. For the *Washington Evening*

This article, in a slightly different version, originally appeared as *Project Camelot: An Autopsy,* in *The Public Interest* (Fall 1966), 45–69.

Star, whose political reporter, Walter Pincus, first broke the story, Camelot was another episode in the unending conflict between the Departments of Defense and State. For the United States Army, under whose auspices Camelot had been conceived, it was a research project concerned with conditions of social unrest, riots, and insurrection, that would, in the words of General Dick, "help us to predict potential use of the American Army in any number of cases where the situation might break out." For more than a few Chileans, in whose country Camelot first came to international light, it was a flagrant and odious intervention in the domestic affairs of a country with which the United States was at peace. Secretary Rusk saw Camelot as a less than brilliant intrusion by the Army into the always delicate sphere of Latin American foreign relations. Most members of the House Subcommittee on International Organizations and Movements saw Project Camelot as a sad consequence of the dispersed, unfocused, and inadequate role of the behavioral sciences in the Federal government. This last view, as we shall see, comes perhaps the closest to revealing the whole elephant.

For many social scientists, the most conspicuous feature of Camelot was its summary cancellation by the Army, an act widely held to unfold yet another chapter in the government's discrimination against the behavioral sciences. (This view, as we shall also see, was perhaps the most self-serving, the least founded in reality.) For some university administrators across the country, and also a few behavioral-science project tycoons, the reaction to Camelot was, or might have been: "There but for the grace of God. . . ." For American social scientists at work in the field abroad, especially in those political areas where national patriotisms tend normally to be on trigger, Camelot was dynamite that might easily spell disaster for future foreign area research. And so it went.

There was one other reaction to Project Camelot that we must mark for the sake of the record: the reaction of many liberals and non-Establishment social scientists. What they learned from Camelot, others have learned elsewhere: the wages of sin is death. One of the most ironic—let us say, Camelotian—aspects of the Project was the utter absence from its operational staff of those social scientists who are most commonly the targets today of the Outsiders: those for whom the sesquipedalian "Establishment" has come to replace all four-letter words in the lexicon of Outsider profanity. Think of it! Here was a huge behavioral science project sponsored and financed by that most establishmentarian and hoary of all Establishment agencies, the Army; a project created—to cite the words of the high chief of Camelotians, Dr. Theodore Vallance, Director of American University's Special Operations Research Office (SORO) —as "an outgrowth of continuing interest in the Government in fostering orderly growth and development in the newer countries in the world," an Establishment objective if there ever was one. Add to all this the fact that Project Camelot was probably the most richly endowed (up to $6,000,000 had been allocated) single project in the history of the behavioral sciences. And, *Gloria in Excelsis Deo*, it was a project at long last in which Outsiders were Insiders— most of the social scientists involved were, to one degree or another, on the liberal-left of the political spectrum, and it is not likely there was a single supporter of the Viet Nam war among them. Across the River Styx, the shades of Plato and all his descendants down to C. Wright Mills must have danced in joy at the sight of this final ascent of the pure in heart to the very citadel of modern power.

What were the incentives that attracted and the motives that inspired such social scientists to a project, the official nature of which was a kind of unclassified intelligence enterprise to permit the U. S. Army easier tactical footing? Irving Louis Horowitz, who had no part in Camelot but whose article is the most informed and the most clarifying of all that have appeared, tells us that a glittering range of motives was to be found among Camelot's participants. The following is drawn in paraphrase from Professor Horowitz's "collective self-portrait of Camelot as the social scientists who directed it perceived it."

First, there was the joy of being able to do something Big in social science, something to wipe out memory of the picayune, to obliterate the remembered tedium of what C. Wright Mills had once called "abstracted empiricism." Second was the intoxicating sense of freedom that came with a position at the pinnacle of power; this in contrast to the unfreedom of ordinary academic existence where peers could examine one's work for merit and substance. Third, there was the Platonic prospect of educating an elite, of moulding the minds of that most ancient and reactionary of ruling groups, the generals, and of perhaps endowing the Army, for the first time in history, with peaceful and constructive aims. Fourth was the hope of accelerating man's ascent to perfectibility through the humanization, if not immediate capture, of military power: a dream that had heretofore been confined to utopians in history but was now part and parcel of the newest men of power, the behavioral scientists. Fifth was the intoxicating sense of living dangerously while other poor behavioral scientists remained within university cocoons.

These are a few of the motives that Professor Horowitz was able to uncover in his investigation of Camelot. From them it is easy to conclude that a sense of millennial excitement must have seized the minds of Camelotians during the stirring days of 1964–65; a sense of excitement generated by the realization that minds incorruptible and imperishably humanitarian were in the halls of power, at the ramparts indeed, able to look down upon those lesser social scientists, the Establishmentarians, who had sold their souls too early and too cheaply.

Then all hell broke loose. After months of Camelotian repose, of contemplation, of thought and planning, of endless cost-plus consultation with the favored, months in which dreams were dreamed and then coded and punched, the whole thing (oh, cursed spite!) had to end. End not with a bang but a whimper. It happened this way.

One of the Camelot consultants, an assistant professor of anthropology, of Chilean birth but American citizenship, who was on his way to Chile for the summer on personal business, offered—for a fee, of course—to sound out Chilean social scientists on their possible enthusiasm for a project in which the United States Army, working through behavioral scientists, would undertake—in a strictly basic science sort of way, naturally, and with only the highest of motives—to investigate the conditions of social unrest, of insurgency, and means of counterinsurgency, in foreign countries; not necessarily in Chile, understand, but in other Latin American and foreign countries. This seemed like a dandy idea to the Chief Camelotians in Washington, and off went the, if not very first, the very last of Camelot's Intrepids.

The rest is history. Chilean social scientists, for some reason, did not take kindly to the thought of their country or any other being investigated by behavioral scientists who, however pure in heart and in methodological design, and however many echelons removed from tanks and flame-throwers, were nevertheless inescapably acting as agents of the United States Army on foreign ground. We are informed in the Chilean Select Committee Report to the Chamber of Deputies that the initial slight interest of a few Chilean social scientists in the project came from their having been assured in writing that such study as Camelot envisaged was sponsored by private or civil agencies and that it was not until they began reflecting on the implications of the use of a code name and, even more revealing, had received a full and documentary account of what Project Camelot was in fact from another of its consultants—a man of pacifist inclination unable to bear longer the weight of guilt—that they were able to respond in ways appropriate to the occasion.

One of the ways was to turn the whole thing over to a left-wing newspaper which, after months of the usual dreary leftist copy, had, for a change, something of Stop Press significance. It is not difficult to imagine the theme: American diplomacy, after a century of working through banana royalists had now turned to behavioral science royalists, that is, from industrial to academic tycoons, etc. etc. In any event, the news of Camelot was out—in Chile at least. Domestic uproar was predictably immediate and substantial, reaching the Chamber of Deputies which, as I have indicated, saw fit to receive a report on the whole matter from a special committee. All things considered, the Chilean report is remarkable for its temperateness, but it spares few details of Camelot, its operating structure, personnel, contacts with Chileans, and so on. In these respects it is a more useful document than the report on Camelot of our own House Subcommittee on International Organizations and Movements which protects the identity of Camelot scientists and the nature of all the details of the project—in a way that would probably not have been allowed had Camelot involved business or government figures rather than academics.

But if the Chilean Select Committee report was relatively moderate in temper, public and governmental opinion was not. The backlash produced by Camelot caught at least one American social scientist that I know of, leading to his summary eviction from Chile, with months of important research left dangling. He was indeed a victim, hardly qualifying as a bystander, for he was not only unconnected in any way with Camelot but totally ignorant of its existence. His protests were unavailing. The odium of Camelot was inclusive so far as American social scientists were concerned.

It was not, however, Chilean but Washington reaction to Camelot that proved decisive and of great long run significance to the behavioral sciences. Our Ambassador to Chile, Ralph Dungan, stung by his ignorance of something that (given U. S. Army sponsorship) understandably seemed part of his proper business, sent a sharp cable to Rusk after reading the details of Camelot in Chilean newspapers. Rusk went to LBJ, LBJ went to McNamara, McNamara went down gracefully (and gratefully, no doubt), and out of it—in one of the fastest actions ever recorded in official Washington—came a Presidential directive prohibiting *Government-sponsored* foreign area research that in the opinion of the Secretary of State would adversely affect United States foreign relations. Without the loss of a measurable instant, Defense put Camelot to rest; or, to stay within the lovely imagery of it all, sentenced its inhabitants to return to the world of reality.

And the saddest of all the sad little ironies in the whole story is that, as one of the principals was to say, almost plaintively, Chile had not even been marked for Camelot study, had not been brainstormed, programmed, coded or punched! Of such, alas, is the city of man.

II

But Camelot's memory lingers on. Its real importance in the history of the social sciences begins indeed with its death. As nothing in the life of Macbeth's Thane of Cawdor became him as did his manner of ending it, so nothing in Camelot's life was as fertile to the social sciences, as pregnant with issue, as its corpse; the corpse that was ordered exhumed for Congressional autopsy almost before its last breath. From the hearing conducted on Camelot by the House Subcommittee on International Organizations and Movements came a Report, and I can think of nothing more edifying for social scientists than a reading of this two-hundred page document; edifying and flattering. If any further medicine is needed to wash away the minority-group syndrome that still characterizes the self-evaluation of so many of us in the social sciences, that still leads us to feel despised, discriminated against, and disliked by society and government, it is to be found, free, in this Report. Let it be trumpeted far and wide: the Federal government, starting with the Subcommittee whose job it was to look into Camelot's coffin, and going all the way across town to Secretaries Rusk and McNamara, loves the behavioral sciences.

In fact, one discovers, as he reads through the text of the Report, that the behavioral sciences are miraculously found free of sin. The Military's *use* of the behavioral sciences is not free of sin, but that, as we shall see, is a different story. Twice only could I find, in comments of individual members of the Subcommittee on the behavioral sciences, undercurrents of the ironic, but these were prompted by testimony on the behavioral sciences that has to be read to be believed. Let me cite the two instances. At one point, the Director of SORO (the administrative structure within which Camelot was hatched) was explaining to Subcommittee members the importance of American behavioral science "know-how" being exported to the underdeveloped nations; his illustration is the account given him by a friend who, while traveling in Africa, had once seen an automobile on an African highway stopped because of a flat tire, with its occupants standing about helplessly, as it seemed. To this one of the Subcommittee members could only gently recommend that the Director drive down any American highway. The second example was offered by a representative of the Military. He pointed, when pressed by the Subcommittee, to behavioral science's "discovery" that the Viet Cong frequently travel in village groups, with women and children along, and that they eat their meals at fixed times of the day. This intelligence, he noted, has made possible easier exterminatory actions by the American forces. One of the Subcommittee members, his patience by now somewhat tried, wondered why batteries of behavioral scientists were required to discover what presumably would be within the powers of any scouting detail, something that Julius Caesar had found out through simple legionaries in his Germanic campaigns.

But these, I emphasize, are the only such examples I can find in the Subcommittee Report, and their real butt was not the behavioral sciences but, rather, the Military and its use of them. Reading the Report one finds himself, as a social scientist, almost literally holding his breath as he progresses through the testimony, for if ever a single behavioral science project lay exposed—in professional judgment, in design, in execution, quite apart from heavy expenditure of money (several hundred thousands of dollars had already gone into it)—to the possibility of merciless caricature by a Congressional committee, it was Project

Camelot. But, far from caricature or hostility, there is only respect, courtesy, and seriousness of interest in the contributions of the behavioral sciences and in their proper status in the Federal government. After all, where else in a Congressional document (or professional document, for that matter) can one find the behavioral sciences characterized as "one of the vital tools in the arsenal of the free societies," with concluding recommendation made that funds for their subvention be greatly increased and their official status honored by inclusion in the Executive Office of the President as well as in a national foundation?

III

Not once in the Subcommittee hearing was the matter of professional ethics raised with respect to the behavioral scientist participants of Project Camelot. It was, however, in Chile, where apparently a different standard of conduct is expected of academic scholars. Reading the Chilean Select Committee report and some of the expressions of opinion in Chilean newspapers, one finds little if any of the censure of the American military that our own Subcommittee confined itself to, for in Chile, as in Latin America generally, nothing but the worst is usually expected from the military. What bothered, and still bothers, Chilean social scientists is, first, the fact that American academics could have allowed themselves to become involved in something like Camelot and, second, that no acts of censure toward Camelot social scientists have been taken, or even voiced, by American social science organizations. From a Chilean perspective it seemed incredible that social scientists could have given themselves, in the first instance, to a project under the auspices of the United States Army involving research into "the most intimate details" of Latin American institutions and personal lives; equally incredible that in their earliest communication with Chilean social scientists, American

social scientists had camouflaged Army sponsorship by referring vaguely to private foundation and National Science
Foundation support. To this day there are Chilean and
other Latin American social scientists who believe it the
responsibility of American academic professional organizations to render apology in some form; even to register censure
for the conduct of the Americans. But anyone who knows
the reluctance of American professions, medical, legal, or
academic, to voice censure of their own kind knows that the
Chileans will wait a long time.

The ethical aspects of Camelot have received some attention by American social scientists, but it has been chiefly
in the form of letters to the editor of one or another
journal, and these seem, on the whole, superficial and
tangential, frequently self-serving, with the Military and
State Departments made the scapegoats, and are largely
concerned with the question whether or not the behavioral
sciences have any business working for the Military. The last
seems to me a baseless question, except on grounds of personal ideology. I happen to believe that there was a major
ethical responsibility that Camelot's technicians flouted by
acceptance in the first place of *the nature of this assign-
ment.* But that has nothing to do with what would appear
to me to be the unquestionable, the almost axiomatic,
propriety of the behavioral sciences entering into *certain
kinds* of professional engagements with the Military.

If the behavioral sciences are what their prime representatives say they are—non-ideological, objective bodies of
hypothesis and conclusion drawn from dispassionate and
controlled study of human behavior—then there is nothing
intrinsically wrong with their conclusions being used by,
or given to, the Army. Why should not the behavioral
sciences contribute to military and foreign policy as they
contribute to community organization, urban renewal, race-
relations, and other areas of society? Whether behavioral
scientists make this contribution to the military directly—
as employees on a military-designed project—or through
quasi-autonomous foundations or universities is, as I shall

emphasize below, a matter of profound operational and organizational significance. But it is hardly an ethical matter.

The right of the individual, whether he be a sociologist, chemist or engineer, to hold back from the Military, to the best of his abilities, the efforts and contributions he has made as a scientist is, I should suppose, incontestable, however vain and illusory it might be. But the grounds for this have nothing to do with the nature of the sciences and everything to do with personal moral values. I do not see how we can argue on the one hand that the behavioral sciences are *sciences*—that is, bodies of knowledge which reach beyond individual caprice and moral preference to the level of empirically validated conclusions—but that on the other hand their principles should not be given to the military or some other established, recognized part of American society and government.

Where the issue of professional ethics entered most significantly in Project Camelot, it seems to me, was in the initial acceptance of the mission of the project by social scientists *acting in their role as social scientists*. Let us, for sake of emphasis of this one point, dismiss the feelings of the Chilean social scientists and others who felt put upon by the Americans; it is always difficult to prove who said what, when. Let us, for the same reason, dismiss the ethical matter of the motives Professor Horowitz's interviews uncovered among principals of Camelot—motives which, I have to confess, shock in me what I had thought was an unshockable sense of propriety; for, motives, after all, are elusive, tenuous, and probably irrelevant. But what cannot be overlooked is the fact that a group of American social scientists, acting as social scientists, allowed the American military to believe there was nothing *scientifically* wrong in an American social science project, *under American Army sponsorship,* entering the historically sensitive areas of Latin America for the express purpose of discovering, through every possible penetration of culture and mind, the conditions of social unrest, conflict, and insurgency.

Here is a cross-cultural consideration that one might justifiably assume to be understood by every sophomore in an introductory sociology or anthropology course, one that might occur to any lay American who has been reading the news over the past decade or two. Was there no one in the administrative organization of SORO, no one among the social scientists who were appointed as *professional* men, not as simple technicians, to say in effect to Lt. General William Dick, Chief of Research and Development, Army: "Your objective is your business and no doubt admirable from the point of view of the Army; as behavioral scientists we desire to be of such help as we can; *but everything we know as behavioral scientists suggests the monumental, possibly catastrophic, unwisdom of such a project.*"

Not five minutes would have been required to acquaint the good general with the most elementary aspects of Latin American ethnocentrism, especially when the American military is involved. Was not the raising of such a question necessary and fundamental? I do not mean "ideologically" fundamental, but *professionally, scientifically,* fundamental. Is not the physician *as physician* professionally bound to refuse the order of a patient to prepare a compound that medical knowledge tells the physician is injurious? Does any sociologist believe that the physician can properly take refuge in the implicit statement: I am a behavioral scientist and if my sponsor orders it, it is not mine to reason why?

To say that the social scientists have no right, as scientists, to question a mission, even to refuse (still as scientists) cooperation, is not only to miss the nature of professional ethics but also to be blind to the view that has come to prevail in the larger scientific community today, where the scientist's duty to pronounce on matters of research policy, to pronounce as a scientist on the feasibility, economy, and wisdom of research policy, is not only unquestioned but, as Don K. Price has documented in admirable detail in his *The Scientific Estate*, is a matter on which Congressional and Executive opinion has come to depend.

But this, from all I have been able to read, was not a consideration in the minds of the behavioral scientists of Camelot or their consultants. Theirs not to reason why, theirs but to do or die—an epitaph more fitting, however, for cavalrymen than for professional scientists from whom judgment of feasibility is a recognized part of any contract.

IV

But if the behavioral scientists and the Military never saw the underlying, constitutive question, the members of the House Subcommittee assuredly did. Over and over during the hearing, the question was raised by one or another member as to the wisdom of the Military undertaking the kind of research contained in Camelot's objective. No one asked the question more tersely and pointedly than Representative Roybal: "Wouldn't the mere fact that the Army was heading the Project itself create a problem in many countries?" That is indeed the question: How does the military get into this act? To which General Dick replied that, when American soldiers go into a foreign area, it is useful for them to know about the mores, customs, and also possible internal conflicts of that area; hence the Army's long standing custom of issuing handbooks to its entering troops. But this was hardly an answer to the real question which pertained, not to handbooks issued soldiers in areas in which the United States maintained troops, but to the multi-million dollar "basic science" project that was Camelot. Representative Fraser conceded the necessity of handbooks in Viet Nam or Korea. "But," he went on, "when you try to create a model of a developing society for purposes of predicting what is going to happen in that society, for purposes of trying to figure out what kinds of things can be done to affect decision making, and the social processes, I do not see the Army in the game."

Nor would a good many other persons, but so far as one can infer from a reading of the transcript, neither Dr. Vallance, representing Camelot's behavioral scientists, nor General Dick and Mr. Seymour Deitchman, representing the Army, ever got it into his head that some gross stupidity or—looking at the matter "methodology-wise"—some scientific anomaly lay in the U. S. Army having commissioned behavioral scientists to go into Latin American countries like Chile. It was not a behavioral scientist connected with Camelot but, once again, Congressman Fraser who uttered the following words—this time following some rather pious testimony from Dr. Vallance:

"[T]here is throughout your whole presentation a kind of—an implicit attitude or relationship that this country bears to the rest of the world which, if I were not an American, I would find perhaps most highly offensive, but it suggests somehow we are the ones to find out the dynamisms that are at work in these countries for the benefit of our Military Establishment. If I were a Latin American, I wouldn't find this a particularly happy arrangement."

With Camelot to spur them, Subcommittee members could have entered into the record that just as war has long been held too important a matter to be left in the hands of the generals, the behavioral sciences are too important to be left in the hands of project titans. But the Subcommittee didn't. With the kind of luck that, as Arthur Guiterman described it many years ago in his famous jingle, God grants to children, fools, drunkards, and citizens of the United States of America, the behavioral sciences emerged from this potentially devastating hearing with their luster untarnished, their prestige, if anything, higher, having been treated to the always joyous spectacle of the military being spanked, and the clear prospect ahead of Federal organization and funding of the social sciences beyond anything that might realistically have been dreamed of once the Pandora's box of Camelot had been opened.

Nor was this all! We are treated also in the Subcommittee report to something that social scientists can rejoice in almost to the degree of their pleasure in seeing the military made the scapegoat. This is the spectacle of the State Department being told by the Subcommittee to commence making more use of the behavioral sciences in the formulation of foreign policy. In some ways, this is the most Camelotian byproduct of the whole weird enterprise, for if ever there was a time for the State Department to shore-up its traditional dislike of the behavioral sciences, this was it.

It is an old story that between State Department policy sections and the American academic community there is, and for long has been, distrust founded upon the State Department's lack of confidence in the concrete results of social science research and the academic community belief—best expressed by Professor Gabriel Almond to a reporter for *Science*—that the State Department is a "conservative institution dominated by a foreign service which is trained largely in the law, in history, in the humanistic disciplines. They believe in making policy through some kind of intuitive and antenna-like process." According to official estimates gained by *Science*, of the $25.3 million spent by government agencies on social science research abroad during fiscal 1966, the State Department spent only $200,000. The Defense Department spent $12.5 millions or half the total.

Despite his generally candid and impressive testimony before the Subcommittee, Secretary Rusk did not appear eager to go into reasons for this disproportion. When pressed by Representative Frelinghuysen as to why, given the large amount of money that Defense got from Congress for behavioral science research, State received, and asked for, only pennies, and, more to the point, why such research as that represented by Camelot was not in State's hands rather than the military's, Rusk indicated only that he preferred not to get into the "question of criteria by which one or another Department might accept responsibility for certain types of research." To be sure, Secretary Rusk did, at this juncture, make the important point that such research "might be better left even to private agencies." I shall return to this in the final section of my article, for it is probably vital to the future of foreign area research by American scholars.

But if Secretary Rusk did not choose to explain the gulf between the State Department and the academic community, others with equal experience in both the foreign service and the universities have. Louis J. Halle, writing in *The Virginia Quarterly Review* (Winter, 1964), has put the matter illuminatingly. "There was a period after the [Second World] War when various departments of the Government tried to marry themselves to the universities. This worked in the case of the Pentagon and the faculties of science and technology, a wartime precedent having already been established at Oak Ridge and Los Alamos. In the case of the State Department it did not work. Professors of diplomatic history, professors of Latin American history, professors of economics and of sociology were brought to Washington for meetings at which the men in the State Department tried to explain their troubles. But the gulf could not be bridged. The professors tended to confine themselves to the general nature of the problems that the officials hopefully set before them, often speaking about the need to maintain the traditional idealism of our international conduct. When confronted by the direct question, 'What shall we *do?*', they fell silent. They could answer every question up to that last, but that last was the one question for which the men in the State Department had to have an answer. The experiment, abandoned at last, left the State Department men in a mood of disenchantment tinged with bitterness, such as often follows a frustrated courtship or a broken engagement."

One guesses, however, that in the future the State Department, under the prodding of the Subcommittee (formal prodding, contained in its official recommendations), will engage more actively in research partnered with social scientists. Not the kind that is expected to produce an answer to each *ad hoc* question that crosses a desk during a State Department day, but a kind that, when carried on long enough, and, hopefully, with a degree of discrimination lacking in Camelot, could be the context or seedbed of decisions of policy.

V

We cannot conclude discussion of Camelot's impact on the State Department without reference to one development that for awhile led to considerable agitation in the social science world. This was the memorandum from President Johnson, hard on the heels of Camelot's exposure in Chile, directing the Secretary of State henceforth to screen all Government-sponsored foreign area research for its possible adverse effects upon United States foreign relations. Heaven knows, given the blunders of Camelot, there was every good reason for such a directive. But the first response of social scientists, including those who had been involved in Camelot, was to cry "censorship." By what right, it was asked, did one department of government take to itself the function of scrutinizing research projects sponsored by other Government departments in which American social scientists were participating?

The answer could have been stated simply: by the same right under which today, though still imperfectly, the State Department screens "projects" of American industry that involve entry into Latin American countries. The once odious spectacle of American businessmen entering the banana republics of Central America and then calling for the Marines when the going got difficult should not be repeated, it would appear obvious, when it is large scale social science projects that are involved. Despite the myth of Immaculate Conception that obtains among American behavioral scientists—under which the most aggressively intimate forays into human privacy are held miraculously pure—the rape of national dignity by American academic enterprise is as repugnant to foreign feeling as rape by American business or government. The Chilean Select Committee Report makes this very plain indeed! On a hot day one can chill himself by reflecting on what might have happened in Chile—or any of the countries marked by Camelot for invasion—had the project had "good" luck; had it been "successful"; had unforeseen exposure not led to premature death. Several regiments of Marines would have been necessary to salvage American research capital and protect American researchers' lives.

The blessed wonder is, given all the considerations of national dignity involved, considerations that, as the Select Committee Report specifically emphasized, could not be waived "under the pretext of the scientific character of Camelot," that the President's directive did not include *all* foreign-area research. For what can be more important than preservation of good feeling in Latin America, good feeling that for years was jeopardized by American commercial arrogance and that American academic arrogance jeopardized in 1965? But the President's memorandum did not make this mistake. It properly confined itself to *Government-sponsored research*. It excludes altogether from its scope private research—of universities, foundations, and of individuals. Secretary Rusk made this emphatic in his testimony before the Subcommittee. Almost equally important, the Foreign Affairs Research Council that was established by the State Department to give effect to the President's memorandum, has, in practice, excluded also from its jurisdiction domestic grants of the National Science Foundation, the National Institutes of Health, the National Defense Education Act, and the Fulbright program. The Council's range thus is restricted to Federal departments— Defense, Commerce, Treasury, etc.—in the more customary sense. Finally, in the year's experience with the new procedure, it would appear that nothing of legitimate concern to the social sciences has arisen in the Council's actual administration of its responsibility. It is difficult to understand what the executive officer of the American Psychological Association had in mind when, according to *Science* (8 July), he declared that the new risk review procedures "have eroded confidence in the government's understanding of how science goes about its business. . . . You would prefer that your peers look at your work. This is the way science is advanced, by having your critical colleagues look over your shoulder."

Such words are as irrelevant as they are pious. Returning to Camelot, it may be assumed that dozens of scientific consultants looked over the shoulders of dozens of Camelot principals. But if there is any record of their having looked critically enough to get at the core of this monumental blunder, I have been unable to find it. To talk serenely about the holy ground of science in the aftermath of Camelot, a project that, above anything that has ever happened, has weakened the confidence of Latin American intellectuals *in the American academic and scholarly community,* is a little like talking about the rights of free private enterprise in the predatory contexts of dollar diplomacy.

As I indicated above, the members of the Chilean Select Committee were unmoved by the "scientific" objectives of Camelot. It is useful to quote the words of the Committee report: "We wish to say that this foreign intervention in our internal affairs may not be defended on the pretext that the social investigation which was proposed has a scientific character." I shall have more to say below of the mounting implications to American foreign policy of large scale, corporate research in search of foreign areas. Here it suffices to emphasize only that when a major Federal department—be it Defense, State, or Commerce—sponsors a scientific project, even one composed of dues-paying psychologists and sociologists, it is elementary that not even the elixir of scientific method is sufficient to wipe away the fact of sponsorship.

VI

We come now to what are surely the most far-reaching episodes in the aftermath of Camelot: the Congressional hearings and bills which, if approved, will result in a Na-

tional Social Sciences Foundation and an Office of the
Behavioral Sciences in the Executive Office of the President
—not to mention a White House Conference on the Behavioral Sciences.

I do not mean to imply that Camelot was the sole
cause of these momentous events. After all, proposals along
their line have been in the minds of social scientists for
years. There was, moreover, the effect on academic and
government consciousness of disclosure that Michigan State
University had had for some years a project, under Federal
financing, for the training of police in South Viet Nam, a
project in which individuals were employed "who had
background in intelligence work for the United States,"
according to President John Hannah. It was charged that
CIA under-cover agents were among these individuals, and
although President Hannah declared that none "was known
by the University or its representatives to have affiliations
with the Central Intelligence Agency," such a statement,
with all respect to its maker, is a little hard to assess. In
the nature of things the University *wouldn't* have known,
wouldn't have been permitted to know, officially at least, if
some of those "with background in intelligence work" were
agents of the CIA.

But the Michigan State affair was only a tempest—with
rather limited consequences, a few being cancellation of
some potentially sensitive university projects around the
country with CIA and other agencies of the American
military apparatus. Camelot, on the other hand—in terms
not only of ensuing governmental action but also of ethical,
intellectual, and academic issues—was, by comparison, an
earthquake, one whose repercussions will continue for a
long time. Let us examine a few of these.

There is, in the first place, the vital matter of Federal
policy with respect to the social and behavioral sciences.
As I noted above, the House subcommittee, in its autopsy
of Camelot, made strongly evident its dislike of military
sponsorship of foreign area research. This is explicit in the

Subcommittee's official recommendations. And while there was an inclination among Subcommittee members to see such research under the State Department, the most significant recommendation (with but one member dissenting) was toward the establishment of a separate agency in the Federal government for sponsorship of the social sciences. The official recommendation of the Subcommittee did not go beyond an Office of Behavioral Science Advisor in the White House. Subsequently, however (in June, 1966), the Chairman of the Subcommittee, Dante B. Fascell of Florida, introduced bills in the House to give formal effect, not only to this recommendation, but also to the establishment of a White House Conference on the Behavioral Sciences and, most important, to the establishment of a National Social Sciences Foundation. At the present time (August, 1966), the Senate Government Research Subcommittee under Senator Fred R. Harris of Oklahoma, is holding hearings on these and related matters. The preponderance (though by no means all) of academic testimony has been in favor of such a foundation, and we are told that Senator Harris' own sentiments in the matter are favorable. Still another hearing on the social sciences and their use by the Government is currently being held by the House Research and Technical Programs Subcommittee (of the House Committee on Government Operations), under the chairmanship of Representative Henry S. Reuss of Wisconsin.[2] Again, of Camelot, one can only say reverently, never have so few so unintentionally earned the gratitude of so many!

Whether a National Social Sciences Foundation, not to mention an Office of Behavioral Sciences Advisor in the White House, is desirable at this juncture in the history of the social sciences is a difficult question even for those of us whose immediate interest is the welfare and prosperity of the social sciences. There is no doubt much to be said for both agencies. Some embarrassments and difficulties might be obviated. But there are others that, far from being obviated, might easily be created by such agencies. I am surely not alone in my belief that formal and heralded establishment of these agencies could well lead to a burden of expectation by government and public opinion that the social sciences are ill-prepared to shoulder. I say this not from belief that nothing or little of scientific character exists in the social sciences. Far from it. There are areas in the social sciences today where work of more genuinely scientific nature (using the word in its strict and hard-core meaning) exists than in certain areas of the biological and, for all I know, the physical sciences. This is not in question. The major difficulty would come, I believe, from the heavy likelihood that the Federal government—which already tends to be largely and increasingly "mission-oriented" in its conception of science—would place upon such a Federally-sanctioned office responsibility for massive *policy* questions and problems that the social sciences neither can, nor should, be expected to answer.

Over the past generation, the social sciences have made contributions of considerable value to society and to social policy. This is incontestable. That, given current tendencies, they will make even greater contributions in the future is almost certain. But this is not the essence of the problem. The essence is whether, given the monumental policy *expectations* of the social sciences that would be created by establishment of such agencies as those envisioned in Representative Fascell's bills, the social sciences (or, for that matter, *any* sciences) could meet them in a way not leaving a gulf between expectation and reality so wide as to promote disillusionment in government and society. Stating the matter briefly, one can say the danger consists in the ever present temptation of government to see the social scientists as *physicians*—called upon to answer *ad hoc* questions today, yesterday if possible—when they are, at their best, *physiologists*, still concerned with vital matters of the nature of human behavior.

There is another disturbing aspect. The social sciences contain today a great diversity of not merely *kind* of work done, but, equally important, of conceptions of kind of work that *should* be done. Beneath the crust of apparent unity in the phrase "the social sciences" lie fissures of extraordinary depth in self-conceptions by social scientists. Orientations here vary much more greatly than among natural scientists. The almost inevitable effect, it would seem, of the establishment of a social sciences foundation would be to create an all too visible hand in the eventual resolution of their conflicts. A national foundation means a powerful director, not to mention vast funds. Everything we know as social scientists about bureaucracy and about the informal but potent pressures on bureaucracy, from inside and out, suggests the prospect of an external shaping of the development of the social sciences that one cannot contemplate with equanimity.

There is, finally, and from the strict point of view of social science research the most important of all considerations, the inevitably fragmenting, not to say segregating, effect that such a foundation would have upon the science of human behavior. The root is still man, and one of the most fascinating and encouraging of all tendencies today in the behavioral sciences is the synthesizing of strains of social, psychological, and physiological (and, who knows, physical in the next generation) research in the study of man. If there is anything that makes the elusive term "behavioral science" different from the "social sciences," it is the closer concentration, it would seem, upon *human behavior*, as the rigorous point of departure, in contrast to the plethora of problems, issues, values, and ideologies that the long history of moral philosophy and the social sciences have bequeathed to us. There are vital problems that are neither social nor biological in character but both—problems on which important research is now being conducted. To seek, in effect, through separate funding and design of problems, to disengage the social from the biological would be to reverse present healthy trends.

It seems to me that it would be far better to widen, through appropriate legislation, the present social science area of the National Sciences Foundation. (A bill now before Congress proposes exactly this.) Experience of recent years with this agency has certainly been encouraging from the viewpoint of the social sciences. Having for years protested, as many of us have, the arbitrary distinction the public makes between "science" and "social science," why, now, seek to institutionalize this distinction, risk perpetuating it forever, through establishment of a separate foundation?

VII

Important as it is, the matter of a new foundation may be of less vital relevance than still another question—one also dramatized by Camelot—and that is the continued usefulness of the whole "project system" that has been in vogue in the Federal government's relation to the sciences ever since the years just following the Second World War, when a group of outstanding scientists in Washington were able to give it the wise guidance and control that the project system so plainly needs. But such wisdom cannot be taken for granted. The opportunities, on the one hand, for bureaucratic direction and misdirection of scientific research and, on the other, for political (I mean intra-scientific politics as much as other) considerations to govern, are all too rife. There is much to be said for the abandonment, or at least sharp cutback, of a system which not only permits, but encourages scientists to go to Washington as individuals or in small groups and receive grants for projects with scrutiny too hurried and too much governed by pecking-order considerations. The system, moreover, promotes disaffection within the universities.

Dr. Frederick Seitz, President of the National Academy of Science, has uttered some recent, important words to this effect. "I think that the whole process of supporting academic research with federal funds would be improved substantially if a larger fraction of the money granted by the government came to universities in the form of institutional grants that were handled on the basis of decisions made jointly by university administration and faculty."

Dr. Seitz makes clear that one of the primary reasons for his recommendation of this change in policy is that of restoring strength to the inner governments of universities— to department chairmen, to deans, but also to constituted faculty committees and councils; strength they have lost under a project system in which they are either bypassed altogether or reduced to mere clerical or clearing-house status by individual scientists whose own power and mobility are guaranteed by the independence of their project from the university in which their primary identity (and tenure, and high salary, and perquisites) are rooted. As Dr. Seitz emphasizes, such independence helps explain the kind of disintegration of academic community on a campus that Berkeley experienced two years ago.

The second reason Dr. Seitz gives for his recommendation is the fatal affinity that seems to lie between the project system and the *size* of projects that take residence on university campuses. No bureaucracy likes to administer funds for an infinity of small, individual projects. It is so much easier to grant one distinguished man large sums of money in a single project. Knowing this, scientists make application accordingly. Add to this the fact that Congress can most easily be pleased, on the occasions of its examination of how funds for science have been spent, by projects that are "mission-oriented," that have a high degree of applied flavor. The result of this is to encourage proliferation of types of scientific project of a practical or applied nature that could as easily be handled by non-university bodies—Federal, state, or private—and a subtle but puissant downgrading of appeal of those smaller, more open-ended, even amorphous "projects" that fall in the basic or theoretical areas of science.

There would be, it is clear, still another gain, and that is to the steadily enlarging field of American foreign-area research. If Project Camelot teaches anything, it is the crucial importance of *sponsorship* when a team of American social scientists goes abroad to conduct inquiries into social structure, culture, and values which, by their very nature, run the risk of offending foreign sensibilities. There is, among many foreign scholars—quite apart from government officials and citizens—a certain suspicion of, not only the United States government and its agencies, but of government agencies in general: a suspicion founded upon frequent conflicts between their own governments and the intellectual communities in these countries—especially in the new and underdeveloped areas. Research projects which go abroad from the United States under the aegis of a governmental department, even departments as generally "clean" as AID or NSF or NIH, will increasingly encounter suspicion of, or will at least be subject to partisan political charges of, clandestine military penetration.

Universities, on the other hand, would appear much less susceptible to such suspicion or charges, especially when their research enterprises abroad are based, from the start, upon full cooperation with universities in the areas to be studied. In almost all countries of the world, the university is, and is most likely of all institutions to remain, trusted. One need think only of the large numbers of scholars, scientists, and public servants in the Latin American, Asian, and African countries whose higher educations have been gained in whole or part in American universities—quite apart from a generally distinguished record of American university scholars in these foreign areas.

It can be said, of course, that Camelot is evidence of the contrary. After all, this project was conceived within SORO which is itself administratively connected with American University. But from all one can gather, SORO has virtually independent status; it would appear to be only nominally a part of the University, in it but not really of it; its ties with the Army come closer to being those of RAND's to the Air Force. It is, in fact, a research center of the Army that, for various reasons which must once have seemed good to officials of American University, is housed there instead of in the Pentagon.

This is surely a very different thing from university-spon-sorship as we generally and rightly understand it. And if Latin American scholars were, unhappily for us all, justified in placing some of the odium on a university in the United States, sober analysis nevertheless requires the differentia-tion I am making. But there is a hard lesson, nevertheless, in Camelot. If the system of block-grants to universities should be adopted by Government foundations, in prefer-ence to the present project system, then much is properly owing these Government foundations by the universities in the way of *guaranteed administrative machinery* within the universities through which all such block-grants will be handled. Federal foundations should insist upon, at a mini-mum, proper academic-administrative bodies of review within the universities, composed of faculty members, as well as of administrators, which would have something of the same overall responsibility for research conducted under these block-grants that faculty-administrative councils and committees have immemorially had over curriculum, courses, and over internally-financed research in the universities.

Let us make no mistake. Such a system, replacing the twenty-year-old project system in this country, will have its bitter enemies among scientists themselves; among those, at least, by now well accustomed to the free-wheeling possi-bilities, the independence, the sense of titanship, that go with the project system. Nevertheless, both for the reasons given by Dr. Seitz and for reasons inherent in the special nature of the social sciences—especially inherent in the na-ture of foreign-area research—I think the block-grant sys-tem, making the universities rather than Federal agencies acting through *ad hoc* projects the true principals, will work to the long run enhancement of research. There will be, I should think, far less probability of a Project Camelot again occurring. But this will be true only if a *bona fide* university "infrastructure" for the allocation and handling of these funds within the university exists. To turn such vital matters over to an agency like SORO, where university ties are only nominal and those between it and the Army (or any other Federal department) are decisive, could be ruinous.

VIII

But no matter what the "infrastructure" of American foreign-area research, it would be naive to suppose that the future can be made free of the threat of impact upon foreign relations that Camelot represented in so egregious a way. Even if Camelot had never happened, there would still be what Camelot assuredly intensified: the problem of retaining (not to mention increasing) the hospitality of foreign nations toward American research in the behavioral sciences. Granted that Chileans, Nigerians, Ceylonese, English, French, and Germans would be more hospitable to a project of Camelot's general type emanating from Harvard University than from the Department of Defense, the question remains: how favorable? For we are dealing with research orientations in today's behavioral sciences in the United States of a mass, and of a type, that increasingly pose problems of potential conflict with foreign sensibility.

It is well to be reminded that some of the animus toward Camelot found in the Chilean Select Committee Report has to do with the basic type of problem that was buried beneath the Project's more manifestly absurd pretensions. From the Chilean point of view, there was gross impropriety in the fact that, irrespective of Army sponsorship, Project Camelot proposed (I am quoting almost verbatim here) to investigate not only isolated and innocuous aspects of Chilean life, but to make an X-ray of the nation, including the most intimate aspects of human beings: what they think, feel, believe, or hope. And all of this without the consent or authorization of either the Chilean government or the Chilean universities.

It is a fact worth stressing that personal and institutional privacy is still taken more seriously in Latin American and many other countries in the world than it is in the United

States, where Gallup and Roper Polls, Kinsey reports, behavioral science and/or FBI bugging of juries, class rooms, offices and conference halls, not to mention the oceans of questionnaires that go forth daily from social science centers, industrial personnel offices, and civil service agencies, inquiring into every intimate and sensitive aspect of one's political, sexual, financial, and dream life have, over a period of a quarter of a century, made Americans the most nakedly exposed—and in this vital sense, perhaps, unfree—people in history. Even under the military dictatorships of Latin America, a freedom of individuality and of personal privacy is known and cherished that we in the United States may be beginning to forget.

There is a further reason for possible distrust among intellectuals and social scientists abroad of American foreign-area projects. That is the slightly uneven record of preservation of research confidence by individual American social scientists. There have been instances, as is well known, in which full entry into a community, a sect, a club or gang, or a file of documents was granted a social science project *only* under the guarantee of absolute confidentiality and anonymity of respondents: confidentiality and anonymity which were ruthlessly violated by one or more individuals of the self-same projects acting, despite the best efforts of the principals to restrain such violation, under the cloak of individual academic freedom to publish the truth, however gained. The recent cancellation, by the U.S. Air Force, of a project funded by the Air Force Office of Scientific Research, but administered at the University of Wisconsin, is possibly a case in point. Although the Air Force gave no official excuse for cancellation, there is reason to believe that when some of the detailed and intimate questions that were to be asked of selected Air Force officers were examined, the conclusion was reached that such a questionnaire would be inimical to service morale, given the ever-present possibility of future leaks of community-, group-, or individual-identity.

Here again, as with so many of the issues raised by

Camelot, the immediate, instinctive reaction of the academic-research community is a curious one, to say the least. We find one professor declaring that the prime lesson to be learned from the Air Force cancellation is that we, the social scientists, must educate the public into understanding that the same kind of personal intimacy of question is to be expected and accepted from social scientists as has long been accepted from physicians and lawyers. But at least two aspects of the matter render this comparison decidedly suspect. In the first place, the physician's "intimacy" stems solely from diagnosis designed to cure. Intimacy of the social scientist stems from research designed for publication. There is, second, the matter of responsibility and sanctions. A physician found guilty of broadcasting or leaking the identity of a patient with, say, a venereal disease or an advanced case of alcoholism or nymphomania would be broken professionally. There are no such sanctions in the academic profession. It is possible, indeed, to be promoted and to draw excellent royalties in the behavioral sciences for actions that would lead to suspension from the legal or medical professions.

This may seem a tangential matter. I am suggesting, however, that what is an increasingly complex and uneasy matter for American conscience is bound to be, given the less than perfect record that the behavioral sciences have for preservation of confidentiality, a matter of considerable moment when the subjects are Chilean or French instead of American. As I noted above, one of the responses of the Latin American academic and intellectual community to Camelot has been precisely that of asking what acts of censure have been taken by American social science associations toward the individuals involved in Camelot.

More important, however, to the future of American foreign-area research than type of research project and question is its potential volume. Here we have something that can, not inexactly, be put in Malthusian terms. The number of foreign research areas will increase (through dropping of barriers) *arithmetically*, but the population of American behavioral scientists with questions to ask of foreign areas will increase *geometrically*. Where once American foreign-area research was confined to a tiny handful of anthropologists and geographers who learned, the hard way, the exceeding importance of tact, trust, honesty, and limits to questions when dealing with foreign peoples, and who went in as individuals, not as members of formidable projects, such research now, as we know, engulfs all the behavioral sciences. Given its rising popularity among social scientists who once could not have found their way to a passport office; given the shrinking (in the sense of yielding diminishing returns) domestic supply of political attitudes, religious beliefs, social aspirations, dreams, orgasms, etc., against the voracious requests of domestic behavioral science titans for ever enlarging masses of subjects; and given, finally, the hordes of graduate students writing dissertations, junior professors on the make, senior professors in struggle for project titanship, not to mention the tens, the hundreds of millions of dollars for such research that will inevitably come from formalized Federal assistance—given all this, it could hardly be a matter for wonder if more and more foreign governments (and also foreign academic communities) began to take the hostile stance toward American social scientists that was once reserved for American businessmen. The bland and righteous belief among American academics that any degree of invasion of privacy, any degree of public exposure of the human psyche, is justified so long as it is in the name of science rather than, say, the TV industry, is no more likely to win popularity in the long run than did the medieval Inquisition when it defended *its* invasions in the name of piety and protection of the faithful. To assume that all will be well if only investigation of natives abroad is done by an American NSSF or a university is, I fear, naive. There will be, all too certainly, other considerations—of foreign relations, national policy and so on—when the American knowledge industry really gets tooled up for foreign markets, and its production rolling.

Does such language offend? We had better get used to it. The relevant model of behavioral science research is fast ceasing to be the scholar—he of "furrowed brow in bookish corner"—and fast becoming the brisk executive, at home, equally, in institute, business, and government. We still use the beguiling image of the scholar and his natural right to freedom of inquiry. It is to today's large-scale, corporate research what the image of the small individual businessman and his natural right to profit is to corporate industry: a compound of honest nostalgia, guilty conscience, and camouflage. The structure, the incentives, and even the language of contemporary large scale research have more in common with business than with the academy. And it matters little, substantively, whether we have reference here to "academic" or "nonacademic" research.

It is possible, I think, to apply to today's knowledge industry what Berle and Means wrote thirty years ago of the modern corporation. "Just what motives are effective today, in so far as control is concerned, must be a matter of conjecture. But it is probable that more could be learned regarding them by studying the motives of an Alexander the Great, seeking new worlds to conquer, than by considering the motives of a petty tradesman of the days of Adam Smith." Substitute "petty scholar" for "petty tradesman" in the foregoing words, and the relevance is immediate.

Foreign-area research is bound to become massive and, potentially, invasionary. If one were a Marxist-Leninist he could say that the American research industry is just beginning to enter its imperialist phase. Diminishing returns, a falling rate of profit, are encountered in the American market. Smalltown, Midcity, Big City have been entered too often; the middle, upper, and lower classes are beginning to be sucked dry. New worlds are needed for conquest if the already frenzied competition for returns within the United States is not to result in civil war. (A sometime business executive, now financial vice-president of a great university, said recently: "Nothing I saw in fifteen years of business compares with the gut competition, the dog eat dog, that I see in the university. God help the natives abroad when the academics get at them in full force.") There must be, at this moment, literally tens of thousands of American behavioral scientists—Ph.D. aspirants in search of dissertations, professors of all ranks, not to mention the hordes of nonacademic researchers in business and government—poised, computers oiled and at the ready for the Big Leap across all oceans, once long-dreamed-of capital is available.

IX

The time is 1984. Dispatches from the Latin American country, Bralivia, have just been received, reporting thundering headlines and editorials in Bralivian newspapers, riots in the streets, and the government in mortal danger of collapse. The American Embassy and consul offices are being stoned. A vast Project Shangri-La in Bralivia has just been discovered; funded by the United States Foundation for the Behavorial Sciences and led by eminent American behavioral scientists in secret cooperation with Bralivian scientists under American salary. Confidential permission of access had earlier been given by the Bralivian government in return for an 87 percent administrative override, payable in dollars, the going rate in American universities for projects Federally funded. Project Shangri-La, according to Bralivian newspapers, had been organized years earlier—immediately after the mistakes of Project Camelot had been counted and assessed—for the objective of Saturation Inquiry of an unsuspecting (and, hence, research-pure) foreign population. With the permission of the Bralivian government and the aid of Bralivian scientists, Bralivian confessional boxes, juries, schoolrooms, household kitchens, and brothels had been bugged. Through recently discovered computer techniques of Simultaneous-Total Assault, all Bralivian institutions—church, family, political party, local community, trade union, school, mental asylums, infant nurseries, business enterprise, and bureaucracy—had been engaged. Depth interviews of new intimacy had been made possible through psychodelic techniques that destroyed all possibility of suspicion on the part of the Bralivian subject. Project Shangri-La, it is learned, has been in existence in Bralivia for more than three years. Although no American behavioral scientist could be found who professed knowledge of Project Shangri-La, a member of the Project administrative staff made the following statement: "Shangri-La was only a feasibility study; we were not really interested in Bralivia at all; it was not among the 24 countries marked for intensive study. The tragedy is that we were just on the verge of the greatest methodological breakthrough in the history of science. Now it is all for nothing." It is understood that exposure of Project Shangri-La came from a leak by one of the American consultants when he learned that the results of Shangri-La would be made available to the Department of Commerce.

NOTES

1. The bare details of Project Camelot are as follows: the Project was conceived in late 1963 by some officers in the Army's Office of Research and Development. Detailed planning was turned over to American University's Special Operations Research Office (SORO), an organization that had been established a number of years before under Army funding for the express purpose of conducting social science research for the Army. The objectives of Camelot were declared to be (1) the systematic identification of the symptoms of the breakdown of a society and (2) the identification of actions that might forestall breakdown. The major national areas of Camelot research interest were chosen from countries of Latin America, the Middle East, the Far East, Western Europe, and Africa. Project Camelot was activated in late 1964 by SORO with a special group of social scientists under the direction of the late Rex Hopper, a sociologist with Latin American interests.

Advising the Project, with varying degrees of directness and continuity, were some thirty-three consultants, many of them among the most distinguished behavioral scientists in the United States. Project Camelot was terminated in July, 1965, by order of Defense Secretary McNamara, following a chain of events described briefly in this article.

2. These matters remain under official consideration as this book goes to press.

(14)

Conflicting
Academic
Loyalties

I

If there is a single transcending challenge before university presidents and faculties today it is that of somehow keeping the university in vital relationship to society and its insatiable demand for expert knowledge and, at the same time, protecting and nourishing those more fragile activities within the university that are not primarily concerned with giving professional advice and that require relative autonomy as the condition of their creativeness.

I say *relative autonomy*. There are those—of whom Robert Hutchins is perhaps foremost—who see the answer to academic complexity and to conflicts of academic loyalty in a monastic retreat to organizations of a type so opulently exemplified by his Center for the Study of Democratic Institutions in Santa Barbara. Mr. Hutchins seems to think that such an organization is related more closely than is the present university in America to the great university tradition of Western Europe that began in the twelfth century. Mr. Hutchins is wrong. He is thinking of the monastic tradition;

This article, in a slightly different version, originally appeared in *Improving College Teaching*, Calvin Lee, ed. (Washington, D.C.: American Council on Education, 1967).

one which—whatever its pietistic graces, its value as a haven for the tender-minded, its role in the ritual perpetuation of texts and ideas—has been generally sterile in furthering intellectual advancement. The odium under which the words "monk" and "monkish" lay for many hundreds of years in the minds of intellectuals in Western society had almost nothing to do with the fact of religious identification and almost everything to do with the monastery's sequestration from the powerful currents which were altering European thought and life. The university, in contrast to the monastery, beginning with the great Bologna in law and Padua in medicine and Paris in theology, has ever been in the thick of things; ever related to the professional needs of society, be these legal, medical, and theological, as they were in the beginning, or scientific, administrative, and industrial as they have come also to be in our age.

I cannot agree that the answer to the contemporary university's problems, to its academic conflicts, lies in making it more like a monastic center aimed at contemplation and criticism of the world. I cannot agree, first, because for the university to retreat from active engagement in society's professional needs would be to fly in the face of a tradition of professional service that began almost a thousand years ago at Bologna and Paris and, second, because I cannot help believing that such disregard would result in the kind of social irresponsibility that breeds, not creativeness and leadership, but inanition and irrelevance. The great minds in the history of Western thought have been minds concerned first and foremost with intellectual problems *drawn from* the practical needs of society, with their own individual relation to these problems and needs frequently that of professional consultant. This was as true of a Plato and Aristotle, who never disdained to draw philosophical problems and principles from their practical consultantships in the service of kings, as it was fifteen hundred years later of the powerful Roman law teachers in the medieval university who, in their own consultantships with struggling monarchs, helped to found the national state and create, incidentally, the basic problems of modern European moral and political philosophy.

Immaculate conception and fastidious separation from the hurly-burly of society have never been elements in the historic university, not, at least, during its great and creative periods, of which the present is surely one. There have been, alas, ages of inanition and stupefying ritualism in the history of the university, and these have been (such as in the eighteenth century in Europe, extending through most of the nineteenth in England) ages when the university was indeed an autonomous center for meditation, reading, and dialogue, when it was sheltered from political, economic, professional, and technological currents in the surrounding society. Then the torch of intellectual leadership in society passed from the university to the hands of those like Diderot, Gibbon, Voltaire, and Bentham for whom the university stank of dry rot. The makers of the great *Encyclopédie* in eighteenth-century France had very professional objectives indeed and their work was specifically described in its title as being an encyclopedia of *sciences, arts,* and *crafts.*

It is, I believe, a point worth emphasizing that the really outstanding academic centers in twentieth-century United States—those centers where, by common assent, the foremost creative minds in the humanities as well as the sciences have existed, centers such as Harvard, Chicago, Columbia, and Berkeley—have been set within contexts of vigorous professionalism. The American university may indeed be—as Mr. Hutchins has for a third of a century been charging it with being—shot through with professionalism (a term that in his usage seems to include everything not reducible to instant dialogue). But it would not be hard, I think, to show that within this third of a century more creativeness— in the arts and letters as well as in the sciences and the professional schools—has come forth from the university campus than during any period preceding. It might also be emphasized that it is within this same third of a century that the university in America has reached a type and level of distinction that has made it the object of respect and even emulation in Europe (where the professional nature of the university has always been understood).

I shall indicate below some grounds for apprehension regarding the long-range effects on the university of some of the massive research and training projects now entered into so often and so uncritically by universities at the behest of government and industry. But this is a reflection of lack of discriminating judgment and of magnitude of the projects, not of professionalism as such. On the evidence of history, it would appear to be insulation of the university from the evocative forces of polity, economy, and profession that periodically plunges it into irrelevance and inanition or pushes it to a level of abstraction that reaches pure sound.

II

All of this does not mean, of course, that the problem of conflicting loyalties is not a real one at the present time. Even if the university in America is today closer to its historic type than some of its critics believe, we still cannot be blind to some extremely difficult problems, the result of major changes that have taken place in the relation of the university to society.

Change in any institution is, at bottom, change in the social roles that are held by individuals. We often speak of political, economic, or social change as though it were a matter of supra-individual processes in large institutions and social structures. But genuine social change is never present until the roles, habits, attitudes, and life styles of *individuals* are irreversibly affected. This is as true of the university as it is of family, church, or state. Social change thus inevitably precipitates conflict among allegiances, meanings, and roles.

Equally true and vital, however, is the fact that the *source* of major change is almost never to be found in forces within the institution but rather in the tensions that develop *between* the institution and the surrounding social order;

tensions which are caused by significant alterations in the organization's functional relation to the social order. The family is an obvious example of this. It was only when, as a consequence of the impact of the industrial and democratic revolutions in the last century, the social function of kinship was sharply modified that conflicts of role and allegiance within the family became a cardinal aspect of the American social scene. This is not to say that role conflicts had never before existed; only that under the external impetus of major economic and legal changes they assumed unprecedented intensity.

It is not different with the university. Behind the present intensity of role conflicts in the academic world lie two structural changes of profound importance, both aspects of the history of the university in America since the second World War. The first is manifest in the increasing *directness* of the university's relation to government and industry; the second is the spreading *professionalization* of academic disciplines. Although both have been widely commented upon, it is useful here to describe each briefly before taking up some of the conflicts which arise from the changes.

Down until approximately a generation ago, the university's contribution to society was essentially *indirect*: expressed almost exclusively through the time-honored functions of teaching and scholarship. It is difficult to recall, even as recently as the 1930's, more than the barest number of instances in which the university contributed directly to the working machinery of society—to government, industry, agriculture, and the professions. There were, to be sure, the agricultural experiment stations and, here and there, fact-finding bureaus for the assistance of state and municipal governments. But these were rare, confined to some of the public universities and, it is amusing now to recall, kept rather carefully segregated from the main academic community. Seldom did even professional schools of law, medicine, and engineering offer direct service to government or industry. And in the area of the liberal arts and sciences such service was unheard of except, starting with the first World War, from a few chemists. Governmental agencies and industries supplied their own research. That fields such as mathematics and physics, much less economics and political science, had anything of importance to give directly to government and industry would have been as appalling a thought to professors as it would have been hilarious to politicians and business tycoons of the day. Professors should be seen in the classroom, not heard in the market-place; so might the homely maxim have been paraphrased. All of this is not to imply that universities were either ghettoes or feudal enclaves of privilege. Their concern with the problems of society was deep, as is evidenced by the textbooks written, by the kinds of courses taught (often more "vocational" than today), and by the prime importance on university campuses of professional schools and colleges.

Far from being fastnesses of monastic contemplation, they were, as I have already suggested, thoroughly in the thick of things: things religious, political, and economic. Conflicts of power and ideology within them could be titanic, as the Second Battle of Princeton, with President Wilson and Dean West as opposing generals, made splendidly evident. But such conflicts were personal, not of role or function. By everyone it was understood (and by no one more clearly than Woodrow Wilson) that the "university in the nation's service" was emphatically not a service station, not a department store, but a setting within which teaching and scholarship would seek to *inspire* to service, not provide it—at piece rates!

Very different, of course, is the contemporary university; the institution that Clark Kerr has so well called the "multiversity." Nothing in the recent social history of the United States is more remarkable than the bridging of the gulf that once lay between the university and the practical machinery of society. There is no university today that is not involved in a wide variety of direct services to government at all levels, to industry, to the professions and arts, and to the mass media. If such involvement were strictly institutional—that is, *sponsored* by the academic institution but kept separate from academic activities as the agricultural experiment station was once kept separate—the change would be perhaps minor in its impact upon academic life and loyalty. But, as is only too evident, involvement reaches down to the very heart of the university: to the professor, to the nature of research done, and inevitably to the character of the teaching done.

"Service station" and "department store" as terms to describe categorically and undiscriminatingly the contemporary American university are unfair. As I indicated above, it is difficult to see how a society as large and complex as ours could possibly maintain itself except by a use of university resources that is bound to be more direct than it was in other ages. The problem, however—and it is, I believe, the major problem of academic policy in our society—is that of making sure that government and industry, in the process of *using* university resources, do not also *shape* university resources. For neither society nor the university will have been well served if the relationship between them proves in the long run to have diverted the university from furnishing society that type of knowledge for which it is uniquely fitted. It is a dangerous misconception to suppose that the university is the proper scene of *all* types of knowledge, research, and teaching. For the university to establish—even worse, take over—research that can be as well, if not better, done in governmental or industrial laboratories must inevitably, through a kind of Gresham's Law, harm the kind of work that it can uniquely do.

There is a conflict today that may seem now no larger than a man's hand but that is bound to become major. It is the conflict between the scientist's role of autonomous and free-ranging investigative mind, obeying the ancient maxim that he goes farthest who knows not where he is going, and his very different role which, however carefully its "independence" is guaranteed in the fine print, is nevertheless *not* autonomous (not in the crucial psychological sense) if only because in application for funds a title had to be seized upon, and in seizing upon a title a mission constructed and because, with each passing month, one's commitment to this mission becomes ever greater. The difference, in purely creative terms, between "basic" and "applied" science seems to me of less moment than the difference between "open" and "mission-oriented" science.

III

The second major structural change in the contemporary university is a consequence of the increasing professionalization of scholarly disciplines. This is most notable, of course, in the natural sciences, but it is becoming ever more characteristic of the social sciences and even the humanities. Whereas, as recently as a generation ago, physics, biology, mathematics, economics, psychology, or sociology had disciplinary identity only insofar as each drew it from the larger and encompassing profession of university teaching, today each has its own professional identity. Once, to be a physicist or sociologist meant, beyond any possible question, that one held academic rank in a college or university. Today each is more like engineer or physician. To be a sociologist at the present time means that one is *probably* in a university (more probably, on the statistical evidence, than if one is a chemist) but he may easily be in government, private industry, or even, with shingle out, in practice. From being primarily and essentially a university member whose field was, more or less incidentally, sociology, one is today a sociologist whose job is, more or less incidentally, in a university. More and more academic fields now conceive of themselves as professions, with university connections incidental, more a matter of housing than umbilical tie. In fields like law, medicine, and engineering, the tension between academy and profession has, on the whole, worked itself out. There is at least a working arrangement. The role issues are clearer. After all, the overwhelming majority of lawyers and physicians are nonacademic, and few organizations in modern society are more potent and more prestige-conferring than the American Bar Association and the American Medical Association. But in many other academic fields the tensions are great because of the relative recency of the change.

These are the structural changes that, above any others I can easily think of, lie behind present conflicts of academic role and loyalty. Two preliminary points should be made about the contexts of these conflicts before we turn to their detail. First, for individuals, such conflicts are likely to be difficult only in proportion to one's eminence as scholar or scientist. The greater a man's value to the university as the master of a learned discipline, the greater his value as a professional man to government, industry, foundation, or profession. That these conflicts of role and loyalty are not merely abstract or potential is attested to by the frequent decisions, often perplexing, sometimes agonizing, that the individual must make through the period of his greatest creativity; decisions concerning alternative careers or, within the single career of academic man, decisions of allocation of time toward the varied demands which his own eminence brings upon him from profession, government, and research institute as well as academic department.

Second, just as the intensity of role conflicts varies among individuals in the measure of their personal distinction (and also, to be sure, in the "hotness" of the special fields they have chosen), so does intensity vary with the type and distinction of academic institution. A recent year spent in one of the great Ivy League universities, supplemented since by some random questioning of others, suggests clearly to me that the intensity of academic-professional conflict is less—both for the man and for the university—in a Harvard or Princeton than it is in even such justly renowned public universities as Berkeley and Ann Arbor. However distinguished the public university may be in eminence of its faculty and wealth of capital resources, it has not yet reached the point where it seems to provide the same anchoring sense of identity and to promote the same overriding loyalty to academy, that we find in some of the greater private universities. I am not, needless to emphasize, suggesting that the factors "public" and "private" are the crucial ones.

European experience alone would cast doubt upon such a conclusion over the long run. And the spectacle of Berkeley makes plain that aggregations of scholars and amassments of financial resources as imposing as any to be found in the greatest private universities are perfectly compatible with public status.[1]

But aggregation does not a community make nor capital riches an aristocracy. The line between even Berkeley and a Harvard or Princeton is a clear one when we turn from human and financial resources to the subtle but potent matters of internal academic structure, hierarchy, and professorial role. In older universities, as in older aristocracies, internal processes of dislocation, of status anxiety, and of role conflict are, on the whole, more moderate, under the impact of external change than they are in the newer social strata or universities. When we move down the scale of institutional eminence from a Berkeley or Ann Arbor to those public universities (and a few of the newer private ones as well) which, through recent effort to catapult themselves upward, must bear some of the storied marks of the *nouveau riche*, internal strains of structural dislocation, status mobility, and role confusion can be deadly.

Obviously, in this differentiation among universities, we are dealing for the most part with factors over which neither faculties nor administrations have present control: sheer historical length of university eminence, number of academic luminaries reaching back for many decades, number of distinguished alumni, the social prestige that even for academic man attaches to private and endowed—in contrast to tax-supported—wealth, and a cultural style that only centuries can form. To pretend that the internal life of universities, any more than that of aristocracies, is not affected by such matters would be to pretend nonsense. But I am convinced that this differentiation of universities, and the difference in incidence and intensity of role conflicts and strains, is also the result of factors over which faculties and administrations *do* have some control. Among these are type, magnitude, and sway of university involvement in extramural ventures, and, second, the degree to which the purely *professional* attainments of faculty members outweigh, as values, internal contribution to the residual functions of the university.

But whatever the causes of this differentiation—historical and social, academic and administrative—it is a real one, to be seen in the varying intensity of the conflicts within the contemporary university.

IV

Unquestionably the major conflict of loyalties on today's campus is that between teaching and research. Such conflict would appear inevitable, given the scope and nature of much of the research done. We are still prone to say, as did our academic forebears, that there cannot be, at bottom, conflict, for good teaching requires the insemination of ongoing research, and good research requires the stimulus of ongoing teaching. But these words have, increasingly, the ring of incantation. For plainly, much that passes under the name of research—including most of the consultative activities that today spring from the university's altered role in society and from the professionalization of academic discipline—does *not* require teaching, in fact, finds teaching to be avocational at best, distractive at worst. The reason lies in the massiveness and character of more and more of the research that is today done in universities.

The university, in taking over research activities that once existed (to the degree that they existed at all) in the U.S. Department of Agriculture, Bureau of Mines, Ordnance or Quartermaster Service, or in General Motors or General Electric laboratories, has increasingly taken over projects that do not at all require the ambience of teaching or the physical presence of graduate students for their successful prosecution. And we do little service to teaching or the nature of the university when we pretend that students are required for such projects. Assistants, yes, but not students. This is, I believe, the single most impressive difference between research today in the universities and the research of a generation ago.

No doubt there were conflicts of a sort between teaching and research before the multiversity entered the scene. But these, if they existed, were relatively few and small. They had to be. For, quite apart from the fact that teaching was, even in the major universities, incontestably academic man's first moral obligation, if not love, the invariable and unyielding pivot of one's contractual relation to the university and membership in the academic community was the teaching role. Teaching was as much the essence of one's academic image of himself as it was of society's stereotype of the academic profession.

But the major reason for the relative lack of conflict before the present generation was the character of research done in the universities and colleges. It was small in scope, personal in character, finite in aspiration, and, on the whole, optional. It was not, as it so often is today, immense, heavily bureaucratized, infinite, and compulsive. Let me use one example—admittedly extreme but far from unrepresentative: the multibillion dollar industrial-military research enterprise that is the University of California's atomic energy research project—spread out in three gigantic locations in Berkeley, Livermore, and Los Alamos. It is useful and sobering to recall that this vast project began in the late 1920's in the hands of one man, the late Ernest O. Lawrence, at Berkeley, without technical assistance beyond what was given by graduate students, without so much as a secretary, much less administrative assistant, and the whole of it housed—I recall vividly—in a room that would be too small today to take care of a departmental typing pool. Apart from teaching— that is, of graduate students—it is difficult to imagine Professor Lawrence's Nobel-prize-winning achievement ever having got off the ground. And apart from his own research genius, directly impressed upon students, not diffused through layer upon layer of technical-administrative staff, it is equally difficult to imagine the teaching impact that he made upon a generation of physicists.

The point is, the principal criterion of university-level research, down until a couple of decades ago, was its adaptability to the function of teaching. Such was the small, personal, and interactive character of research (in science as well as in the humanities) that it could properly be regarded, for graduate students at least, as but another mode of teaching. And in an age when research budgets were minuscule, when they rarely allowed the employment of research technicians, graduate students were as indispensable to the research function as professorial research was to their own education.

I am not suggesting, of course, that the *only* function of university or college research was instructive. Far from it. Beginning in the late nineteenth century with Eliot at Harvard, Gilman at Johns Hopkins, Jordan at Stanford, Benjamin Ide Wheeler at Berkeley, Harper at Chicago, and Wilson at Princeton, research came in for its own due. The difference between the university, properly called, and the more typical American *academy*, however it was called, lay in the increasing emergence of research as a legitimate activity of the university. But the truth remains: research then was given primary justification by what it did for teaching, for a level of teaching that had not previously existed on the American campus. And such research, in any event, depended for its audience on, was indeed exclusively addressed to, fellow scholars and scientists—*not* the men of affairs in government and industry whose primary interest in its operational or practical character has become increasingly directive in the academic community.

The major cause of present difficulties—of conflicts in academic role and loyalty that sometimes threaten to drive the university's historic and still essential functions underground—is not, therefore, the mere fact of the university's taking on the operational problems of society. It lies in the widening, undiscriminating, often frenzied, tendency to take on *any and all types* of research problems. The really serious and responsible criticism to be leveled at many universities today is that in the understandable and laudable act of making their resources available to a society desperately in need of knowledge, they have taken on not only the kinds of research project for which the university alone is adequately fitted *but also types of research project and development that could more easily and appropriately be placed in nonuniversity settings.* In some universities it is, alas, the second type that shows signs of proliferating the fastest and most widely. And, I would argue, it is in these universities that academic conflicts—between teaching and research, between university and professional affiliation—are most vivid and, often, wasteful of intellectual resources.

Professor Harrison Brown of Caltech has recently estimated that at the present time 1.3 billions of Federal dollars are invested in ongoing research in American universities and colleges and that this sum is two-thirds of all the university research funding in existence. In an age of cold war it would be folly, of course, to pretend that much of this does not serve military objectives, and, in passing, it might be observed that if occasionally some of it is embarrassedly discovered to be going into CIA activities, this means merely that it is serving the needs of *invisible* rather than *visible* war, a difference that would not, in all probability, have seemed of much moral consequence to earlier generations of university scientists and scholars.

The essential problem is not, however, that of the source and application of research funds; and it will not be met by recommendations which as seriously misunderstand the nature of the university as they flout the needs of a complex society. The university, to re-echo Woodrow Wilson's words, must certainly be in the nation's service. But it must serve *as it is uniquely fitted to serve*: through research that is compatible with university ends and structure, research small enough in scope to permit not only the utilization of students *as students*—rather than as technicians—but professors *as professors* rather than as project supervisors, first, second, and third grade.

V

There is today a blurring of the academic image, one that is the direct result of the kind of forces we have been describing. If this blurring is less obvious at a Princeton or Harvard than it is at a Berkeley or Ann Arbor—let alone at universities long content with mediocrity but now striving with every possible million dollars to achieve instant greatness—it cannot be missed even in the Ivy League. The difference between academic and nonacademic on the campus becomes ever more tenuous under the spur of professionalization of field and of a Faustian conception of the university. It used to be said that there was more difference between two professors one of whom was an administrator than between two administrators one of whom was a professor. This may still be true in a few areas of the university, the sciences included, but in more and more instances it is not. How could it be? For the physical or social scientist engaged more and more typically in large-scale research, more and more visible as *professional* physicist, biologist, or sociologist, working on an around-the-calendar schedule, housed in special institute or laboratory quarters (sometimes with Do Not Enter, not merely on his door but on the fence around his building), equipped with staffs of secretaries and technicians formidable enough to frighten away all but foundation executives or Federal supervisors, with budgets to prepare, applications to make out for further funds, and payroll sheets to sign—given all of this, it is hard for the individuals involved not to look like civil servants or businessmen. Add to this the man's constantly rising number of consultantships, incessant "site visits," and almost ceaseless travel to meetings and conferences, and the traditional image of academic man often seems less real than that of business executive or bureau chief.

Elsewhere[2] I have suggested that it becomes steadily more difficult, given this momentous change in academic role, to justify to nonacademic intellectuals the iron protection, the differential privilege, that is enjoyed by academic intellectuals in the form of tenure. In a day when academic man lacked the occupational mobility that his present professional identity gives him—with ready entry into government, profession, and even business—when he was the victim, so to speak, of a specialization that was as fragile as it was narrow, with life made precarious by hostile winds that all too often blew across the academic landscape, when, in short, he was literally and exclusively academic man rather than professional man, there was much to justify tenure even when its costs could be measured, as they still can be, in mummification. But that day is departed. Other grounds have to be found today on which to justify the differential privilege of tenure, academic freedom being the commonest and certainly the most respectable. But to plead necessitous or fragile circumstance for today's affluent man of science or letters is to plead a case that is at best naïve, at worst cynical.

Professionalization and the vast increase in research activities have inevitably led to a change in the criteria of achievement within the university. It is almost impossible today for a faculty member to win prestige in an academic environment on the basis of the largely moral or "human" qualities that in decades past gave certain individuals influence on the campus even when their scholarly or professional fame was slight. The sociologist Max Weber, in his treatment of a typology of educational systems, pointed to two opposite types of teachers: the one primarily able at "awakening charisma," the other at "imparting specialized expert training." It is reasonably clear that the second has become overwhelmingly dominant, though I would not wish to suggest that the two types are as irrevocably separated as Weber seems to imply.

The change in criteria of achievement and promotion can make for minor tragedies today, especially in some of the smaller colleges that have traditionally emphasized qualities in a professor that might be expected to "awaken charisma." Consider the plight of the professors in a certain celebrated liberal arts college that I have been told of. Tradition requires that the faculty member's office door be open to students all hours of the day except when he is at class. Students, I am told, are relentless in their insistence upon this open-door policy. But with inconsistency verging on downright betrayal, the same students will ridicule their professors because they lack the research reputations held by faculty members at a neighboring university.

Administrations might take warning. The same criteria of success that have become operative in faculty minds become, within a few years, and in different intensity, the criteria that students themselves apply to faculty. There is a rising tendency on the part of even undergraduates to rate their teachers less upon qualities that traditionally have counted and that undergraduates might be presumed competent to judge, and more and more on what filters down to them about a faculty member's professional eminence or national visibility as creative mind. Is the day too far off when one can expect to overhear an undergraduate saying, "Take Jones's course; he just got half a million from NIH" instead of the more familiar type of recommendation? Fortunately, probably a long way off. But students are nonetheless alive to the research reputations of their teachers, and nothing is more pathetic on campus today than the plight of a man who, after the bulk of his career has been spent at teaching alone, and with little if anything accrued in the way of professional reputation, suddenly awakens to the fact that in today's academic setting the man who has *only* his teaching to offer to students does not even have that.

The once familiar characterization of a faculty member as a good teacher but a poor research man is very likely to be fatal in the university today. Awareness of this has led many a naturally good young teacher to hide his light under a bushel lest he thereby run the risk of this currently invidious tag being applied to him. As one very candid assistant professor once put it to me in a letter: "I hope I never get labeled in any student or faculty evaluation as a good man with undergraduates. Until my research record is unchallengeable, I can get farther by dull teaching of undergraduates. This will at least leave open the *possibility* that my research promise may therefore be high." Students—

and, of course, notably graduate students—are quick to absorb shifts in values, and one detects a certain suspicion among the more sophisticated students of that faculty member whose teaching scintillates through possession of older graces.

If the changed role of the university professor—that is, his increased professionalization and prominence as expert in national service—were accompanied by a decline in attractiveness of the university to undergraduate students, the conflict between research and teaching, between professional and academic roles, would be less intense; would certainly be less obvious. But, plainly, the university becomes ever more attractive to high school graduates and to their parents. Hordes of undergraduates, seemingly unfrightened by rumors of grim impersonality and bureaucratization at State U, pour through its gates each year. Once there, they adapt themselves astonishingly well despite the reports of alienation, of political activism supposedly founded upon curricular discontent, of defiant sexual experimentation, and escapist use of narcotics[3] that the public has come to read with all the delighted horror that, in a more innocent age of our history, went into the reading of missionary reports on the outrageous customs of the heathen. Moralistic tractarianism, it may be accepted as a principle, does not vary in amount from generation to generation; only in content and medium. Undergraduates, for the American reading public, have succeeded Polynesians and Nigerians, just as *Look* and *Life* have succeeded the good old *Missionary Review*.

Why undergraduates like large university settings (and my own view is that for the rest of this century such settings will become more, not less, attractive) is not altogether clear, but it may have something to do with Cardinal Newman's pregnant observation in his *The Idea of a University* that what students do by way of educating each other— through mere rubbing of shoulders together for four years— within an *exciting atmosphere*—is of more importance, both morally and intellectually, than what is done *for* them by a faculty. (This can be paraphrased by saying that students, in the long run, like to be where the action is, not where new umbilical cords are provided.) In any event, it might be noted that the fall-off in applications for undergraduate admission at Berkeley the past two years has been infinitesimal by comparison with what it could have been, given the rather horrifying yellow journalism (written by academic as well as nonacademic) in newspapers and magazines about Berkeley.

But while the university's popularity with undergraduates seems to be undiminished, the kinds of conflict we have noted between academic man's role as teacher and scholar, on the one hand, and his role as a corporate executive in research project, as industrial adviser, as government consultant, or even as independent intellectual in arts and letters remain nonetheless obvious; and galling to academic man himself.

Academic prestige today, on and off the campus, depends, to a degree never known heretofore, upon intellectual qualities that are not merely distinguishable but actually separable from older academic functions. This may be vivid only in the physical and social sciences (humanists are fond of saying it is) but I think it is scarcely less real in arts and letters. The university's prestige in the literary and artistic marketplace is today quite as great as in the industrial or governmental marketplace. Witness the increasing efforts of nonacademic literary editors and other impresarios to "capture" professors in the humanities. The enlargement of the humanist's national image—reflected in his widening appearance in magazines and at White House parties—has come to mean as much to him as the enlargement of the scientist's national image, and with similar results upon the more prosaic and routine duties on the campus. This reality is often overlooked by the humanist, convinced as he is that he alone today keeps the vestal flame aglow. In the same way that the substantive difference between academic and nonacademic science has become less significant—the result of nonacademic centers allowing more individual research autonomy and "mission-oriented" contracts within the university allowing, in fact, less—so has the line between academic and nonacademic humanism grown less distinct. Thus, the national visibility that was once enjoyed only by the nonacademic humanist—by a T. S. Eliot or an Edmund Wilson—is now, increasingly, enjoyed by the academic, whose contributions to nonacademic prestige journals often seem to matter more to him than those he submits to strictly academic journals. Both in the humanities and the sciences academic minds today enjoy a national visibility that is distinct from their academic habitats.

It is this extraordinary professional visibility and renown in the republic of letters, arts, and sciences coupled with the diminishing appeal of such traditional university functions as teaching and academic fellowship with students that creates the notable conflict on all campuses between the Locals and the Cosmopolitans. Except for transient periods of moralistic fervor on the part of the Cosmopolitans, attention to matters of curriculum and academic policy is left to the Locals. The Cosmopolitans—too deeply engaged in more profitable or prestigious work at the professional or national level—care little for such duties; that situation can sometimes result in the chairman, the dean, and the president getting their advice on curriculum, educational policy, and other vital matters from those whose chief qualification is availability rather than insight or wisdom. Worse than this, however, is that indifference of the influential and notable toward time-honored curriculum and policy committees has something of a downgrading effect on these committees, on their intrinsic function and their attractiveness to the less notable of the faculty. There is inevitably a perceived stratification of academic-administrative functions on a campus, and it requires little vision or shrewdness today by a faculty member on his way up to sense that those committees most directly concerned with teaching, especially undergraduate, are less desirable than those concerned with, say, research and external relations.

Here, as in other spheres, however, it is possible, I believe, to differentiate between private and public universities. While the attraction of service on curriculum and internal policy committees has declined at a Yale or Princeton, it

has not declined as much. Just as the image of the undergraduate teacher still glows more brightly, so does the appeal
of activities directly concerned with teaching. We come
back to the point made earlier: such is the continuing
prestige of a Harvard or Princeton as an autonomous community that external research and consultative work at even
highest professional levels can oftentimes seem less gratify-
ing to ego, less important somehow, than the unsung, relatively invisible, and wholly unpaid duties of intramural
character.

No doubt to many a veteran professor of the Ivy League,
remembering how it used to be, the differentiation I am
drawing will seem tenuous. I am far from claiming that even
at Princeton teaching holds undiminished luster. But there
is no question that the status of the student, undergraduate
as well as graduate, and the general esteem in which teaching is held, are higher in the Ivy League universities and in
private universities generally than in the public universities.
And among the public universities there is, I am convinced,
a scale of faculty regard for the student that is roughly in
proportion to the scale of institutional excellence. That is,
there is more interest in, more effectiveness and distinction
of teaching at, say, Berkeley or Ann Arbor than at certain
other institutions where, in recent frenetic attempts to
achieve quality overnight, contracts have been made with
eminent individuals which in their heavy and public emphasis upon research have had the predictable effect of
downgrading the status of teaching. When, however, as not
infrequently happens, one of these eminent individuals
shows that he is keenly interested in students and in teaching, and that isolation from curriculum is the last thing he
is interested in, the consequences can be extraordinarily
fruitful.

There is also, apparently, a reasonably high, positive
correlation between an academic man's excellence as scholar
or creative mind and his respect for teaching. Not every
form of teaching, to be sure. But when, after all, did *every*
form of teaching ever interest all members of a faculty?
Teaching is many things. It is research conducted with stu-

dents (in contrast to hired technicians). Teaching is the excitement that can be generated in a student's mind by mere presence on the same campus with faculty minds known to be creative and to be esteemed by the profession. Teaching is the random suggestion, however inarticulate, conveyed perhaps osmotically, that a certain problem is important to investigate. Teaching is casual conversation. Teaching is lecturing to large audiences. (In how many academics is there not something of the actor *manqué*, something that is stimulated and gratified by the mere existence of an audience?) Teaching, above all, is something that is important to say. It may be safely assumed that in ancient Athens or in medieval Paris large numbers came to hear Aristotle or Abelard not primarily because either was reputed to be a "good teacher" but because he was known to have something to say worth listening to. Teaching is many things. And the only possible prescription for it at university or college level is to see that somehow, in some way, active junior minds are in some kind of contact with active senior minds. We are told that Enrico Fermi took as much pleasure in his freshman class in introductory physics at the University of Chicago after the war as he ever had in any of his signal contributions to theoretical physics. We do not know *how* he taught; only that, like Mt. Everest, he was *there*, to be, so to speak, scaled by students.

For either administration or faculty to take method or organization of teaching too seriously is, of course, fatal. Several years ago I saw a list prepared by someone in the U.S. Office of Education of what purported to be the "twenty-three indispensable qualities of the good teacher." It was computer-based. Good grooming and pleasing manner were placed just behind "clear organization of subject matter" in importance. Let us, however, overlook that particular juxtaposition of the computer mind, and fix attention only on "clear organization of subject matter." I think irresistibly of three or four great teachers of this century I have been privileged to know: Gilbert Lewis in chemistry, Edward Tolman in psychology, Carl Sauer in geography,

A. L. Kroeber in anthropology. Not one of them would have passed muster on this item any more than on most of the other items so solemnly listed. Seminal minds are almost never very clear in their organization of subject matter. How could they be and at the same time leave generations of students—undergraduate and graduate—with the feeling that in knowledge as in a woman's beauty there is something wonderful and beckoning that eludes precise classification?

Today, in too many quarters, we are bedeviled by the image of Old Chips—a good fellow, kind to students, interested in their personal lives, a "character," and "who may not have been a scholar but was a real guy" in the bleary memories of older alumni. But the first step in any rational view of the present situation is to forget Chips. Modern students—the better ones, at least—have little interest in his resurrection and would have little time for him were he to suddenly appear. He would simply embarrass them.

There is a widespread belief today in higher education that a foremost task is that of somehow making large universities seem like small colleges. But this is dangerous business, for there is tyranny implicit in all efforts to make large organizations—be they nations, corporations, or universities —seem like small communities. My own unabashed view is that a more important task, given the complexity, the quality, the style, of twentieth century American culture, is that of making many small colleges seem more like universities. And this means—in addition to the first requirement which is that of *greater intellectual creativeness* from the faculty, with freedom from classroom routine for its expression—the formation of a scene in which some of the cosmopolitanism, the excitement of diverse numbers, and the social freedom of the large university are somehow made present. Many of us would echo Dean DeVane's belief that a large college of liberal arts set within a university has, on balance, advantages over the small independent college, and most of these advantages flow from exposure of liberal arts students to a setting that is more variegated professionally, richer in number of opportunities offered, and generally more stimulating and more maturing than that to be found in the small college.

VI

The present intensity of conflicts of academic loyalty would appear almost certain to lessen in the years immediately ahead. There are several reasons for this. In the first place, the university is an institution, and institutions (in contrast, say, to sects) have their own mechanisms for the assimilation of change and of the conflicts induced by change. An institution is, after all, multipurpose, and it is not therefore as vulnerable to sudden modifications of environment as are social entities whose specialization of function leaves them less adaptable. This evolutionary principle is, I believe, as likely to be applicable to centers for research or dialogue as to biological organisms.

Second, change of an internal, academic-administrative nature may be expected. Administrations (and faculty members), profiting from some recent embarrassing experiences in contract research, will almost certainly begin to make sharper and more critical distinction between types of research congenial to the nature of a university and types that are not congenial. Further, the incidence of student revolts of the kind Berkeley memorably began in 1964 will surely aid in this much-needed academic change. Whatever the dubious credentials of some of these student revolts, however often their academic value has been distorted by extraneous political ideology, they cannot help but stimulate a re-examination of the functions proper and improper to the historic university.

Third, while the heady wine of professionalization is now indeed a major influence on the academic scene, nothing can withstand the long-run appeal of the university itself as the primary loyalty of those fortunate enough to be its members. I use "fortunate" advisedly. Even in the great, long-established professions of law and medicine, one cannot but be struck by the continuing magnetism of the university law and medical schools and by the sacrifice in income that will be gladly endured for the assured intellectual stimulation (also, not to be missed, the social prestige) that come from faculty status. The university is, and is likely to remain for a long time, the bearer of more intellectual influence and of more social status in the United States than any other single institution. It holds much of the position once held by the church and clergy. It is as easy, we should not forget, for an aristocracy to be founded upon academic merit (reinforced by tenure, to be sure) as upon land or military prowess. The professoriat in the United States today comes closer than either the business or governmental class to resembling a feudal nobility. It has its barons and lords (Nobel prize winners, National Academy members, Guggenheim fellows, *et al.*), its immense influence on nation, its unique *esprit*, its honor, its *noblesse oblige*, its unrivaled sense of mutual aid and corporate protectiveness, and is even, apparently, becoming more and more endogamous. Nothing in the world mattered so much to the late President Kennedy, or would mean more to President Johnson, than support of the professoriat.

Finally, there is the sheer, unquenchable love of teaching (in whatever form) that lies in the heart of not merely academic man but of man in general. The impulse to inform, to instruct, to mold, to indoctrinate, is a powerful one in the human race. Whether teaching is a variant primarily of gossip or of the sermon is not clear, but the same impulse that leads to each of these leads equally to teaching. There is evidence, as I said above, that a positive correlation exists between excellence (institutional and individual) and faculty interest in students. This correlation is not likely to diminish, and it may be taken for granted, I believe, that its implication will become more, not less, vivid in the academic world at large.

NOTES

1. It is a point worth emphasizing, however, that Berkeley, partly through heavy endowments but chiefly through the unique constitutional position held by the University of California, has come the closest of all the public universities to being "private."

2. See "The Permanent Professors: A Modest Proposal," pp. 225–245.

3. A large percentage of the public seems to think that the same students are involved in all of these modes of reactive behavior. Quite apart from simple observation, mere common sense would suggest, however, that this, if true, would be what the *New Yorker* used to call the neatest trick of the week.